How to Restore Your Motorcycle

How to Restore Your Motorcycle

WITHDRAWN

Mark Zimmerman and Jeff Hackett

MOTORBOOKS
INTERNATIONAL

Dedication

This book is dedicated first to all of the people who taught me what little I've learned about motorcycles and mechanics—you know who you are—and since I'd need an entire book to list you by name, I'll just say thanks. Secondly, I'd like to dedicate this to all of the guys (and gals) slaving away in their garages on some old motorcycle. No one who hasn't been there can appreciate all of the hard work, busted knuckles, and long hours that go into the restoration process. I do, and so do your brethren. Here's a well-earned pat on the back, it may not be a "Best of Show" trophy, but believe me it's the next best thing.

This edition first published in 2000 by Motorbooks International, an imprint of MBI Publishing Company, Galtier Plaza, Suite 200, 380 Jackson Street, St. Paul, MN 55101-3885 USA

© Zimmerman/Hackett, 2000

The information in this book is true and complete to the best of our knowledge. All recommendations are made without any guarantee on the part of the author or Publisher, who also disclaim any liability incurred in connection with the use of this data or specific details.

We recognize that some words, model names and designations, for example, mentioned herein are the property of the trademark holder. We use them for identification purposes only. This is not an official publication.

Motorbooks International titles are also available at discounts in bulk quantity for industrial or sales-promotional use. For details write to Special Sales Manager at Motorbooks International Wholesalers & Distributors, Galtier Plaza, Suite 200, 380 Jackson Street, St. Paul, MN 55101-3885 USA.

Library of Congress Cataloging-in-Publication Data

Zimmerman, Mark.
  How to restore your motorcycle / Mark
  Zimmerman & Jeff Hackett.
    p. cm.
  Includes index.
  ISBN 0-7603-0681-8 (pbk. : alk. paper)
    1. Motorcycles—Conservation and restoration—Amateurs' manuals. I. Hackett, Jeff.
  II. Title.

TL444.2.Z55   2000
629.28'775—dc21   00-057853

On the front cover: Louis Paris and Bobby Brown work on Brown's 1976 Honda CB750, while Paris' 1978 CB750 Supersport (the last of Honda's single-cam in-line fours) awaits their attention.

On the back cover: Top: A Hodaka sits atop a simple stand. A good, sturdy stand is essential for surviving any restoration project. **Right:** Kawasaki's W-2 650 has become a desirable Japanese classic motorcycle, and makes a great restoration project. **Left:** The author recommends you loosen the fork caps before removing the forks, unless there happens to be a half-inch-drive impact gun handy.

Edited by Lee Klancher
Designed by Bruce Leckie

Printed in the United States of America

Contents

Acknowledgments

Nothing happens in a vacuum, especially a book like this. Without the assistance of our friends we never could have done it. Jeff and I thank you for your patience, your help, and your encouragement. I'm certain we missed a few of you and for that I apologize; to all of you a heart felt thanks.

In no particular order thanks to Jaye Strait (Britech), Sean Lazzotte at Connecticut Cycle Refinishing, Phil Cheney, Ted Tine (Essex Motorsports), "Uncle" Hugh Weaver (Hugh's Bultaco), Sean Reynolds (Reynolds Racing), Ray Mancini (Mancini Racing), Alex Gifford (Branchville Motors), Pete Daitch (darkroom) Mike Davins (printer), Paul Stannard (Strictly Hodaka), Tommy Pirone (T.P Engineering), Rod Pink, and Dave Scheffer.

A special thanks to the guys at MBI, for whipping my scribbling into some semblance of order especially Jim Miller, Paul Froiland, and Lee "no more excuses" Klancher.

The following made their restored, treasured, and valuable motorcycles available to us for photos—usually on very short notice. Paul Miller, Charlie Mello, BMW N.A., Allan Chalk, Lindners Cycle Shop, Cal Reynolds, Jim Cooper, Karl Duffner, Rick Seto, and Robin Markey.

Thanks guys, we couldn't have done it with out you!

Foreword

I had a lot of fun putting this together. I hope the reader finds the information helpful. I'm sure that I'll be second-guessing it for a long time: thinking of items I should have included, people I should have mentioned, and finding a mistake or two I shouldn't have made.

If this book serves no other purpose, I want you to realize that anyone, anywhere should be able to restore a classic bike. I also want you to always remember that most of us got into riding motorcycles because it was fun. Restoring one should be at least as much fun. So get out there, find a bike, and have as much fun as you possibly can.

—Mark Zimmerman

Introduction

Restoring classic motorcycles is a challenging, rewarding pastime. It can also be time-consuming, expensive, and frustrating beyond belief. Restoration will teach you a little bit about history, a lot about mechanics, and fair amounts about frustration, patience, and determination. Occasionally and unfortunately, you might even learn something about first aid.

Until a very short time ago most riders—including yours truly—felt that motorcycles fit into one of two categories: new or old. For those with well-endowed bank accounts, new was always preferable to old. I began riding motorcycles in the mid-1960s. Since my income was derived solely from an after-school job pumping gas, I was solidly in the "old" category whether I liked it or not. A succession of motorcycles, all of them pretty tired, began passing through the family garage, much to the dismay, I might add, of my poor mother. I didn't so much restore these as resuscitate them.

In the process I learned something about mechanics, something about motorcycle design, and a lot about myself. I also swore that someday I'd earn enough money to buy a brand-new motorcycle, but that's another story. I hung around the local motorcycle shop so much that I was finally offered a job—in part I'm sure because they felt guilty about not paying me for all of the time I spent running errands for them. I progressed from "go-fer" to mechanic to service manager and eventually to a dealership of my own.

Along the way I witnessed the evolution not only of the motorcycle but also of motorcycling itself. The pushrod twins and lightweight two-strokes of my youth gave way to sophisticated multicylinder motorcycles that didn't leak, break, or require constant attention. While motorcycling was once considered an avocation of hooligans—at least in the United States—it began to acquire a mantle of respectability, thanks in part to Honda's "You Meet the Nicest People" ad campaign.

Along the way some of us began to realize we were losing an important aspect of motorcycling's heritage. (Not that we considered hooliganism an aspect worth saving.) As riders noted the passing of venerable marques, some became interested in preserving them, and the vintage movement began to grow. In truth there have always been clubs dedicated to the preservation and restoration of old motorcycles, such as the Vintage Motor Cycle Club in England and the Antique Motorcycle Club in the United States, but it's only been since the mid-1970s that the hobby of motorcycle restoring has really taken off.

This book is intended to help the novice restorer avoid some of the pitfalls that the rest of us have encountered. You won't avoid all of them—in fact, you'll probably stumble into a few new ones. But that's part of the fun, overcoming challenges.

This book is not intended to be a version of Motorcycle Mechanics 101. For better or worse, I'll assume that you have at least a passing knowledge of the basics. By the same token, if you were an expert mechanic/restorer, you presumably wouldn't need this book and I'd be going hungry. Nonetheless, armed with this book, some common sense, and the manufacturer's service and parts manuals you should be able to restore any motorcycle you set your heart on. I'll walk you through the general methods and procedures that are commonly used. I'll introduce you to specialists who can provide everything from the odd decal to a complete restoration. I'll even tell you when to farm out a job that requires special tools, knowledge, or talent.

Along the way I'll try to make the whole procedure as painless as possible. Hopefully you'll have a lot of fun doing it, learn something in the process, and ride the finished product with pride and enthusiasm.

WHY WE RESTORE

Why even bother to restore a motorcycle? I'm usually tempted to give the answer often printed on T-shirts: "If you have to ask you wouldn't understand." But that really doesn't explain it, does it?

Motorcycles are restored for a variety of reasons—nostalgia, for instance. Nostalgia can be insidious, in part because we so often view the past through rose-tinted goggles. I restored a BSA B25 once because I had so much fun on that model when I was still a leaky kid. I had forgotten what a truly terrible motorcycle it was, and soon after the restoration I disposed of it. I did have fun restoring it, though. If you want to restore a model simply because it brings back fond memories, by all means do so.

Some riders just like to be different. After all, being a little different is a big part of motorcycling in general. Restoring mainstream motorcycles—while challenging—is hardly as ambitious as tracking down and returning to "as new" a motorcycle as rare as, say, a 1939 Dollar 750. (Dollar was a builder in France between 1925 and 1939; only one of its shaft-driven 750s is known to exist. If you run across another, call me—collect!)

My own tastes, bankroll, and level of patience run more toward the mainstream. If you're interested in something more quirky, go for it. There are lots of odd bikes out there and they all need a loving hand to save them.

The "savior syndrome" is another reason to restore, and I confess I suffer from this myself. The savior syndrome means you just can't stand to see a bike, no matter how dubious its heritage, languish and die. Otherwise-rational men will spend hours devising a way to drag some rusting hulk 20 miles out of the woods to the nearest road and into their garage. Once it's in the garage they'll work morning, noon, and night on the bloody thing until it's perfect.

Subspecies of the "savior" will only try to save every model of a particular marque. For

Some guys "dream" about Hondas (sorry, I couldn't resist).

instance, I once decided to collect and restore one of every model of twin-cylinder Triumph. Ambitious, to say the least: that was 20 years ago and I'm still working on it.

Some guys (and girls) just want a bike they couldn't have or afford when it was new. Now that they've achieved a measure of financial stability and independence they can afford to relive their youth, this time on a 1967 Bonneville. When you're 45 or 50 and decide to buy a motorcycle, it's tough for Mom and Dad to say no. If that is still a problem, you obviously have some unresolved issues you need to deal with.

Some restorers just like to tinker, and nothing lends itself to tinkering like an old motorcycle, although I imagine a steam engine comes close.

Finally, some of you might be tempted to restore a bike in the hope that when it's done you'll be able to sell it for a big wad of cash and then buy something you really want. Bad plan. Very few restorers turn a profit—even the pros. If that's your aim I can tell you from lessons hard learned, that, in the end, chances are you'll finish in the red.

In short, while there are no wrong answers—save maybe turning a profit—there are lots of right ones. Perhaps the one most right is also the shortest: because it's fun.

WHEN TO RESTORE

That, as they say, is the question. Often a good case can be made for keeping a bike in its original, "as-found" state—particularly if it's in good running order and looks presentable. As a rule of thumb, original unrestored bikes are worth more as a collectible than restored ones. While I don't advocate collecting bikes for financial gain, the inescapable fact is that a lot of horse-trading goes on. Few of us are content to restore a bike and keep it forever; if you're one of those few, God bless. The rest of us, for various reasons, like to barter, swap, and buy.

Fact is, an unrestored version, in good repair, is almost always preferable to one that's

This fully equipped 1972 Moto Guzzi is used by its owner as his go to work/Sunday bike ride. It's still wearing the original paint. After 28 years it still looks great.

This decidedly nonstandard Commando has the complete go-fast package bolted on, including a dual Lockheed front brake setup and a Dunstall exhaust.

been restored. Why? The short answer is that the unrestored original is the real thing, and a bike is only "original" once. After the bike has been restored it's something less than that, no matter how perfect the restoration. An unrestored bike bears its scars proudly; it's a battle-hardened veteran. In my opinion it should be appreciated as such.

What constitutes good condition? That's something we all must decide for ourselves. It's one of those nebulous concepts. For one fellow it may mean a bike in showroom condition, for another it may simply be a bike that starts and runs. For the rest of us it's somewhere in between.

The other side of the same coin might be called the partial or incomplete restoration. Occasionally you'll find a bike that's cosmetically acceptable, but mechanically flawed or vice versa. It's perfectly acceptable to restore one or the other. But be forewarned: If, for instance, you do a full engine overhaul with powder-coated barrels and polished cases, the rest of the bike can suddenly get very shabby looking. Conversely, if the bike now looks immaculate but the engine leaks oil, runs rough as a cob, and clanks and bangs like an old harvester, it's probably not going to be much fun to ride.

The major argument against riding an as-found motorcycle would simply be that you have no practical way of assessing the bike's reliability—or rather, the lack thereof—short of riding it. In which case you may find yourself doing a lot of roadside mechanical evaluation and repair, the first time might make for an interesting story; the second, third, and fourth time it just gets old.

One of the incontrovertible truths in restoration is that no project is ever as simple as it seems. My advice is this: If it's a repair that's needed, fine. But if you're going to paint the frame, for instance, it hardly makes sense to remove all the components and reinstall them without giving each a thorough examination. What you should strive for in a partial restoration is simply a sense of balance. When you're done, no part of the bike should stand out from the rest.

Obviously there are lots of machines out there that require a complete and thorough restoration. These bikes include (but certainly aren't limited to) basket cases, bikes that have been thoroughly neglected, and bikes that are mechanically suspect. A full restoration in these cases might not only be the most practical way to get the bike up and running, it may well be required—and end up much cheaper in the long run.

Full, ground-up, or frame-up restorations afford certain advantages. For starters, they allow you to "learn as you go." For example, let's say that during the disassembly process you get a little overexuberant with that 36-inch adjustable wrench and wind the better part of a bolt off flush at the engine mount. No problem—you keep going, and once the motor's been removed and stripped, you do what you must to extract the broken bolt (don't worry we'll show you how).

Total restoration may also be the easiest route to take. If the frame and running gear look like hell, and the motor needs rebuilding why not do it all at once? Besides, once a total restoration is finished you should have a reliable, good-looking motorcycle that can be ridden anywhere.

There are a few downsides to a total restoration. It goes without saying that you'll probably be tying up your motorcycle for an extended period of time, perhaps a year or two. Obviously you won't be doing much riding on it until you're done. Which, of course, gives you a perfect excuse to buy another one to ride in the meantime. Your better half might not see the logic in that decision, but the rest of us certainly do.

Total restorations also cost a lot of money, but there are two sides to this. During a total restoration you can dole the cash out in small doses, which is somewhat less painful. By doing the brunt of the work yourself you can also keep the overall cost down to the minimum.

A REALISTIC LOOK AT YOUR ABILITIES

Let's be honest: We're all familiar with the old saying that the road to hell is paved with the best intentions. So it goes with motorcycle restoration. Many would-be restorers start out with the best intentions. Over time they start to lose interest. Eventually another bike hits the want ads: Basket case, partially restored, lost interest, cheap. Another potential show winner heads into the black hole of basket case hell. I'd estimate at least half of the restorations started are never finished.

Before taking on any type of restoration project you'll need to take a hard look at three things. Can you afford the cash outlay required to see the project through? Do you have the mechanical ability (or are you willing to acquire it)? And finally, are you willing to make an overall commitment to a project that could take several years, involve thousands of dollars, and frustrate you beyond all reason? Or would you rather just buy an already restored bike and ride off into the sunset?

DECISIONS, DECISIONS

At some point you're going to have to decide just what you want to do with your bike. Are you going to restore a bike to ride or are you going to restore one to catalog specification that will only be shown? While I think most of us assume we're going to ride our restored treasure, that's not always the case nor is it always practical. For the sake of argument, let's assume you've just finished a no-expense-spared, no-holds-barred restoration of an early Norton Manx. In a word, it's perfect. Obviously, the only fit place to ride the Manx, in fact the only legal place to ride the Manx, is on the racetrack. Since you have no intention of racing the Manx you have, in effect, created a static display of art. A trailer queen, so to speak. Its sole purpose is to be shown, usually as a testament to the owner's skills as a craftsman, or his wallet. While I enjoy vintage racing I can understand the Manx owner's reluctance to use his bike on the track, especially when there are so many replicated Manxes being raced.

Here's a similar situation—only this time it's a Norton Atlas built just to ride. While in both cases the mechanics must be done properly, (there's no excuse for a bike that doesn't run right, even if it's show only) the Atlas owner isn't bound by any particular need to slavishly re-create a bike in showroom condition. To that end he can replace the original bars, for example, with a bend he likes better. Since practicality takes precedence, he's free to powder-coat the frame, the better to withstand the rigors of daily use. Rather than rechrome or replace the original and hard-to-find Dunlop rims, he can opt for a set of alloys.

What do you want? is the question. Since I place a high value on having fun, I like to restore to ride, which I consider more fun. For starters, you can build what you want rather than what the factory delivered. Fancy a flamed paint job on that 1970 Bonneville? Go for it. Want a café racer sand-cast 750 Honda? It's yours for the building. Like lots of chrome

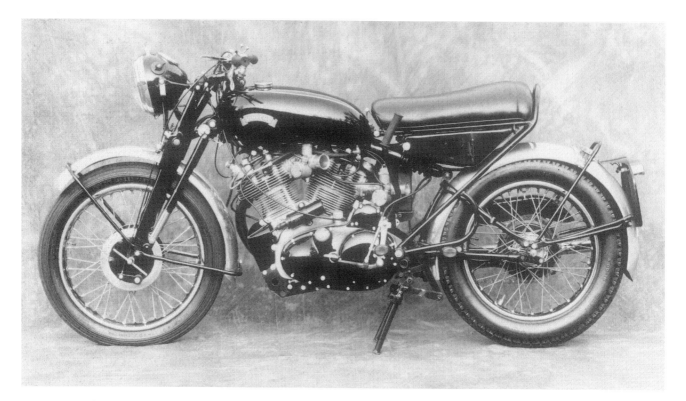

The mighty Vincent Temperamental, a challenging restoration, and exhilarating to ride.

and a powder-coated frame, or perhaps high handlebars and open megaphones on a 1968 Sportster? The sky, as they say, is the limit. A bike that's restored with an eye toward riding can be restored and/or modified any way you want, and there's a lot to be said for that. Not the least of which is that both time and money are saved.

On the other hand, it can become an obsession to restore bikes strictly to show. Original parts must be found or repaired. The restoration process can become extremely tiresome, ("Now exactly where does that low oil level decal belong?") and in many cases money flows like water. The fit and finish must be perfect—in almost every case far better than when it left the factory, and that costs money. The other side of the coin is that when the bikes are judged, someone is always disappointed. I have literally seen grown men cry when their bike and by extension their handiwork was judged and found wanting. No imperfection is tolerated. I've seen bikes lose concourses for everything from the wrong wiring harness clips to powder-coated frames. I once—and I swear I'm not making this up—heard a judge state that a Gold Star Catalina Scrambler should be eliminated because when the owner walked it across the wet field mud stuck to the tires

and "everyone knows, that's the wrong kind of mud." I presume he meant that only California or English mud was acceptable but I'll never know, 'cause I packed up at that point and rode my bike off into the sunset. The bottom line is that if you are preparing a bike just to show, prepare for a fair amount of heartache as well.

When I restore a bike I try to keep faith with the designer's intended purpose, but I also restore my bikes to ride. That means I upgrade the brakes and suspension if I feel it's required. I install the handlebars I like, and if I want I hang the exhaust system I like. If I feel like changing the color scheme, I'll do it. After all that's what I would have done had I purchased the bike new. Every once in a while I'll even enter a show and sometimes take home a trophy.

Building a bike to show and to ride are not mutually exclusive purposes. If you want to work to show standard, do so. It certainly won't prohibit you from riding the bike. But if you build a bike to ride, perhaps with the intent of occasionally showing it, you will have a little more leeway in the way you do it. For what it's worth, I've restored bikes to "catalog" and to ride. I've enjoyed doing it both ways, but in all honesty the bikes I've built as riders were always more fun.

What It's All About

Getting Started

WHICH BIKE IS RIGHT FOR YOU?

Which bike is right for you? Wow, talk about a loaded question. Picking a bike for someone is a lot like picking a wife (or husband)—it's just about impossible.

Instead, let me lay out some criteria you can use to decide which bike is right for you. Of course you might already have your mind made up—in that case, I'll try to either confirm you in (or dissuade you from) your choice!

Restorers may specialize in marque, model, era, or country of origin. Some like the challenge of restoring one-off race bikes or competition models. A few like to restore mundane utility bikes such as the BSA Bantam or Honda Super 90. And there are those that seek out the exotic, the esoteric, and the plain old weird.

As a novice restorer you must first decide where your interests lie. For example, you might be turned on by BMWs—perhaps you even own a current model. An older model BMW would be right up your alley—or so you think. Maybe you've always had the hots for one of those rorty British twins, perhaps a Triumph Bonneville or BSA Lightning would be just the ticket. Maybe a two-stroke hot rod like a Kawasaki H1. Or a popular choice: why not find and restore your first bike and return to the days of your youth? Pretty soon your head explodes and you decide to take up model railroading.

Actually, exploding heads—at least exploding human heads—are fairly rare. In fact, most of us already have a reasonably clear

A flawless example of a 600CC BMW R66 built between 1938 and 1941. The R66 makes a rare and challenging restoration. The finished product is well worth the effort.

idea of what kind of motorcycle we want to restore. The next question is, how practical is our choice?

Let's use the example of the BMW rider. He's decided that he'd like to restore an older BMW to go with his current street ride. He's looked around and decided that he wants one built before 1969. In fact, based on conversations with other BMW aficionados, he's decided that what he really wants is a 1961 500-cc R50 S. How practical is his choice, considering that it's his first restoration?

On the face of it, not too bad. Older BMs are fairly easy to work on, parts are readily available, and there is a wealth of easily accessible knowledge out there. Unfortunately, however, there is a slight drawback. The R50 S was made only from 1960 to 1962, the total production run a mere 1,634 bikes. Finding one will be a challenge, and finding parts peculiar to that model might prove even tougher. Furthermore, because the 50 S is so rare, our friend will pay a premium price for one.

A better choice would be the 600-cc R60, the 500cc R50 or even the sport version of the R60, the R69 S. Even the R69 S, the rarest of the aforementioned bikes, had a production run of nine years and 11,316 units. It's still an expensive project, but at least there are a few of them around.

There is another side to the coin. Let me recall a lesson hard learned. If, after all the pros and cons have been sifted through, our hypothetical friend still wants to restore an R50 S, then that's exactly what he should do. In my experience he won't be happy with anything less.

My advice, for what it's worth, is this: Start with a bike you have a genuine and abiding interest in restoring. Restoring a particular model because "it seemed like a good idea at the time" often turns out to be not such a good idea after some reflection. In truth, I've restored several bikes because they popped up when I had either the cash or the inclination (seldom at the same time) to take on another project. They were, however, all

Coming under the heading of "I had one of those," this 1968 Kawasaki W-2 650 is a desirable Japanese classic. Since I owned a 1967 version, the W-1, I've always had a soft spot for one.

This 1979 Triumph Bonneville just needs a little tidying up. Though not perfect, it's all there and—except for the aftermarket Dunstall mufflers (desirable in themselves)—almost 100 percent stock.

The "rolling basket case." This early YZ 250 needs a complete rebuild before it'll be race ready. But it looks to be complete with all the important parts intact. It runs, which is a plus, and the missing parts are easily replaced.

motorcycles that for one reason or another I had always wanted.

OLD WHEELS AND DEAD PRESIDENTS

Call it what you will: green, moolah, or plain old cash. A substantial amount of it generally changes hands during a restoration. One of the objects of this book is to keep that exchange to a minimum. Unfortunately, money makes the world go 'round, and you'll have to part with some of it.

Let's start with the actual buying of the bike. In many cases the purchase of the motorcycle turns out to be the least of your worries. It stands to reason that a rare bike will be more expensive than a common one. To a point that's true; just because a bike is scarce, though, doesn't mean its worth a big bag of dead presidents.

The 175-cc WSK, made in Poland, is relatively rare—it's also relatively worthless, in part because it's not much of a motorcycle. Conversely, 1970 and earlier Triumph Bonnevilles are reasonably easy to come by, but that doesn't

make them cheap. They command a good price because they are good motorcycles. Truly rare and desirable motorcycles such as the MV Augusta 750 Sports change hands at high enough prices to give us mere mortals a nose-bleed—at last count, upwards of 75 grand.

My advice to the neophyte restorer: Keep it in perspective. Lots of first-time restorations don't make it past the first lap. If you lose interest halfway through that BSA Thunderbolt, it's no big deal. If you throw in the towel on a Velocette Thruxton, however, it's going to cost you big bucks.

Other expenses will accrue at an alarming rate: parts, machine shop work, paint and chrome (even the beer and pizza tab). The list goes on and on. At some stage reality will rear its ugly head: You'll realize that either you've spent way more than the bike is worth, way more than you've intended, or way more than your spouse suspects you've spent. Usually it's a combination of all three. You have rather limited options at this point. You can rationalize ("But look how much fun I'm

The author's latest find: a complete, original 1972 Montesa Cota 247 Trials bike. This bike, in mint condition, was found at Hugh's Bultaco, semi-rare and in excellent condition. It was reasonably priced simply because not many people collect vintage Trials bikes.

having!"); you can bite the bullet ("It's expensive, but it's what I want."); or you can whine and bitch—which, while annoying, is a fairly popular option.

You can also follow my lead and simply destroy all the evidence. I'd like to tell you that you should prepare a budget and stick to it. You and I both know that it's not gonna happen. Basically you'll spend what money you have, when you have it.

There are two schools of thought at work here. Some restorers like to spend like drunken sailors until the project is done, and then pay the consequences. Some (and I include myself in this category) disburse the cash as it becomes available—pistons this week, bearings and valve guides next week. And of course there's always the ever-handy credit card when things get tough (resto by plastic). When it's all said and done, try not to miss too many mortgage payments, or let the kids go hungry for more than a week at a time. Other than that, you're on your own.

THE PAPER CHASE

The next step is to rush right out and buy a bike, right? Wrong. The next step, my friend, is probably the single most important aspect of motorcycle restoration. In a word, research. You're about to turn into a paper junkie.

Before you do anything more than contemplate your choice, you've absolutely, positively got to learn as much as possible about that particular motorcycle. Every motorcycle ever made has warts. Some are minor idiosyncrasies, others are major flaws. Better to discover now that your handsome prince (or princess) is really a toad than after umpteen dollars and untold hours of labor.

By the same token, you want to be sure that the bike you're considering is as correct and complete as possible. Motorcycles that have passed through several pairs of greasy hands are inevitably modified. It's not uncommon to find major differences between the original version and the "mildly customized" one. Forewarned, as they say, is forearmed.

Few serious collectors hold the 1971 Triumph- (BSA) 250 Trailblazer in high regard. That didn't stop this enthusiast from doing an outstanding job. These bikes are relatively inexpensive and make a good first effort.

Complete familiarity with the model you want minimizes the possibility that you'll be unpleasantly surprised at a later date.

Start by acquiring the appropriate buyer's guide. Quite a few good ones exist—in particular the Roy Bacon series. Bacon, a prolific writer if ever there was one, has covered most of the classic market with titles such as *Illustrated BSA Buyers Guide, Illustrated Norton Buyers Guide, Triumph Twin Restoration Guide,* etc. Bacon's buyer's guides provide you with a thumbnail description of each particular bike, technical features peculiar to each model, an overview of the marque, and an investment rating of each bike. The end papers contain an enormous amount of useful information as well: everything from motor/frame numbers to paint and trim options. His books are by no means the only ones out there, but in general they provide an excellent starting place.

There are also narrow-focus publications available, for instance David Gaylin's *Triumph Motorcycle Restoration Guide Bonneville & TR6 1956–1983,* or *How to Restore Your Vintage BMW,* by Roland Slabon and Steffan Knittel. Filled with tips, minutiae, and hard facts, books like these are a must-have for anyone planning a catalog restoration—one that brings a bike

back so it's exactly as it appeared in the maker's catalog.

Obviously, books are not your only source of information. They are convenient, though, and nothing looks better in your living room than a shelf of titles dedicated to classic motorcycles—at least that's what I tell my wife.

Motorcycle magazine articles, especially road tests, can be extremely helpful. In many cases they provide a look into the technical aspects of the bike, what the bike was like to ride when it was new, and how it was viewed in the context of its day. The photographs of the machine as tested are invaluable when it comes to detail items like cable routing, decal placement, and paint schemes.

Original magazines are available through specialty dealers and the back issue department of most of the periodicals themselves. There are also several reprint services available that can provide information on a specific model. Over the years *Cycle World* magazine has collected the road tests on a particular make or model into monographs titled, appropriately enough, "Cycle World on Triumph," or "BSA," or "Harley-Davidson," or whatever the case may be. These are collected road tests bound into one volume, and they generally cover a span of years such as, BMW from 1963 to 1973.

The Roy Bacon series of buyer's guides are invaluable. They contain lots of photos and all of the detail information you'll need to appraise the bike's originality or lack thereof. Bacon also rates the bikes as to their overall value, which may prove useful at bargaining time.

19

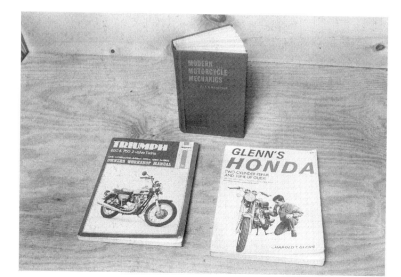

Service manuals are invaluable aids to restoration. Modern Motorcycle Mechanics covers many popular American, British, and Japanese models from the 1920s to the 1970s. It also has a great section on generic repairs, rebuilding generators, making cables, and so on. The vintage Glenn's manual is over 30 years old. It contains more info on vintage Honda twins than any manual I've found since. The Haynes manual is outstanding; it assumes you have no special tools or abilities. It walks you through repair procedures from start to finish.

Service and Parts Manuals

Manufacturers' service and parts manuals are invaluable aids in restoring your bike. In fact it's a pretty dim bulb that attempts a restoration without one. They also make for great late night reading, especially when you can't get to sleep. Most of us wait until we've already started to work on the bike before acquiring the shop manual. There is a certain amount of logic in that.

If you are in the market for a given model, having the service manual along when shopping for the bike makes identification and assessment that much easier. Unfortunately, in some cases they simply aren't available. I'm thinking here of very old or rare bikes—for example, I doubt that any parts or service manuals exist for the 1926 Eisenhammer 206cc TS (Germany 1923–1926). But if you've decided on a particular model, the service manual will help you determine if in fact the bike you're looking at did come with a 23-inch front wheel.

Factory service manuals contain everything you need to know about a particular model. Specifications and repair procedures, special tools, and the occasional production line modifications are laid out in a clear and (generally) concise manner. If you need to know piston-to-cylinder-wall clearances, connecting-rod length or fork-spring diameter, the service manual should list it.

There is one fly in the ointment, though: Factory service manuals are written for professional mechanics. They assume you possess a

Vintage wall charts like this Triumph suspension and engine blow-up make great shop decorations. They also help the visually impaired (such as yours truly) make certain that all the right pieces get put back in all the right spots!

certain degree of skill and knowledge. For the novice they can be needlessly complex. They also assume that you have access to factory tools and have been to factory service schools. If you're an experienced mechanic, they are invaluable. If not, they can confuse the hell out of you, especially when you get to the part that says damage to the frammis pin can occur unless special tool X-234 is used to secure the refractor fitting. Huh? It really gets interesting when the manual goes on to state "assemble in the reverse order of disassembly."

A better choice, particularly for those who "don't speak tech" might be one of the aftermarket manuals such as those published by Haynes. Haynes manuals are written specifically for the nonprofessional. The editor actually works on the motorcycle as the owner would. If a generic tool can be used to replace a factory one or an alternative method used, Haynes manuals spell it out. They also supply large blow-up diagrams and lots of photos. They usually provide an excellent alternative to the factory manual and are quite a bit cheaper to boot.

Parts manuals go hand in hand with service manuals. A parts book is simply a blown-up diagram of every single piece that makes up the motorcycle. The appropriate part number and a brief description identify every piece. They also show you where each part fits in relation to its neighbor—very helpful when whatever it is you're taking apart goes "sproing" in the night and a zillion pieces fly across the shop. Parts books are great for showing what the other guy left out as well. They also list the pertinent decals, stripes, and options for your bike. In fact, the parts book might well become your best friend.

Occasionally even the guys at the factory get it wrong, and when they do they issue a service bulletin. These describe where they went wrong, how they went wrong, and how to fix what went wrong. If you're lucky, the service manual might have these printed either as part of the text, or grouped together as an addendum. More often they will be found in a separate collection, usually a notebook.

Service bulletins can be hard to track down. Normally they are only sent to the dealerships, and quite frankly a lot of dealers typically threw them out, lost them, or filed them away, never to be seen again. If you can latch onto a set, great. If not, don't worry, most if

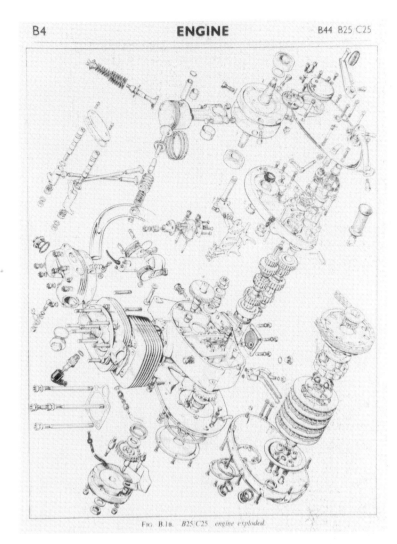

FIG. B.1B. *B25/C25 engine exploded.*

not all the info contained in them is probably common knowledge by now.

Sales Brochures and Magazine Ads

Over the years I've had a potential buyer insist that my 1967 BSA Spitfire never came with a fiberglass tank (it did), and a potential seller that was equally insistent that the 1970 Triumph TR6R came in metalflake blue (it didn't). In both cases I produced a color ad. The BSA was sold. The price of the Triumph substantially reduced (I still didn't buy it).

Because color sales brochures are a collectible in their own right, they can be tricky to find and expensive to buy when you do. Frankly, since they were a giveaway designed to entice buyers into the showroom, not many were put aside for posterity. In fact as soon as the new models came out, last year's brochures were generally tossed. Fortunately, a few pack rats always squirrel away such

I had to include this page from the BSA B-25. Former owners will know exactly why when they read the caption!

things for future use (or profit?). Today, several dealers carry old brochures, usually as an adjunct to other printed material. Full-color brochures are a terrific help—they clearly display color schemes or decal placement and often list options.

If the particular brochure you need can't be found, don't panic. Magazines are also an excellent source of full-color advertisements. Often these ads displayed the full product line in vivid colors and overwrought prose. It may take some detective work, but you can find many popular bikes from the 1970s displayed in full-color magazine ads—particularly the British bikes. (Who can forget the "Norton girls" or "BSA babes" of the late 1960s and early 1970s?)

As the quality of their bikes dropped, the British manufacturers began a full-court press on the advertising front.

Owners Clubs: Help When You Need It

When the Beatles sang, "I get by with a little help from my friends," I doubt they had motorcycle owners clubs in mind, but they might as well have. An owners club is very likely to become your largest single source of support.

Owners clubs provide a source of collective information, helping hands, advice, and in some cases a periodic newsletter—another excellent source for want ads, by the way. Many of the clubs hold regular meetings and group outings at which you can meet like-minded individuals. No matter what your particular problem, chances are someone, at some time, has been in the same pickle. At the very least you'll have a sympathetic shoulder to cry on.

Several larger owners clubs manufacture their own parts, and a few have a common tool crib, where special tools may be borrowed. An owners club may also provide a steady source of used and new parts, not to mention motorcycles. Besides it's fun to hang around with a bunch of folks who share the same obsession. ("Gee, I'm not so weird; there's 30 guys in the club and they're all as nutty as I am.") Kind of gives you a warm, fuzzy feeling, doesn't it?

Finding the right club is a pretty straightforward task. For instance, if your interest is Triumph, you join the Triumph International Owners Club. If it's old BMWs, look up the lederhosen-clad lads of the Vintage BMW Owners Club. While these are national or even international associations, you might also find a club that's somewhat smaller and closer to home, or local chapters of the national organizations.

Clubs are always on the prowl for new members; after all, there's strength in numbers. Finding one that suits your interests shouldn't be too difficult. Most clubs advertise in the various magazines, *Classic Bike, Old Bike Journal, Cycle News,* and so on. Finally, most marque clubs don't require you to own a bike to join; they require only an interest in that particular motorcycle.

Chapter
Two

Acquiring Your Bike

Now we're going to get serious. First let me disabuse you of the notion that lots of collectible vintage bikes are lying around in barns, basements, and garages waiting to be picked up for a song. They aren't. Twenty-five years ago this might have been true. Currently, it seems as if the pendulum has swung the other way. Acting on their "knowledgeable friend's" advice, it seems as if every yahoo with an old bike thinks it's classic, collectible, and worth a ton of money—sorry guys, Honda 400 Automatics are neither. But I digress.

THE BUDDY SYSTEM

Over the years at least half of my projects have come to me by word of mouth. Friends both in and out of the vintage motorcycle community always seem to know someone who wants to unload an "old bike" cheaply. Start there, and don't be afraid to make your desires known. If their efforts bear fruit, send them a bottle or two of their favorite adult beverage, smile, and say thank you.

YOUR FRIENDLY, LOCAL DEALER

The best place to start is a dealer either specializing in vintage bikes or one who's been around long enough to simply have accumulated lots of them. Why start at a dealer? To begin with, dealers are a lot more likely to either have what you want in stock or know where to get it. Secondly, because they are in

My friendly local Bultaco dealer is Hugh's Bultaco. If you need a Bultaco, or a part for one, he's got it. This photo is from the "Sherpa Stall."

This Guzzi dealer had a nice selection of T3s and Eldorados nestled among his new Sports and Bassas.

business, and typically intend to stay that way, they have a vested interest in keeping the customer—in this case, you—happy. And finally, while the dealer might charge top dollar, he usually has a very realistic idea of what top dollar is for a particular model.

The obvious also suggests that a specialist dealer will be able to provide parts sources, restoration services, and—if he's good—the occasional shoulder to cry on. And finally, bear in mind that should things go really wrong, at least you have some legal redress when doing business with a legitimate dealership.

There are literally thousands of vintage and special-interest motorcycle shops in the world—what the hell, there are probably a thousand right here in the United States. Whenever I'm in the mood for a new toy, that's where I start. Look for them in magazines catering to the vintage market, such as *Old Bike Journal, Walneck's Classic'fieds, Classic Bike,* and so on, as well as in the Yellow Pages,

or simply by word of mouth. Don't be put off by appearances. If you're used to modern dealerships, some of the old timers' shops can be a little disconcerting, although just as many look like NASA assembly bays, too.

Modern shops might seem like the last place to look for vintage project bikes, but remember, they are usually run by motorcycle enthusiasts. They take trade-ins, and if they've been in business for any length of time might have accumulated a considerable stock of motorcycles. A fair number of modern dealerships also price their "old crocks" very reasonably.

On a recent trip to my friendly local Honda dealership, for instance, I came across a pretty decent 1972 GT 750 Suzuki (with a four-leading-shoe front brake!). When I mentioned to old friendly local that the GT was fairly rare and collectible, he replied that he'd sat with it all summer, and collectible or not, if he didn't show a profit on it, it was just taking up space. A quick swipe of the old Visa card, and it was on its way to a new home—mine!

Don't misunderstand; I don't mean to imply that every dealership hides untold and reasonably priced treasure. But I can say that they are out there. Besides, where else can you use your credit card to buy an old bike?

WANT ADS

OK, you've haunted the local shops and nothing you've seen turns you on. There's always the want ads. I check the want ads religiously. In fact I check them every day. Not so much because I think I'll find anything of great value but simply because something odd or interesting might float by.

Don't limit yourself strictly to the motorcycle section, either. I check the estate sales, "tag" or lawn sales, and even the "free if you haul it away" section. You never know what might pop up. I also check the weekly shopper magazines with fervor. Occasionally you can find some real bargains in these. In fact, these are generally where you'll find that real deal. Aunt Tillie cleans her garage and decides to sell dear departed Uncle Buck's old motorcycle, cheap. Well Dear Old Auntie might not know what she's got to sell, but she does know that the "Want Ad Press," "Bargain News," and "Penny Saver" don't charge for their ads and that everyone seems to read them.

Still no luck? Well then it's off to the magazine rack. *Old Bike Journal, Classic Bike, Hemming's,* and *Walneck's* are your basic sources of supply. If you can't find what you want in one of these magazines—and there are a dozen more just like them—then you aren't half trying. These magazines exist to sell vintage bikes.

The downside is that most magazine advertisers want top dollar, and since many of them are spread across the country, it's tough to just hop in the car and go take a quick look. "Honey, I'm taking a quick ride to Arkansas to look at a bike" might prove problematic, especially if you live in Maine. Nonetheless, there are ways of dealing with the long-distance buy.

LONG-DISTANCE BUYING

It's a sad fact of life, but the global community really isn't. It often seems like the best deals and most interesting bikes lie on the other side of the continent. Buying long distance might complicate the sale; it shouldn't make it impossible.

Start by requesting photographs of the bike: front, both sides, and rear; documentation of the bike's condition; and a photocopy of the title or registration as proof of ownership. If the bike's a runner, request a short video of the bike being ridden or at least started and run. If the seller refuses to supply either photos or a video, pass on the sale, but understand also that you might lose the bike to someone who isn't quite so demanding.

If you decide to buy, try to arrange a mutually satisfactory compromise for delivery and final confirmation of the bike's condition. Perhaps the seller will be willing to meet you at the halfway point. If a face-to-face meeting is impossible, you'll just need a little trust. Personally, I must admit I'm not crazy about making a long distance deal. I've only been involved in two of them and in both instances the seller delivered the bike. In one case there turned out to be hidden frame damage and the bike went home with the seller. In the second case the bike suffered cosmetic damage during the trip and the seller adjusted the price. If there is any doubt request verifiable references, or pass. While you can certainly get burnt making a deal with your next door neighbor, the likelihood of getting screwed seems to increase with distance.

Also, try to include at least a portion of the shipping cost in the deal. See if the seller will either pay for shipping or deduct it from the purchase price. Occasionally he may even deliver it. Finally, there are a variety of professional shipping services that will pick up and deliver anywhere in the country.

THE SWAP MEET

My personal favorite, swap meets are terrific—a chance to meet old friends and make a few new ones. You can find everything from rough runners to restored concourse winners. Vendors sell new parts and accessories as well as take-off, damaged, and junk parts. It's like a huge treasure hunt. That scruffy guy with six tons of rusted, worn-out junk might have the one widget you've been looking for.

Swap meets are often set up to cater to a specific marque or country of origin. My favorite is the annual Triumph Day (which actually takes place over the whole weekend), held every June near historic Old Sturbridge, Massachusetts. You can find almost any British part or bike your heart desires.

If you can't find it here, don't worry: there's another swap meet somewhere next week. This shot was taken at the AMA's Vintage Motorcycle Days. In the foreground sits what looks like an old Greeves. In the background are enough Kawasaki fours to build your own race team. Swap meets yield an amazing array of bikes, parts, and good times. I know guys who haunt swap meets just to see what's there, and some of them don't even own a vintage bike!

Even if you don't buy anything, swap meets are wonderful sources of information and a great way to spend the day. Bring some cash; few vendors will take a personal check unless they know you. Lately, though, I have seen a few of the full-time vendor/dealers showing up with credit card machines. Oh yeah, don't be afraid to dicker; that's part of the fun.

AUCTIONS

Finally, there's the auction. Personally, I'm not a big fan of motorcycle auctions. The problem with an auction is that you can get

For all of you high rollers out there, the Jerry Wood auction. I suspect this one was from Daytona. Looks like a tasty U.K. Bonneville on the block. Auctions can get a little heated, but if you want a particular model, they may be your best bet. Like they say, though, spend with your head, not over it.

caught up in the heat of a bidding war. I have very little self-control. When the auctioneer says "Do I hear $7,550 for this beautiful, fully restored motorcycle?" I think to myself "Self, that's only $50 more than you were prepared to pay anyway." I trust you can see where this line of thinking is going.

If you rein in your wallet, though, auctions are fun to attend. You'll get to see what a wide variety of bikes are going for in the real world. Auctions are also where lots of high-end bikes are traded. Entire dealership inventories, memorabilia, tools, and anything else you can think of are also traded at auction. Several years ago the contents of Flint Indian Sales were auctioned off when the owner died. Flint was the Midwest distributor for Indian, Norton, and AJS motorcycles and also ran a huge retail store. Some of the lots up for bid included brand-new Norton and AJS motorcycles, new Indian frames and parts, and everything else needed to run several motorcycle shops. Needless to say, the sale generated millions of dollars over a three-day period. Big fun, if you can afford it.

Auctions: Let the Buyer Beware

While auctions all differ in detail, for the most part they run the same way. In general you'll arrive to find a large selection of bikes on display, with numbered tags and a brief description hanging from the handlebars. In some cases the owner may be standing near the bike to answer any questions. Depending on the auctioneer and the venue, you may be able to start the machine and hear it run.

The auctioneer usually lays out the ground rules right at the start. He'll establish the sale conditions and any buyer's commissions. A bike may be listed as having a "reserve"—the lowest price the owner will accept. Bidding should start at the reserve price and work its way up. If the bike you're interested in fails to sell, it's usually worth trying to make a private deal with the owner; after all, he's at least saving something on the auctioneer's commission. (It pays to be discreet here. Auctioneers tend to frown on these types of deals—and who can blame them?)

HUNTING WE SHALL GO

Part of the fun is in the chase. Once we've tracked our quarry down, we still have to capture it. In theory you've done your homework: you at least know what you want and what kind of money you're prepared to spend for a bike in a given condition. Of course, some particular bike may just catch your fancy at an opportune time—for me that would be when I had some expendable cash. Now that you've got it in your sights, you'll have to nail it down. In some ways this is the most difficult part of the restoration process, the negotiation.

At the risk of my becoming redundant, don't delude yourself. If it's a restoration project, can you handle it in terms of finance, time, and ability? A resounding YES is what I'd like to hear. Next, do you really want the bike, at any price? If you don't feel 100 percent comfortable with the machine, take a pass. It's neither the only one of its kind, nor the last one you'll ever see. If, after a quick look and a brief discussion with the owner, the answers to the above are all affirmative, it's time to get serious.

The first step I'll call Q&A: Get to know the seller. You're not going to marry the guy, but it's nice to know what his experience with the bike has been. A little diplomacy goes a long way here. You might like to know where the bike came from, how long he's had it, why he wants to sell it, and how firm he is on the price. His comments may be quite illuminating and the basis for your continued interest or an out-of-hand dismissal.

Remember knowledge is power—the more familiar you are with the bike, the better off you'll be. A snotty remark that no Norton ever came with such a ridiculous seat and those ridiculously high handlebars might be a real ego booster—until the owner points out that you're looking at an original 1973 Hi-Rider. At that point you may have to buy it just to save face!

Caveat Emptor: Buyer Beware

Now is also the time to determine if the bike in question is as represented. While true counterfeits are rare, they do occasionally surface, usually at the high end. For instance, it's relatively easy and—at better than $20,000 a copy for an original—economically worthwhile to convert an early round-case 750 Ducati twin into the Super-Sport version, complete with Desmo head. That doesn't, however, make it a true 750 SS, and an expert can tell the difference.

I have also seen mundane street bikes purporting to be historic race machines.

The frame number or vehicle identification number, stamped into the steering head, had better be there. The cellophane sticker may be missing. If the sticker is still there it should match the VIN number.

While Wayne Rainey's 1983 Championship winning Kawasaki Superbike might be out there and might be for sale, whoever owns it had better be able to provide plenty of documentation. By the same token, there are a fair number of race bikes for sale supposedly ridden by notable heroes. The legendary Mike Hailwood once commented that if he'd ridden all the bikes he was supposed to have, he'd have had damn little time for anything else. Take any claims of an illustrious history with a grain of salt unless the owner has sufficient documentation to back it up.

At the low end of the spectrum you may well run into a BSA Thunderbolt that's been converted into a Spitfire, or an A10 that has miraculously metamorphosed into a Rocket Gold Star. These bikes, as with the Ducati, can be tricky to spot, particularly if the bike is partially assembled or being sold as a basket case. Again, knowledge is your best defense. Usually the frame numbers will tell the truth—but not always, as these can and are altered by the unscrupulous.

THE NUMBERS GAME

The VIN, or vehicle identification number, will provide the basic information on the motorcycle's construction, including engine size, year, and model. Unless you're really familiar with the marque you'll need a buyer's guide, service manual, or parts manual to decode the number. Many (but by no means all) bikes have matching frame and engine numbers. This is where product knowledge really pays off. If the numbers on the bike should match and don't, you can either cut yourself a better

Unless it can be proved otherwise, all modern bikes carry matching engine and frame numbers. Triumph overstamped its numbers with the Triumph logo to prevent thieves from altering the number.

deal, or politely walk away. Obviously, if the bike came with non-matching numbers you can use your knowledge to determine whether or not the frame and engine actually belong together even though the numbers don't match.

It's also a good idea to find out what your state laws are regarding title information. Normally the frame number is stamped on the title. If the frame and title don't match, you've got big problems ahead of you. Find out why they don't and if the explanation won't hold water, pass.

Most sellers are trustworthy, and while they might be misinformed or just lack interest, few of them are out to intentionally screw you. But beware, there are a few bottom-feeders out there waiting to gobble up an innocent victim. Let's assume for the moment that our seller is honest. He's advertised the bike as a complete, non-running 1966 BSA 650cc Spitfire. You've done your research and know that the 1966 should wear a pair of GP AMAL Carbs and 190mm front brake. This one does. It also has the exhaust tie bar common to the 1966 Spitfire. However, it has a finned rocker box cover and a rotor access cover on the primary cover. Your buyer's guide and research tell you that the 1966 should have a smooth rocker box and one-piece primary cover. Is this the real thing or not?

A quick check of the frame number reveals that it is a genuine 1966 Spitfire. But low and behold the engine number doesn't match the frame number. No problem; prior to 1967 they don't. A little detective work reveals that the engine is actually from a later model—for the sake of argument, let's say a 1967. The explanation is easy enough, particularly in light of the fact that early Spits had a real penchant for self-destruction. Someone at sometime dropped in a late-model motor. The bike is still fun to ride. In fact, there might be a case to be made that the bike is still essentially "correct." Unfortunately for the serious collector, however, the bike is flawed. It has the wrong numbers and as such can never be correct.

Collectors place a high value on the "correct numbers." That means matching engine and frame numbers if the bike was so equipped, or the right sequence and serial numbers if it wasn't. Bikes with non-matching numbers are just as much fun to ride; unfortunately, they are also just as expensive to restore and the final product is worth quite a bit less. If the price is right and you aren't in it for the money, don't be put off by non-matching numbers. Be advised, however, that if you plan to show the bike, especially at AMC or VMCC meets, non-matching numbers or numbers in the incorrect sequence practically guarantee a back-of-the-pack finish.

MINT, ORIGINAL, AND READY TO SHOW

OK, you've seen the ad, called long distance, and spoken at length with the owner. Your search is nearing its logical conclusion. You dash to the bank and then make a 200-mile drive. The seller is waiting and the bike is . . . junk, pure and simple. Now what?

It's an unfortunate fact of life but "one man's ceiling is another man's floor." It happens; there really isn't much you can do about it. Avoid recriminations; resist the temptation to come back later and firebomb his home. Get back in the car, stop for a good meal, and chalk it up to experience. Sellers exaggerate—always have, always will. Before you go, pick up the local paper, check out the want ads; you never know what you'll turn up.

HORSE TRADING

I don't know why, but lots of collectors would just as soon swap and barter as sell for cash. I'm partial to it myself. For some reason it just makes the whole deal more fun. Don't be shy. Got something to trade? Offer it up, it just might make the deal.

Very often the seller may also be willing to throw in some "bonus" items if he senses it'll make the deal. These might take the form of spare parts, manuals, tools, or optional accessories. I've seen plenty of deals that included helmets, jackets, and memorabilia as well. Don't be shy, speak up; lots of guys before you have uttered those famous words, "So what else ya got to go with it?"

ASSESSING YOUR FIND

Buying a used motorcycle is an art in itself. Plenty of articles have been written on the purchase and assessment of used bikes. I ought to know—I've written a fair portion of them myself. Most of these have been geared toward the novice buyer. Since I'm assuming that you, gentle reader, have progressed beyond the novice stage, I'm going to gloss over the actual assessment process.

Inasmuch as this book concerns itself with restoring a motorcycle, as opposed to buying and riding off into the sunset on one, I thought we'd take a slightly different tack this time. Rather than writing a lengthy article on what to look for, I'm going to provide a sample worksheet. Use the worksheet to evaluate your potential purchase. Feel free to make a copy to take with you (you will anyway). Please don't hand out any copies to your buddies, however; Mr. Publisher frowns on copyright infringement. (Again, I know you will but the lawyers like stuff like that.)

This checklist applies mainly to a roller or runner. Basket cases are dealt with separately. If I could, I'd assign some sort of grading system to help you assess the bike,s "buyability." Unfortunately, I can't. The problem is that while I might buy a Triumph twin with a bad engine noise, or a bent frame but decent cosmetics, you might find the challenges of restoring such a bike daunting. Therefore, I'll leave the decision-making process up to you. But at least you'll know what to look for.

IN GENERAL

1. Is the bike complete?
2. Does it run?
3. Is it a rider?
4. Do the numbers match/have the right sequence?
5. Are all the parts there?
6. Is the bike cosmetically challenged?

THE EASY STUFF

7. Do the lights work?
8. Does the horn work?
9. Have the switches been replaced with aftermarket items? This might not be a bad idea on some bikes, particularly the Italian marques.
10. Are the levers and throttle straight, or will they need replacing?
11. Do the cables and controls work smoothly?

RUNNING GEAR

12. Is the fork straight?
13. Does it work smoothly?
14. Are the tubes rusted?
15. Do they leak?
16. Are the steering-head bearings worn out?
17. Is the front wheel straight?
18. Are the wheel bearings shot?
19. Is there any evidence of frame damage? Check the frame down tubes and the steering head.
20. Any play in the swingarm bearings?
21. Are the bearings adjustable?
22. Are the rear wheel bearings shot?
23. Does either wheel have missing or broken spokes?
24. Are the wheels in line?
25. Do the rear shocks work?

"Dunno, man; the engine looks a little tired. Got anything else to go with it?"

26. Are they bent?
27. If the bike uses a plunger-type suspension, check any brackets, links, and stays. Are they worn out?
28. Are the sprockets and chain salvageable?

ENGINE AND TRANSMISSION
29. Does the engine start easily?
30. Any odd noises?
31. Will it idle?
32. Does the engine leak?
33. Does the engine smoke or backfire? If possible, shift the bike into gear with the engine running and rear wheel clear of the ground.
34. Does the clutch disengage smoothly?
35. Does the transmission shift without a lot of effort?
36. Do the gears clash badly during shifts? Some bikes typically grind going into first gear, but the rest of the shifts should be smooth.
37. Does it jump out of gear? If you can take the bike for a quick spin, check it for abnormal noises, vibration, or handling quirks.
38. The big question, "What am I prepared to pay for this bike?"

In general if you come up with more noes than yeses, take a hike and move on to the next candidate.

BASKET CASES
Obviously, if the bike's a complete or partial basket case, the above list will probably come up short in the "yes" department. Basket cases must be assessed on slightly different criteria. The primary question, how much work am I willing to put into the bike?

A complete basket case is probably the most challenging and rewarding type of restoration. It's also among the most frustrating. Think long and hard before getting involved with a complete (or more likely, incomplete) basket case as your first restoration. My inclination is to tell novice restorers to avoid basket cases on the first go round. Then again, you're all big boys and girls and entitled to make up your own minds.

If you do decide to tackle a basket case, try to at least determine if any major chunks are missing. That might require some long hours with the shop and parts manuals for company but at least you'll have a fair idea of what's missing and the pieces you'll have to track down.

Chapter
Three

The Workshop

I t is all motorcyclists' right, be they male or female, to have a place they can call their own. For want of a better term we'll call this place our workshop.

Comedian George Carlin used to do a bit about his house. He said he needed a house for all his "stuff." Once he got his house he started to acquire more "stuff"; eventually he needed a bigger house. So it goes with shops. Once you have your shop set up you'll start to fill it with "stuff." Bikes, parts, tools, you know—stuff. Eventually, it will overflow into the basement, the attic, and your gym locker.

Over the years I've seen home workshops that put the average dealership to shame and I've seen sheds with dirt floors. I'd like to say that the quality of restoration is independent of the environment in which it's performed. I'd like to say that, but in my experience it's not true. An individual who takes pride in his tools and his shop will generally turn out better work than someone who doesn't.

It's also much easier to turn out good work if you're warm, dry, and comfortable. Having a safe and secure place to work can also keep tiny inquisitive hands safe from harm. Particularly the type of harm that comes to them when you find that they've decided to turn your precisely laid out and ready-to-assemble gearbox into a display of kinetic art.

Your shop is more than just a place to work. It serves as a secure site to store your bike. It provides a means to organize your "stuff." And it will give you a place to go and relax, to escape from the frustrations of the workaday world and occasionally create a few

new ones! Which is precisely why my shop door has a lock on the inside.

Setting up a dedicated shop is straightforward, and to my way of thinking almost as much fun as restoring a motorcycle. Let's go over the basics: You'll need a way to keep warm and dry. You need some place to store parts and tools in an organized manner. And pleasant working conditions. When you're done with your restoration you'll need some space to store your bike when you're not working on it or riding it.

Now, your shop doesn't necessarily have to be outside your house. My friend Dave likes to work on his projects in the living room. Dave is divorced. The rest of us will probably have to make do with either a garage, basement, shed, or spare room.

Starting at the bottom and working our way up, I'd have to say that the basement is probably, with some exceptions, not a good choice. Basements are below ground, which tends to make them damp. Many basements house the furnace and the water heater. Every time one or the other starts the temperature will rise by as much as 20 degrees in the immediate vicinity. The dampness and the constant rise and fall in temperature—particularly during the winter—can lead to a severe condensation problem.

Basements can also be awkward to get bikes into and out of. And I really don't think that you want to run engines, let alone store anything with gasoline in it, in your home (remember the water heater and furnace?). Considering the potential for disaster I would only use the basement for "dead" storage: i.e., no fuel in the tank and no battery. Besides, lots of basements double as laundry rooms, play rooms, and family storage areas. The disasters that can occur when you mix motorcycle restoration with the aforementioned situations are best left to the imagination.

Another major problem is lack of adequate ventilation: Every vapor, paint, solvent, oil, or whatever will permeate the entire house unless some sort of venting system is employed. It stinks and in fact could prove fatal. My wife threatens to kill me anytime I paint in the basement—expect no less from your spouse.

All kidding aside, the risks of fire and asphyxiation are too great to ignore, and on that basis alone I'd recommend against using your basement for a shop. In short, if your basement is the only realistic choice and you're prepared to make the necessary concessions to safety, then it will have to do. But please be extremely careful.

A better choice is the standard garage or even a small shed. If climatic conditions warrant, the building should be insulated and heated. How you heat it is your decision; however, I'd try to avoid wood stoves for two reasons. The first should be obvious: A wood-burning stove is essentially a steel box full of fire. To keep the fire going you must periodically open the door and add wood. Sparks fly; a gas tank or carburetor leaks, and in a graphic display of caloric energy release, no more shop.

Secondly, a wood stove should also be shut down whenever you're not in the shop. You're away all week, the temperature drops drastically, then comes the weekend. You fire up the stove, the temperature rises and bingo! Condensation: Water is everywhere. Eventually the stove dries everything off again. But some damage is done. A better, albeit somewhat more expensive solution is some sort of thermostatically controlled heat. This can be set low when you're not in the shop and then simply turned up when you plan a little work.

The shop should also be well lit. Double-bulb fluorescent lights are available in every hardware store and lumberyard in the country for around $10. You might also be tempted by the newer halogen shop lights, but be aware that they produce a lot of heat as well as light—great for winter, bad for summer. In ei-

ther case, buy as many as you need. That way when the little "widget" hits the floor you'll at least be able to find it again.

Speaking of light, a coat or two of paint works wonders. You'll be amazed at how bright the old cavern looks after a splash of semi-gloss white hits the walls. Before you paint, though, decide what you want on the walls themselves. I'd recommend a few pieces of pegboard. Use the ones with the [insert number] -inch holes. The larger pegs will support tools and shelves better than those cheap 1/8-inch ones.

After the paint, throw up some artwork to brighten the place up. My personal tastes run toward motorcycle shop freebies and the ever-popular poker-playing dogs. Oh yeah—don't forget the radio and refrigerator; tunes help pass the time and the 'fridge keeps those thirst quenchers cold—useful for chilling bearings, too!

One last thought: You can't have too many electrical outlets. The thought of extension cords running hither and yon, all carrying the potential to trip you, electrocute you, or otherwise ruin your day, leaves a lot to be desired.

SETTING UP SHOP

The rule here is, whatever works for you. You'll need at minimum a solid workbench, some means of supporting the bike, and shelving capable of holding up a few hundred pounds. Shelving and benches can be purchased or constructed. In the long run it seems as if the final cost is about the same.

Of course, when you're in the business, your shelves need to be a little stronger and better stocked.

33

A simple, neat, and efficient home workshop. The benches are constructed of 2x4s with a 3/4-inch exterior grade plywood top. There is plenty of underbench storage available, including a dedicated spot for the compressor. Judging by the selection of tools hanging from the pegboard, the owner appears to be a Triumph enthusiast. Note that air is available at the vise end of the workbench as well as in the center, and that the electrical outlets are centrally located.

For home use I prefer a sturdy wooden workbench to one of those gray industrial steel ones. If you'd rather bolt one together, most industrial supply shops carry heavy-duty steel benches in a variety of forms. They also sell steel legs, you just bolt on the wooden top of your choice. Since my interest in carpentry—as well as my skills—place a distant second to almost everything else, I prefer simple and sturdy designs. Feel free to embellish your workbench with drawers, secret compartments, and other clever features.

The basic bench should be around 33 inches high, from the floor to the working surface. The legs should be a minimum of 2x4 construction, preferably 4x4. Likewise, the rails should be constructed from 2x4s. The top should be at least 1 1/2 inches thick, and as wide as practical. I cover the tops of my benches with a piece of 3/4-inch exterior plywood. Space the legs no more than 4 feet apart. If possible, bolt the bench to both the floor and wall.

Bolt the best vise you can afford to one end—that's another item to look for at swap meets, by the way. If you want, screw down a good size hunk of sheet metal to the bench top. This will give you an easily cleaned, durable area to work on heavy chunks such as engines and transmissions. A piece of angle iron bolted along one edge of the top will give you the poor man's sheet metal brake. When you're done, varnish the whole thing and then build some shelves to match.

Shelves are constructed much the same as a workbench, just taller and thinner. Make

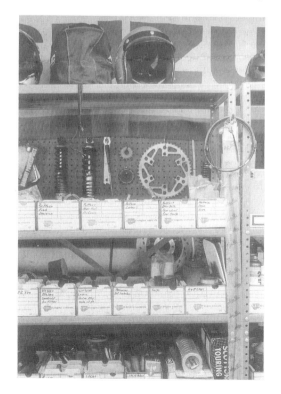

Sturdy steel shelves can be found for under $50.

The author's ancient and sturdy vise. It's been beat on, abused, and hammered to within an inch of its life. It's every bit of 30 years old, and I expect to get at least another 30 years out of it.

A Word on the Vise

them strong and wide enough to hold the largest piece you plan to heave on them, usually an engine. For myself, I'd just as soon buy nice sturdy steel ones. They only cost about 50 bucks, are a lot more durable, and they take a lot less time to build.

Buy the biggest, best vise you can afford—a good one can run more than $300 but will last forever, so swap meets and antique shops are as good a source as your neighborhood hardware store. Get one with pipe jaws for securing round objects, soft jaw inserts to avoid

We cheated a little: The big lift is an electric table lift made by Western Manufacturing. The Hodaka is sitting on a generic motorcycle stand that a friend gave me about 15 years ago.

marring the work, and an anvil so you can hammer away without concern. Bolt it solidly to the workbench. Oil the moving parts occasionally. Use it for a lifetime and then will it to your heirs.

The Motorcycle Stand Dilemma

After working on motorcycles for almost 30 years, I can tell you this: Working on the floor stinks. It's uncomfortable, inconvenient, and downright unnecessary. Before you even think about restoring your bike, buy or build some sort of work stand.

Drive-on stands are terrific for routine maintenance as well as restoration work. The best ones are height adjustable, ensuring a comfortable work level no matter what the task. Unfortunately, they are also fairly expensive. Lifts may be powered by electricity—normally 110 volts. For air, the compressor should be at least 4 horsepower. The leg-powered ones usually require a healthy lad somewhere near the age of 14.

Electric and air-powered lifts start at about $750. Foot pump hydraulic lifts, somewhere near $1,000. You can probably knock together a decent wooden work stand for $100 or less. If you decide to build one, make it about 3 feet high, 3 feet wide, and 7 feet long. Once you've used a bike lift you'll wonder how you survived without one.

If you decide against a lift, an alternative you might want to consider is a simple bike jack. Bike jacks are lifting devices that pick the bike up anywhere from 1 to 3 feet. Designed to slip under the frame rails, a bike jack will allow you to remove the wheels, fork, and swingarm from the main frame without wrestling the bulk of the motorcycle. A few of them have wheel kits, handy for wheeling the semi-finished bike out of the way, but they can be tippy. Normally, bike jacks go for around $300.

If you're so inclined and the bike is light enough, you can probably bang out a simple wooden platform, similar in shape to one of

A small bike lift may be all you need. This version lifts the bike about 2 feet in the air. Both wheels are well clear of the ground. The wheels on this lift let you move it any place you like—a handy feature when the bike is tied up for long periods of time.

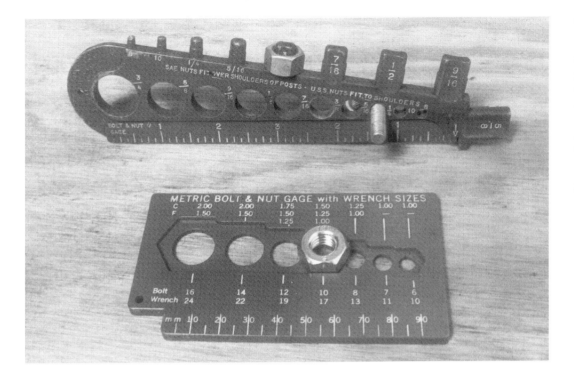

These plastic measuring devices are handy as all get out when it comes to determining what kind of hardware is on your bike. These were hardware store giveaway items, but they can be purchased for a buck or two.

those aluminum dirt bike stands. It'll work fine if you're restoring an ultra lightweight or dirt bike.

TOOLS, BASIC

I confess I'm a tool "junkie," a fool for a tool, so to speak. I like to buy and use tools. Chances are you're one too; you may not even know it yet. Restoring a bike gives you the perfect excuse to go out and stock up on a wide variety of tools, some of which may even turn out to be useful. As I said in the beginning, this book isn't a course in basic mechanics. I don't intend to list every tool you're going to need, but let's touch on the basics.

At the very least you'll need a good set of basic hand tools. By basic I mean enough wrenches, sockets, pliers, screwdrivers, and hammers to get the job done, plus an assortment of specialized tools. If your idea of a basic set consists of a pair of water-pump pliers and one of those four-way screwdrivers, it's time to take a trip down to your local tool emporium.

It goes without saying that the tools should be in good repair and fit the hardware on your motorcycle. If the bike uses metric fasteners, a box full of SAE (known as inch, fractional, or "American") wrenches won't take you very far. British bikes will require a mix of SAE, Whitworth, and in some cases metric tools. While everyone knows where to get met-

ric and SAE-sized tools, some of you might be a little foggy on finding Whitworth stuff. Try British bike shops, foreign car parts outlets, and specialty tool dealers. You can expect to pay a premium from the latter.

HARDWARE: THE WRENCHING EXPERIENCE

Most bikes use hardware peculiar to their nation's system of measurement, i.e., metric, SAE, or Whitworth. Some bikes, however, use a mix-and-match of thread dimensions that will make a strong man weep. For instance, late-model Triumphs will require a set of SAE,

A thread gauge is invaluable when it comes to determining pitch. They are available in SAE, Whitworth, and Metric dimensions.

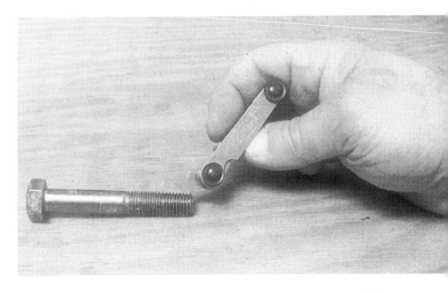

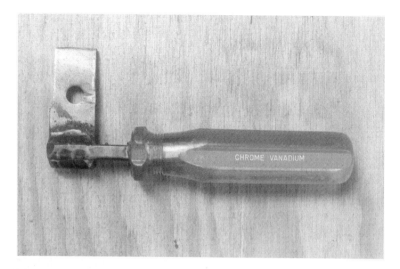

Over the years I've accumulated enough oddball stuff to sink a ship. From left, this Mikuni oil pump gauge is all you need to properly set up any Japanese two-stroke. Oil pump shims are stored under the dome. In the middle is a tool to remove the valve spring-torsion bars on Honda CB and CL 450s. Right is a Kawasaki valve shim tool.

Not all tools need be bought. This tool is one I made to install new clutch hub cush drive rubbers in a Triumph Trident. The tang fits in the drive spline and allows me to rotate the inner hub against the tension of the new rubbers.

metric, and Whitworth wrenches and sockets as well as Allen wrenches and a Pozi-Drive screwdriver. Late-model Harleys use a mix of metric and SAE bolts and screws.

Japanese and European bikes generally stick with metrics, so you should be safe with metric tools. A good habit to acquire is to trial fit the wrench or socket to the bolt before yanking away at it. If the 1/2-inch wrench seems a little loose, try the 5/16 Whitworth or 13mm metric until you find the best fit.

When I said a good set of basic tools, that's exactly what I meant. Craftsmen, S-K,

Husky, and a variety of other manufacturers make good basic tools. They are available at Sears stores, auto parts stores, and discount stores the world over. They are inexpensive and carry a lifetime guarantee. At the other extreme, Snap-On tools are among the best in the world and they cost it. Unless you are a professional mechanic there is little need to go out and spend a ton of money on basic hand tools.

When you're in the restoration business, it pays to have all of the special tools. Britech specializes in British bikes in general, Triumph in particular.

Having made that statement, let me qualify it. There are instances when only a Snap-On socket or screwdriver is capable of loosening a frozen or rusted-in fastener without destroying it. Snap-On uses what it calls (and has patented) "Flank Drive." Suffice to say that it works. There are other ways to remove the offending bolt, nut, or screw, but if you want to reuse it and Snap-On can supply the correct tool to fit it, pay what they want for the damn thing.

Please don't read this the wrong way, Snap-On stuff is first-rate; it's just prohibitively expensive for the casual user. Personally, I'd just as soon buy less-expensive brand-name tools and spend the money I save on the bike.

SPECIAL TOOLS

Occasionally the need will arise for a special tool. Some of these—threaded pullers for removing gears and hubs, for instance—are a must-have and you'll be forced to beg, borrow, or steal them. Others—such as a pre-1971 Triumph fork tube installation tool—can be improvised. Many can be created in-house. For instance, the piston-holding jig shown in the illustration on page [insert page number] can be adapted to a wide variety of uses. The Trident clutch tool, crude as it might be, is invaluable when the hub has to be rebuilt on the T150/160 or BSA Triple.

Some special tools can be dispensed with altogether. For instance, the Norton rocker-shaft puller is easily replaced with an appro-

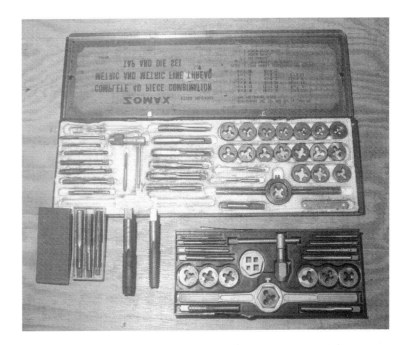

priate bolt and spacer. Likewise, the advance unit on many British bikes is easily removed by replacing the securing bolt with a screwdriver or piece of round stock and giving a wiggle. In general, your service manual will tell you when a special tool is required and when the generic equivalent might be substituted. Specialty shops can also provide you with information about alternatives.

DRILLS, TAPS, AND FILES

You don't have to go overboard here. Buy a small selection to start with and add to it

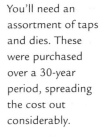

You'll need an assortment of taps and dies. These were purchased over a 30-year period, spreading the cost out considerably.

Yes, there are a lot of files and, yes, I use them all. The jewelers files in the pouch come in handy for polishing out small imperfections, the big bugger on top for roughing out big slabs of metal; the rest fall somewhere in the middle.

when you must. For general motorcycle work a drill index from 1/16 to 3/8 will cover most situations; buy the larger sizes as required. Taps and dies follow the same line of reasoning. Start with a basic set and add the odd sizes when need dictates. Files are generally purchased as a set. You'll need at least one flat, one round, and one half-round. A set of small jeweler's or modeler's files comes in handy for fine work.

THINGS THAT GO WHIR, BUZZ, AND CLICK—POWER TOOLS

The most common power tool is without a doubt a drill. Most of us already own one and use it for a variety of household tasks, not all of them found in the manufacturer's catalog of common uses.

For most motorcycle work a variable-speed 1/4-horsepower drill with a 3/8-inch chuck is plenty, although, at some point you'll start looking for a 1/2-inch drill, or at least a chuck of that capacity. To be honest I probably use the 1/2-inch drill more for light work—drilling mounting holes in the plastic fenders of my dirt bike, for instance—simply because it holds a 7/16ths (11mm) bit. Expect to pay at least $50 for a decent 3/8ths drill, somewhat more for a 1/2-inch.

Next on the most-useful list is a common bench grinder. Bench grinders make short work of most small polishing, cleaning, and shaping jobs. Generally, a grinder is most useful when one side carries a wire wheel and the other a grinding stone. Keep a spare buffing wheel handy and you're good to go. Look for at least 1/2 horsepower, and a 6-inch wheel. Pick up a pair of safety goggles (or a face shield) and a grinding wheel dresser (for dressing and truing the wheels) at the same time. Good grinders start in the $65 and up range.

As far as goggles go, I cannot stress the importance of eye protection enough. Grinding wheels are brittle and have been known to shatter. Average wheel speed is usually around 3,500 rpm. At that speed, I've seen them break and embed the chunks in a concrete wall. Please, for your own safety, wear some type of eye protection anytime you work at your grinder.

A couple other tools fall into the whir, buzz category. While strictly speaking they may not be a necessity, they do make life easier.

If you can swing it, a drill press makes a lot of sense. A press can drill holes with near-perfect accuracy. Drill presses are invaluable when it's time to drill out that broken bolt. Instead of chasing a skittering drill bit across the work surface while you contort your body into some unnatural position, you can place the damaged piece in the drill press vise, position it directly beneath the bit, and bore a true hole.

On the other end of the scale, the hand-held die grinder, the most common of which is a Dremel Tool, is almost invaluable. Its small size lets you cut, grind, drill, and polish in areas that would be inaccessible to anything larger. Plus, the reinforced fiberglass cut-off wheels available for these grinders are a godsend for cutting bolts or light metal pieces.

Most home restorers should be able to get by with a relatively small drill press. I found this one at a tag sale for $25. It has a 1/2-inch chuck, which makes it really versatile.

A small washer tank can be had for about $100. I picked this one up at the local auto parts store. It easily handles a twin-cylinder head.

BIG STUFF

Big stuff includes compressors, glass beaders, parts washers, power washers, and impact tools.

The compressor is more or less a necessity. You might be able to live without one, but once you install one you'll be amazed at how often you use it. Compressed air is perfect for drying off freshly washed parts, cleaning out small carburetor passages, and powering a wide variety of tools. You can always justify the purchase by telling your wife that you need it to blow up the car tires and the kid's basketball.

A decent compressor using between 2 and 5 horsepower is available from about $200 to $600. The size you require will depend on how much air you need and how much amperage your shop's electric service carries. If you plan to do a lot with air tools or spray paint, you'll require a larger compressor than if you're simply blowing off a few parts or inflating the occasional tire. Make sure your choice doesn't overload your electrical circuits, though. I know one fellow who has to shut down every appliance in his house before he can fire up his 5-horsepower unit without blowing a fuse—which is what his wife does every time he fires up the compressor.

Likewise, a parts washer of one sort or another is an absolute requirement. It won't matter if you build one, buy one, or rent one, as long as you have one. Small parts washers suitable for home use are available from auto parts stores, tool suppliers, and specialty manufacturers. Solvent is available through most auto parts stores.

While a practical parts washer can be had for under a hundred dollars, you might decide that you'd rather "roll your own." Resist the temptation to simply pour a few gallons of high test into an old dish pan and have at it, unless of course you like burning down buildings, motorcycles, and anything else combustible in the immediate vicinity.

If you decide to go the cheap route you'll need something to hold the cleaning medium. Before I bought my washer I used an old free-standing laundry sink and five gallons of commercially available solvent. With the stopper in place I'd pour my solvent—which I kept stored in its original five-gallon container—into the sink. I used a small wire rack to which I'd brazed four legs to support the parts. A stiff bristle brush did the rest. When I finished, I removed the stopper and drained the solvent back into its container.

You can also wash down parts with Gunk or some other degreaser—careful, though, the degreaser might eat through your asphalt driveway. As when working with all solvents, appropriate safety attire should always be worn—that includes rubber gloves and eye protection.

If you can afford it, a glass-beading or sand-blasting cabinet is like a gift from heaven. All sorts of parts can be cleaned and de-rusted in a matter of minutes. You'll need a substantial compressor to power up the "beader" and

A small pressure washer will handle most of the cleanup chores associated with restoration. Available at any home improvement center, they can be had for under $200.

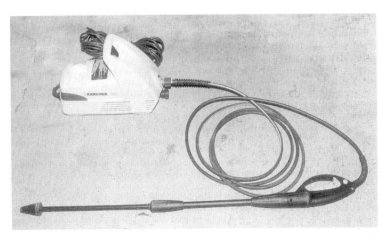

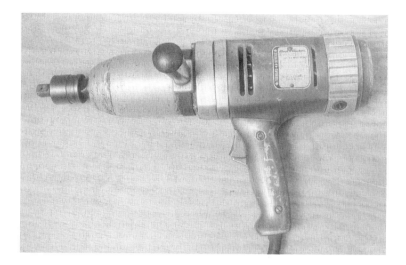

This electric impact gun is so old I can't remember where it came from. It still works like a champ, though. Very helpful for removing large stubborn nuts and bolts.

for a one-time restoration they really don't make good economic sense. On the other hand, if you plan to spend the rest of your life restoring things that might need to be painted, polished, or stripped, a glass beader is definitely the hot setup. There are definite pros and cons to glass beading and we'll discuss those as well as the alternatives in another chapter.

While a pressure washer might not be a strict necessity, it's certainly handy to have, particularly if you decide to restore and ride a vintage dirt bike. It's also useful for cleaning up the driveway and shop floor after you've made a mess of them cleaning up the bike. In fact, you can use it to wash your car, house, clean the gutters, the lawn mower, and so on, which should go a long way toward justifying its purchase.

A 3/8ths "butterfly" or "palm" impact gun is perfect for working on motorcycles. This Chicago Pneumatic has a five-position limit dial that cuts down air pressure (and torque) to avoid damaging small fasteners.

POWER IMPACT TOOLS

By and large I'm not a big fan of using power impact tools for motorcycle work, since they can easily create as much damage as they repair. The exception is the removal of large high-torque fasteners, such as clutch hub nuts, crankshaft and mainshaft nuts, and engine mounts. They're also handy for nuts and bolts that need to be shocked loose, such as fork damper-rod retaining bolts or countershaft sprocket nuts.

In 9 out of 10 cases a 3/8-drive impact gun should suffice—in the tenth case you'll probably need a 1/2-inch gun. If you don't have a compressor there are several electrical impact guns on the market that should accomplish the same task. As with most things there are alternative methods for removing recalcitrant hardware, and I will discuss those at the appropriate times.

Suffice it to say that unless special circumstances prevail, you shouldn't use impact tools to assemble vintage motorcycles.

WELDERS, TORCHES, AND SOLDERING IRONS

Welding, brazing, and soldering are the three most common methods of joining metal together via heat. Soldering and brazing both use a relatively low temperature flame to join two pieces of metal by using a third, softer alloy as a binding agent. Solder is composed of a mixture of tin and lead. Solder might also contain flux at its core. Most brazing rods are brass alloys, although bronze is also used.

The base metal isn't melted when soldering or brazing. Rather, the pieces are literally "glued" together by the introduction of the soft, molten alloy. When the alloy melts, capillary action draws it into the joint. As the parts cool the alloy hardens and joins the two pieces together.

Welding actually melts the pieces together. Normally a filler rod is added to strengthen the joint. Welding rod comes in every style you can imagine: mild steel, cast iron, stainless, and aluminum are a few of the more common types.

While many of us have picked up the basic techniques along the way, some specialized instruction might be required before we start welding on our motorcycles. Adult education classes and welding supply shops usually offer some sort of introductory welding course. Most of the metal joining you'll perform while

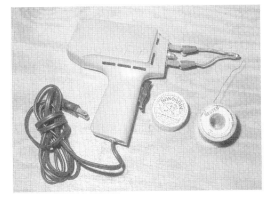

You'll need a soldering iron of at least 200 watts. The flux is used for cables or repairing sheet metal. Never use flux on electrical connections.

The good old propane torch. I use mine to heat up parts that need heating, solder up everything from cables to fuel tanks, and light the cheap stogies that I'm partial to.

The oxygen-acetylene torch can be put to a variety of uses: It'll heat, cut, solder, braze, and weld. If you plan on doing lots of fabrication, the oxygen-acetylene torch should be on your must-have list.

The electric arc welder is a little much for most motorcycle work. It can be useful when repairing heavy pieces or building fixtures, but in general I think it has limited use in most motorcycle work.

The MIG welder, or "squirt gun," is a terrific welder for general motorcycle use. Its forte is welding light gauge metal with a minimum of distortion.

restoring your vintage bike will be of the straightforward, broken bracket, or cracked fender school. Unless you really can weld up the proverbial crack of dawn (that's a welder's joke, son, get it?), I'd leave the frame and exotic alloy repairs to the pros.

As a matter of course, motorcycle restoration work will require soldering electrical connections and possibly leading or building up body parts with solder. You might also need to solder the occasional leaky fuel tank. Brazing is required to attach brackets and mounts. As an alternative they can be welded, but welding is generally used to build up worn parts, or to repair broken ones that require something stronger than a soldered or brazed joint.

Equipment

For soldering, a nice 300-watt electric gun is tough to beat. As is the good old-fashioned propane torch. For common garden-variety motorcycle repair, I'd recommend nothing more sophisticated than a set of torches.

A decent oxygen-acetylene outfit will let you heat, braze, solder, cut, and weld. The whole rig, including bottles, should set you back less than $500. Tell the nice man at the welding supply shop what you intend to do and he'll set you up with the right outfit and probably throw in a free hat. At the most you'll need an outfit capable of welding metal 1/2-inch thick.

I'd avoid electric arc, or "stick" welders, they're much too cumbersome and weld at too high an amperage for most motorcycle work. Likewise, I'd shun those inexpensive AC current "buzz boxes" like the plague. With one of those you can do more damage to a motorcycle in two minutes than you can repair in a day. MIG welders (wire-fed, metal-shielded gas welding) are handy for attaching brackets and repairing sheet metal but you can't braze, solder, or cut with them.

Take the time to familiarize yourself with the various techniques involved at the beginning. By the time you actually need to call on those skills, you'll find you're much more confident and less likely to create additional problems.

EXPENDABLES

By expendables we mean shop supplies that you use up: aerosol sprays, rags, welding gases, oil, grease, rags, and every once in a while, your patience. I'm tempted to tell you to lay in a good supply of everything you'll need and leave you to your fate. But since you've stuck with me this far I'll leave you with a list of what I normally stock and suggest that it's the minimum you'll need to keep from running out to the store every hour or so.

1. Single-edge razor blades, handy for slicing and dicing.
2. Rags—you can't have too many shop rags; use them and lose 'em.
3. Paper towels: plain or fancy, heavy-duty, or cheap generic. You'll use them by the yard.
4. Waterless hand cleaner, unless you like to hear the distaff side yelling about grease on the doorknobs.
5. Sandpaper in various grades. I always seem to run out of what I need at the most inopportune times.
6. Scotch Bright: see above, under sandpaper.
7. Various weights of grease and oil. You'll accumulate these a lot faster than you can imagine. We'll discuss them in the appropriate chapters.
8. Loctite; old bikes do vibrate.
9. Mechanic's and safety wire, for tying and binding—especially handy for those pesky little urchins that always seem to be underfoot.
10. Various penetrating, lubricating, and assembly oils such as WD-40, CRC, Belray 6

in 1, STP, and so on, not to mention anti-seize compound.

11. Polish and wax: see no. 7.
12. Brake, carb, and contact cleaners.
13. Skin cream. Believe me, working on machinery will give you chapped hands that hurt like nobody's business. A little hand cream will keep cracks and bleeding to a minimum.

There you have it. A baker's dozen of the most common expendable items. Of course, you'll add plenty of others to the list as you go—both patience and cash come to mind almost immediately!

FIRE AND TRASH

Trash creates a potential fire hazard. Add oily rags, grease-soaked cardboard, half-empty cans of paint, thinner, various solvents, and moldy half-eaten pizza, and what you have here, son, is a fire waiting to happen. Can you say "spontaneous combustion"? Like they say, "An ounce of prevention is worth a pound of cure."

Rapid and proper disposal of your trash is one way to prevent a fire. As a matter of practicality, however, at least some of it will have to accumulate. Take my advice and use a steel trash can, preferably one with a tight-fitting top. I use an old 25-gallon grease drum; I empty it when it's full and if anything combustible goes in it, I empty it that day; occasionally I'll even wet down the oily rags or whatever.

Overkill, maybe, but I've seen three shops go up in smoke. Two were total losses—tools, bikes, the works. The third kept us closed for a week while we made repairs. A wood stove left unattended caused one fire. One occurred due to a shorted starter solenoid in a personal watercraft, the third by a welder's spark.

If the unimaginable happens, a fire extinguisher might save your shop and possibly your life. Fire extinguisher guidelines are sim-

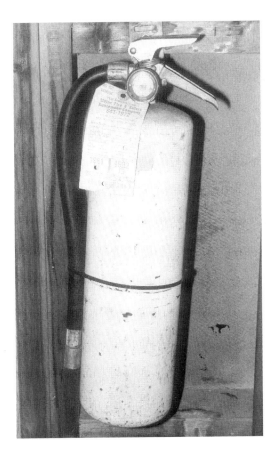

When I saw this photo, I couldn't believe it. Check out the last inspection tag! And this one was in my shop.

ple and straightforward. Buy only an ABC (all fires) -rated extinguisher. Buy as many of the biggest units as you can afford; actually, two 5-pound units should suffice. Have them checked on a yearly basis and mount them where you can get at them in an emergency. I mounted one by the door so I can make a quick exit if I can't put the fire out.

Keep in mind that no bike—or shop for that matter—is worth your life. If you are cursed with a fire that gets out of control, dial 911 and stand back. Material objects can be replaced.

4

Chapter
Four

The Best-Laid Plans

I'm sure the guy who created this jigsaw puzzle knows where everything goes. But will he remember where they go six months from now?

You've found the bike, prepared the work area, and laid in enough supplies, tools, and pizza to equip a small army. Only one more item needs attending to and then we can get to the nitty-gritty.

Lots of motorcycles have been restored by the "seat of the pants" method—in fact I've done a few myself. Fundamentally, the seat of the pants approach to restoring a motorcycle means you take everything apart, throw it in various boxes, and then later attempt to re-

assemble it into something that looks like a motorcycle. In effect you've created a giant and somewhat unwieldy mechanical jigsaw puzzle.

Can you restore it? Certainly. Can you do a proper job? Absolutely. Will it become more frustrating, time-consuming, and expensive than a restoration that was begun with a bit of forethought? Without a doubt.

Before you remove the first component you'll need to consider a basic game plan. Don't get me wrong. You don't have to, nor

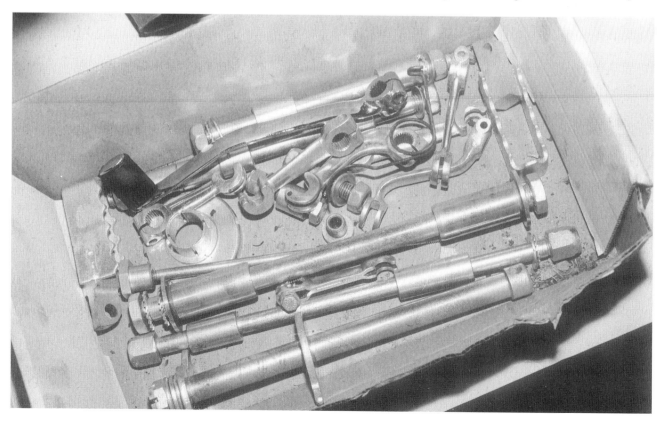

Photos will prevent lots of confusion down the road. It's also nice to have a few before, during, and after shots. It's a good idea to make a few notes as you take the shot. Otherwise, you may forget what the shot was intended to record.

should you, create a rigid and uncompromising timetable or a fully detailed step-by-step schedule. Actually you want to keep it fairly loose and flexible. But you do want at least to know what direction you're going to go.

For instance, if you know the engine is going to require a complete overhaul, your plan might be to remove and strip the engine first. While you're waiting for the various pieces to come back from the machine shop, or you're beating the bushes trying to acquire the pieces, you can remove the various cycle parts and refurbish them as needed.

The actual order in which you perform the work is unimportant. I know of one restorer who likes to finish the frame and running gear completely before he tackles the engine. He claims that seeing the finished bike, sans engine, provides him with the initiative to keep going. Personally, since I consider the engine to be the heart of the project, I like to strip the complete bike and send out the various bits for chrome and paint while I concentrate my energies on the engine rebuild. I try to structure the project so that the frame and engine are done at just about the same time, because I like to reinstall the engine at the earliest possible opportunity.

It's not so important that you blindly follow a particular plan, only that you actually have some sort of plan as a guide. It's also important that you allow for a certain amount of "creativity," lest the project come to a complete halt for want of a crucial part. The key elements in your restoration plan should be adaptability and cohesion.

I'm sure that the obvious has suggested itself by now. During the course of the restoration several operations are likely to be carried on concurrently. Parts are at the chrome shop. Wheels are being re-laced. Paint stripped or applied. Without some sort of accurate record keeping, it's easy to lose track of who's doing what to which! Even if you do the entire job yourself, you'll still need to keep track of what's going on.

KEEPING TRACK

Along with your plan of attack, you need some method of keeping track of the hundreds of little pieces produced by stripping your motorcycle down to the last nut and bolt. Having some idea of their order of assembly might also prove handy.

Before you even wash the bike, the first step should be to take a series of photographs. Apart from the fact that before-and-after photos are always a neat thing to have, the before photos will at least show you where everything should go. The before photos will also come in handy for spotting any discrepancies between what is, and what should be. Keep the camera handy because we'll be using it again during the teardown process.

Once the teardown process actually starts we need some method of storing, identifying, and protecting the removed parts. One solution is to disassemble the offending part, place each piece or subassembly into a muffin tin, (available in any grocery store, or your wife or mom's cupboard) with a label describing where it came from and what it is. I've worked with mechanics that could and often would throw everything in one big box. Somehow they were able to identify each small widget months later when they finally

I pirated these from the kitchen!

These baggies are the cheap ones. You have to label them with tape.

decided to reassemble whatever it was they were working on. Me, I'd have ended up with a box of unidentified widgets.

Obviously, unless you plan to go into the muffin tin collecting business, you can't just leave all the parts lying around in their respective tins. The best solution I've come up with involves another raid on the supermarket (or kitchen cabinet). The ubiquitous Baggie is probably one of the best methods of storing and protecting small parts ever devised—I'm told they're not bad for storing sandwiches, either.

I prefer the freezer type, which has an external label. That way you can spray a little rust preventative on the parts without worrying that the masking-tape label will fall off. Or that the WD-40 covering that clutch release arm will ruin the scrap of paper you left inside

the bag telling you that it is, in fact, the clutch release arm.

Once you've got your small parts bagged and tagged, you can store them in bin boxes (available through any auto parts supplier). Use the bin boxes to segregate the parts by location, i.e., ignition parts, control levers, fuel supply, and so on.

BOXES: GETTING IT ALL TOGETHER

Although bin boxes are relatively cheap and easy to come by, the do-it-yourselfer has a variety of alternative storage options at his disposal. The ever popular cigar box lends a certain cachet to the project. The cookie tin has the added advantage of being full of cookies. Cheese boxes are available through any delicatessen.

Plastic and other somewhat pricey bins and holders are available through the large handyman chains such as Home Depot or industrial supply shops. And finally, you can use old bureau drawers—don't laugh: I knew an ardent Vincent enthusiast who kept his spares in a glass-fronted china case in his living room.

Finally, take notes—lots of notes. I like to use one of those old-fashioned composition books. You might prefer a loose-leaf binder, 3x5 cards, or a brown paper bag. I describe any unusual features I find. I'll list how things came apart, and any odd or mysterious assembly methods I might need to know to get the thing back together again. I also list which parts were sent to the chrome shop, which went to the paint or machine shop, and when they went there. In the back of the book I list phone numbers, parts sources, and contacts who might be able to help with the restoration.

By using your photo records, notebook, and factory manuals, together with accurate storage and tagging methods, I guarantee that you'll eventually reassemble your motorcycle the way God and the manufacturer intended it to be—no matter what pitfalls you might encounter along the way.

To reiterate, organization—of your thoughts, parts, and plans—is one of the cornerstones of a good restoration.

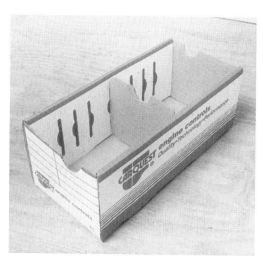

Bin boxes are available from any auto parts store. If you're a regular customer, they may supply them gratis. These cost me 50 cents each!

Let's Get Started

Chapter
Five

Teardown: Separating the Motorcycle into Its Component Parts

Reduced to its component parts, a motorcycle is pretty simple. Of course, this guy has already lost the front wheel and handlebars!

Taken as a whole, the motorcycle is a somewhat complicated device. On the other hand, when reduced to the component level it becomes an entirely different and much simpler kettle of fish.

What we're gonna do here is make our kettle of fish as simple as possible. We'll start by separating the bike into its subsystems, and then reducing those to individual components. Trust me; you'll be amazed at how simple

those components actually are, how they interrelate, and how they reassemble to create an outstanding, fully restored motorcycle. Let's get started.

WASH DAY

"Let the games begin!" or words to that effect. If it's one thing I hate it's working on a dirty motorcycle. Can't stand it; in fact, I loathe it—nope, I just won't do it. If nothing else, I hope the reader acquires the same attitude. Before the first wrench turns you're going to give your bike a thorough cleaning.

Old motorcycles, particularly neglected ones, seem to act as a dirt catalyst. They use heat and motion to turn a variety of oil leaks, chain grease, bird droppings, and road grime into a seemingly impenetrable coating that refuses to be affected by soap and water.

While steam cleaning is probably the most effective way to remove years of accumulated sludge, it's also the harshest and I recommend it only as a last resort. Steam cleaning is a problem because it's so invasive. The steam injected under pressure finds its way into every nook and cranny. It then condenses back into water and might lie for months before you get around to dismantling the now-ruined component.

There are few worse surprises than taking a generator or magneto apart only to find that an accumulation of water inside has been doing its best to return the various pieces to their natural state—iron oxide (rust). Overzealous steam cleaning provides you with a real chance to ruin bearings and electrical components. Steam cleaning also has a nasty side effect of removing decals you might want to save, paint you might need to match, and permeating and ruining everything from instruments to seat covers. Steam cleaning does have its place, especially when the bike has been reduced to a pile of parts. But let's start with gentler methods.

The best way I've found is a combination of degreaser, water under moderate pressure, and elbow grease. There are a variety of commercial degreasers available for cleaning motorcycles (but unfortunately few for chasing away that greaser dude who keeps hanging around your daughter). Gunk, Simple Green, and Silkolene Pro-Wash are some of the better ones. Carefully read the manufacturer's recommendations before using. Some of these

products are petroleum-based, and will eat up your asphalt driveway or attack various types of plastic.

Use a stiff bristle brush, parts cleaning brush, or paintbrush to really work the solvent into the grunge. Then rinse. Repeat as required. A decent pressure washer is the hot tip here. They have enough oomph to blast off the munge without causing damage. Even better is a source of warm water, perhaps a hose run off your hot water heater. You might have to wash the bike two or three times before it's squeaky clean, but try not to lose interest. Trust me; it'll be time well spent.

You'll probably encounter some baked-on crap that just won't come off. Let it slide for the time being. We'll deal with it later. The idea here is to clean the bike to the point where we won't get filthy working on it and we can actually see what we're working on.

Industrial-strength steam cleaners will remove dirt, grease, paint, and decals in short order.

Since it's all coming apart, everything gets a good dose of hot, soapy steam.

Once the bike is clean, snap some more photos, particularly of decal placement, cable and wire harness routing, and external component mounts, fender brackets, engine mounts, or anything else that's external and removable.

REMOVING THE BODYWORK

If you plan to perform a full restoration—and for convenience's sake I'll assume for the rest of this book that you are—you're going to remove the engine at some point in the near future. You'll find that the service manual will provide explicit instructions on engine R&R (removal and replacement). Normally, separating the engine from the frame doesn't require you to remove all of the bodywork. Since we are about to undertake a "ground up" resto, however, we're going to start at the top.

This chapter deals only with breaking the bike down into its constituent groups. From there we'll proceed to component inspection and repair. Finally, we'll reassemble the bike and return to our starting point, only this time with a complete, fully restored motorcycle.

As always, keep your camera and notebook handy. Anything that might seem confusing or out of the ordinary should be documented before brain fade sets in. Take lots of notes as you go. Bear in mind that it could well be a year or two before the bike is reassembled; lots of details fade away. Hell, lots of details fade away after a day or two ("Sure Honey, I know it's our anniversary. Doh!").

I like to start by removing all of the "fiddly" bits first: mirrors, crash bars, all the weird parts that old motorcycles seem to accumulate over time. Save all of it for later evaluation. Some bits might be rare period accessories and well worth saving; the rest might well be junk to you but a swap meet treasure to the next guy.

Seats

Once all of the little bits and pieces have been removed, I pull the seat. Most seats are held on by some combination of hinges, clips, and bolts. In a few cases a side panel or two might have to be removed to gain access to the securing bolts. Remove the seat and any retaining strap, as well as any items stored under the seat—toolkits, manuals, and old fried-egg sandwiches.

Find a safe place to store the seat for the time being; dispose of the fried-egg sandwich in an environmentally responsible manner.

Fuel Tank

Once the seat's out of the way you can pop off the fuel tank. Drain the gas first. Dispose of any stale old fuel in a responsible way. If it's still good fuel, pour it into your lawnmower or car (unless it's two-stroke premix, which can overheat the car's catalytic converter).

Once the tank is empty you can either remove it from the bike or strip it down in place. Since I prefer to work on the tank while it's still attached firmly to the frame rather than wrestle it across the top of my workbench, I strip it on the bike. I like to start with the cap and work my way down. Remove any screw-on emblems and their attendant bits (i.e., screws and rubber insulators) and bag them, as well as any trim strips or kneepads, which might be glued on. Remove any panels, à la "toaster-tank" BMWs. Pay special attention to plastic badges and the older style BMW emblems, which are cloisonné and easily broken.

If you haven't already, remove the fuel lines. OEM British lines use a captive nut you can unscrew; others might be pulled or cut off as the situation demands. If they are or appear to be OEM, save them to serve as patterns during reassembly, but don't reuse old plastic fuel lines.

Remove the petcocks. Keep a small pan handy to catch any residual fuel that spills out when the petcock is removed from the tank. Cut-down oil bottles are perfect. Some petcocks unscrew as a bolt would. Some use a left-handed thread. A few—BMW comes to mind—use a union nut: The nut has a left-hand thread on one side, right-hand on the other. If in doubt as to which type you're about to remove, consult your service manual. Note any obvious defects in your notebook.

If the tank has been repainted in a non-standard color, now is the time to try to find a trace of the original paint. Look under the emblems or petcocks, under the kneepads or around the filler neck—often a trace of the original paint will remain there.

External Oil Tanks

Once the seat and tank are out of the way, drain the oil tank. If the bike is dry sump and uses an external oil tank, remove it. Pay attention to the position of the feed and return lines, as well as any auxiliary lines. Normally you'll find a breather hose, a vent line, and occasionally a drip pipe intended to lubricate the drive chain (and the swingarm, rear wheel, and fender). Some bikes also lube the rocker arms from the oil return. Make sure that all lines are identified and tagged before they are removed. Photos are helpful here, too.

Likewise, before the tank is removed from the frame, pull the in-tank oil filter. Be prepared for a bit of a mess here as some oil is bound to remain in the tank. Once the tank has been removed, flush it out thoroughly and put it aside for paint. Quick tip: When you flush the tank, keep an eye out for any metal debris. If the spent oil is full of chips, fine metal particles, and what feels like gritty paste, plan on the engine's bottom end needing some serious work.

Fenders and Braces

Although it is not strictly necessary, I like to remove the fenders at this stage. That way, if anything gets dropped or bounced, the fenders are out of harm's way. Fender removal should be straightforward, although some of the Brits seem to have gone out of their way to install the most complicated fender bracketry they could devise. Braces and bridges run up and down, spacers are installed, and brackets positioned in the most confusing configuration. Take a few pictures, make a few drawings and notes, then remove, inspect, and set aside.

By now you should have quite a growing pile of parts. I segregate them into parts that need stripping versus parts that must go to either the plater or painter in as-is condition.

The Advantage of "As Is"

Why send painted items to the painter in "as-is" condition? Mainly so he can duplicate the original style and scheme of the factory paint. Photographs, measurements, and color brochures are all terrific aids, but nothing beats having the real McCoy to use as a guide.

Ancillaries

Now that the bodywork is off, it's time to make a few notes, shoot a photo or two, and take a look at the various subsystems that make the motorcycle run. Then you can remove them. Off come the cables, footpegs, exhaust system, and carburetors. Leave the rear brake pedal and the drive chain on the motorcycle and connected for the time being; we may need them later.

Exhausts

Most of the pieces should come off easily enough. Some exhaust collars might call for a spanner or ring wrench—Norton and BMW, especially. Alloy BMW exhaust collars can seize solidly to the head. Trying to force the collar off will ruin the collar, the head, and your day, in short order. Read the sidebar in chapter 8, follow my instructions, and save the head and your day. The collar gets destroyed in the process, but hey, two out of three ain't bad.

Most other exhaust systems unbolt and then come off in a straightforward manner. Some exhausts might show their dismay at being removed from the bike by resisting your best efforts to do so. Heat, carbon, and rust form an incredibly strong bond. Liberal applications of both penetrating oil and a large rubber mallet should persuade the exhaust to abandon ship.

Late-model Triumphs can be exceptionally troublesome in this regard—either that, or

the exhaust systems are so loose that they fall off by themselves, usually at about 60 miles per hour. The combination of the crossover pipe and the push-in exhaust port make them a real pain to remove. It would be nice if you could remove the head pipe and crossover as one chunk. You can't; the frame tube gets in the way. You might well ruin the crossover pipe trying to remove it—but don't fret if you do. Replacements are cheap and easily available. Once the crossover is out, drive the pipes out of the head with a few well-placed shots from your mallet.

Carbs

Drain the carbs before removing them. The carbs will be either bolted in place—à la most British bikes—or clamped in rubber sleeves. Some, like Triumph and BSA, unbolt without a lot of fuss. On the other hand twin-carb Nortons can be a pain if you haven't done it before, because the inner Allen heads are impossible to reach. (Cutting down the correct Allen wrench will speed things up considerably.)

Carburetors might be individually mounted, or they may be hung from a common rack. Rack-mounted carbs come off en masse. You might be tempted to remove the slides from the carbs and leave them attached to their respective cables. Don't. It's a bad

This is a typical problem on most vintage bikes that use a rubber spigot to mount the carb. The rubber has deteriorated past the point of usefulness.

idea—scratched slides, bent needles, and mismatched parts are the end result. Always keep the slides and the bodies together. In fact keep individual carbs in separate boxes. If the bike is equipped with remote float bowls, remove them and store them with their respective carburetors.

All the Other Stuff

Kind of vague isn't it? I honestly couldn't describe the rest of the parts in any other manner.

The rest of the stuff includes the coils, horns, remotely mounted condensers, zener diodes, the wiring harness, and any and everything else including most of the motor mounts that get in the way. There's no need to go into great detail here; work carefully and take note of which way the wires are connected. British bikes with positive ground systems can be exceptionally confusing if you're not well-versed in their quirks.

During removal, label each terminal of the wiring harness and make a drawing showing the location of each component. When working on British bikes, pay particular attention to the rectifier. The bolt holding the rectifier together is also the same one holding it to the frame. The bolt passes through the rectifier plates, which are secured by a nut. The rest of the bolt then passes through the frame; another nut secures the whole shebang.

Problems arise when the novice mechanic tries to remove the rectifier by holding the nut and spinning out the bolt. The plates, which are connected to each other by a thin strand of wire, tend to spin with the bolt, breaking the fragile connections. To avoid any problems, hold the bolt and spin off the nut.

Removing the Engine

At this point we have your basic naked bike. Follow the instructions given in your shop manual for engine and transmission removal. If you haven't yet done so, drain any remaining fluids—engine oil, transmission, and what have you. While you're waiting, take a coffee break. Bag and tag each item that's removed, and don't forget the photos.

Since I usually work alone, I break down the engine as far as I can in the frame. If possible I'll remove the head and barrel*, the sidecovers, alternator, and clutch, as well as most of the other parts that will unbolt. This kills

two birds, so to speak. It makes the engine much lighter, and it makes it much easier to shoehorn in and out of the frame, both major considerations when working alone.

Not all engine designs lend themselves to a partial teardown while still in the frame. To make matters worse, the engines that do are usually quite heavy. The best bet for removing these lumps is to enlist the help of a buddy or two. Buy them a pizza and a beer (or two) when it's out. You'll need their help to put it back in.

*You might want to skip ahead to chapter six, engine teardown, before proceeding for a few tips on head and cylinder removal. Like granny always said, "It wouldn't hurt."

The reason I suggested leaving the rear brake installed is because you might need some means of locking up the engine and transmission. As I suggest, some components are easily removed at this point. The countershaft sprocket nut, the clutch hub nut, and the crankshaft primary sprocket nut are all easy to remove if you have access to an air compressor and impact gun. If you don't, they can be a bear.

There's an easy and safe way to loosen them: Put the bike in gear (if you removed the drive chain, replace it), stand on the rear brake, use a breaker bar and socket, apply elbow grease—off they come. As an alternative, if the head and barrel are off, you can use a piston stop or a drift through the connecting rod to lock everything up. Or you can use a tool known as "Grab-it" to lock the gear or clutch hub. Of course if the engine's seized solid, it's all academic. Your problem isn't keeping the crank from turning; it's getting it to turn.

The Grab-it® tool was invented by Joe Bolger, engineer, motocrosser, and genuinely nice guy. The tool is designed to fit between the teeth of a sprocket or clutch hub. Or anything else it can get a grip on.

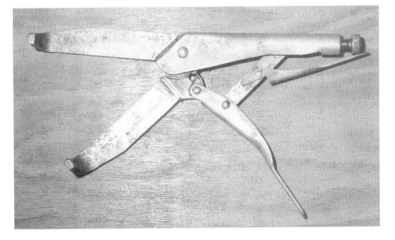

Removing the Wheels

Once the engine's out, the wheels are next. You'll need some way to support the frame—usually a box or milk crate will suffice if you're not using a workstand. While most bikes are stable enough when both wheels are still attached, the bike will probably nosedive like a lead balloon the moment you remove one or the other. Make sure the frame is either blocked up or securely tied down, unless you enjoy juggling one-wheeled motorcycle frames in one hand and a freshly removed wheel in the other.

As you remove the wheels, note the order of any spacers and shims, particularly those centering the rear wheel. If you haven't already removed the brake pedal and footpegs, now is as good a time as any. Ordinarily the order of wheel removal isn't critical, although you might find that a particular bike will balance better on one or the other. If the front is removed first, you can also remove the fork tubes at the same time.

There are several methods of securing the wheels in the chassis. The front might require axle removal or the axle might remain in the wheel while it's withdrawn from the forks as a unit. Rear wheels might be removed as a unit, with the axle, brake drum, and sprocket still attached. The axle can be pulled and the wheel disengaged from the sprocket. In some cases, Norton, for example, you pull the axle first and then unbolt the wheel from the sprocket/brake drum assembly.

Removing the Fork

Remove the fork tubes first, if possible. Japanese and European forks are usually a slip-fit in the yokes, as are post-1970 British models. To remove them, first remove the large fork cap nut and internal spring (if so equipped). Loosen the pinch bolts and try to pull the legs down through the yoke. If they resist, you might need to insert a screwdriver or prybar in the gap of the lower yoke to free the leg—careful: Once the gap is opened the leg might drop like it's shot from a gun. By the way, if the fork cap will slip through the top clamp you might be tempted to leave it in place; don't. It's much easier to loosen the nut with the fork held firmly in the clamp.

The BSA quick-change rear wheel: male splines on the hub engage a matching set of female splines on the brake drum/sprocket carrier. Be sure to lube the splines with anti-seize during reassembly.

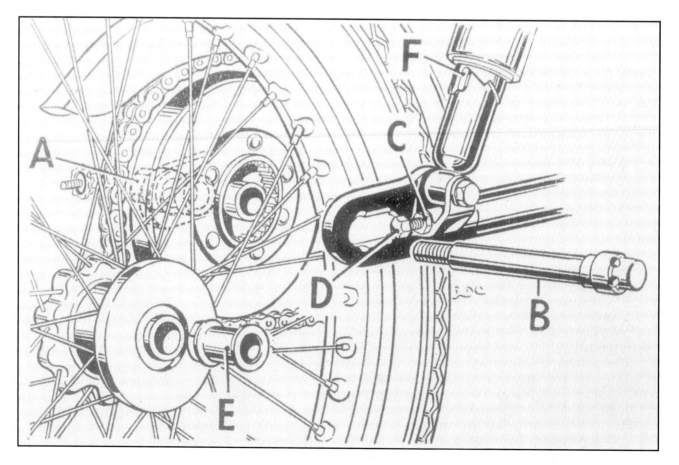

If you're working on a pre-1970 Brit bike, you might find that the fork tube is a taper fit in the top clamp. The solution here is to either procure the special removal/installation tool or improvise. I like to improvise. Loosen the fork cap and turn it out three or four turns, or until you can see a slight gap between the cap and the top clamp. Give the cap a strong whack with a plastic mallet; the tube should break free from the taper. As an alternative, you can loosen the top nuts and steering stem nut, then give the top clamp a good whack from underneath.

You might be tempted to save time at this stage by removing the stem nut and fork caps, giving the top clamp a good rap, and then removing the lower clamp with both fork legs still attached. A good idea in theory, less so in reality. The forks will drop, suddenly, and the top clamp will then launch itself skyward and the forks and clamp will bounce off the floor. Loose, greasy 1/4-inch steering-head bearings—28 to 34 of them—will then hit the floor like so many of Forrest Gump's ping-pong balls. Great fun to watch from the sidelines, not so much fun if you're a participant.

Early, mechanical forks—Harley-Davidson springers, Indian leaf spring, or British girder forks—require a slightly different approach. Before removing the fork from the frame, give it the once-over. Check for twist by sighting from above. Check for bends in the blades by sighting from the side and front. Check for excess play—the technical term is "slop"—in the bushings. Anything you can feel is too much.

Removal procedures vary by manufacturer, but in all cases are relatively straightforward. If the springs are under any appreciable preload you'll need to release the tension before you disassemble the fork. Back off the adjustment a little at a time until the spring is relaxed. And then proceed to remove the fork.

The observant will notice I haven't gone into great detail regarding the removal of the handlebar, levers, and such. First, I figure you can pretty much take care of those items as you come to them. Second, for the most part their removal is so simple that it needs no explanation. There are two exceptions.

Some older BMWs, particularly /2 models with Earles forks, use an eyebolt handlebar mount. Some Triumphs also use a similar mount. On the Triumph, the eyebolt is a large-diameter casting that slides over the handlebar and is then shimmed to fit. The BMW uses no shims; the U.S.-model BMW bar also incorporates a dirtbike-style crossbar in the handlebar.

So how do you remove the eyebolt? Unfortunately, unless you plan on hacksawing through the handlebar, you have to bend the bolt if you ever plan on reusing the handlebar. OEM clamps can usually—and I use the word usually with caution—stand to be bent three or four times. If you plan to install European-style bars, the clamps—sometimes known as "P" clamps—will slip right over the bar.

Triple Clamp

The triple clamp goes by a variety of names: triple tree, fork stem, fork crown, steering stem, and even "the thing that holds the forks." It's also removed in a variety of ways. Some machines use a clamp bolt and top nut to secure the upper clamp to the stem. A few just use the top nut. You might find an adjusting nut beneath the top clamp. If you haven't done so already, remove the top clamp and steering stem.

If the bike is an older one that uses loose balls as steering head bearings—most pre-1970 bikes do—be prepared to catch a few of them and lose most when the tree drops out. Don't fret; 99 percent of bikes use common, over-the-counter, 1/4-inch steel balls. The upper and lower races should be knocked out at this point. Use a drift placed through the steering head; knock the lower race out by sliding the drift through the top of the steering head, and vice versa. Mark and bag the parts. The races might well be two different sizes, so don't confuse them. Likewise note the position of any dirt shields or shims.

Removing the Swingarm and Shocks

The swingarm will be held in by one of three ways. With the simplest type, a long bolt or axle passes through the frame and swingarm, and a large nut secures it. With the second, the swingarm might be held in place with adjustable tapered roller bearings. Bolts are threaded into the frame. One end of the bolt is machined into a stub axle. The bearings seat in the swingarm, the stubs protrude through the bearings' inside diameter and support the swingarm. Adjusting the bolts controls free play.

If the head set bearing races are going to be removed, a long brass punch can be inserted through the steering head. Tap around the circumference to avoid damage to the race.

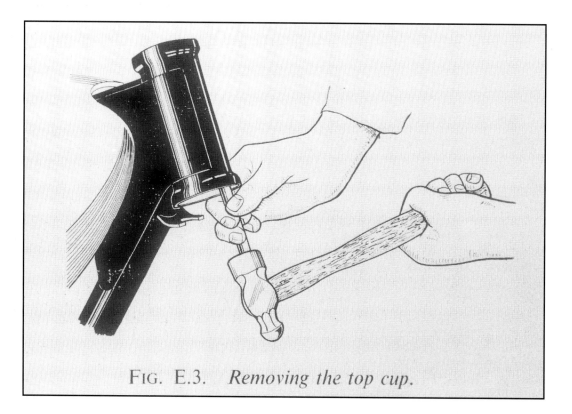

FIG. E.3. *Removing the top cup.*

The third design is rare, but you might encounter it on lightweights and Ducati singles. A pivot tube passes through the swingarm and frame. The frame is fabricated with a clamp at one or both ends, and a pinch bolt secures the tube in the clamp.

To remove a swingarm mounted on tapered roller bearings, simply unscrew the bolts and remove them. The swingarm should drop down. On either the axle or pivot tube style, remove the nut or pinch bolt and drift out the axle or tube. Note any shims or dust seals and their locations. If the bike is equipped with a drive shaft, check the service manual and follow the manufacturer's recommended removal procedure.

I leave the rear shocks attached to the swingarm to keep it from flopping onto the floor as I withdraw the pivot. If you prefer to remove the rear suspension units before the swingarm, by all means do so. If not, remove them now.

If the bike uses a linkage or monoshock rear suspension, you'll find that special procedures might be required; again, consult your shop manual. Since these systems are more commonly employed on newer motorcycles, I'll leave it at that. Similarly, plunger suspension bikes will demand a slightly different approach. Normally the rear shocks are clamped in place and removal is straightforward, if a little time consuming.

Component Inspection and Repair

Well, pilgrim, by now you've got a couple of big lumps, boxes, and bags of small parts, a ton of notes and photos, and a few skinned knuckles. Now it's time to stop fooling around and get serious.

6

Chapter
Six

Engine Teardown

In a perfect world the engine teardown would be a by-the-book procedure. Bolt heads would still be hexagonal. Pistons wouldn't be seized in their cylinders. Bearings would not have spun in their bores, and at Christmas Santa would bring you exactly what you asked for. Nice thought. Reality, though, is a harsh mistress.

In the real world, bolt heads look as if a turtle chewed on them, pistons weld themselves to their bores, "mechanics"—and I use the term loosely—have "improved," "repaired,"

and botched beyond belief. And now you (and I) are going to put it right.

Engine rehabilitation falls into two broad categories. Either you must overhaul the engine for mechanical reasons, or you want to, usually for cosmetic reasons or peace of mind. The rationale here is something like, "Since I'm restoring the bike, I'd be foolish not to open up the engine and at least take a look."

In the first case you have little say in the matter, unless you'd rather push the bike while making engine noises. With rare exception I'd

This homemade universal engine stand was lashed up by the author from 2x2 angle iron, and will hold most single and twin-cylinder engines. The stand uses the engine's rear-mounting bolt hole. The adjustable stop puts enough tension on the engine to keep it from flopping around, while the large tab lets the vise get a good grip on it.

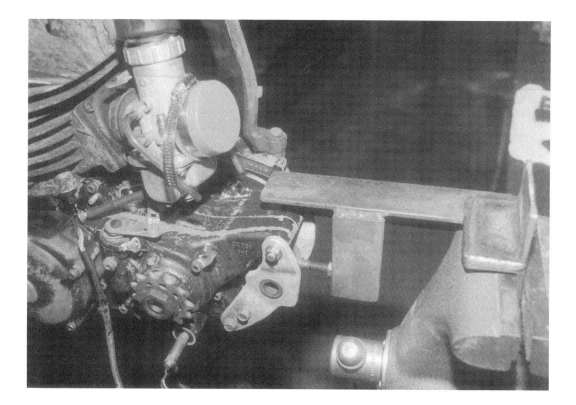

60

have to agree with you in the second case—peace of mind is a powerful motivator. The exception, of course, is that you know exactly what shape the engine is in and feel comfortable with it.

Since the engine is essentially the heart of the beast, no aspect of its repair should be taken lightly. Remember this: If the engine fails at an inopportune time, at the very least you'll face an inconvenient roadside repair, at worst a long and embarrassing walk home.

All engines, two-stroke or four-, single- or multi-cylinder, are disassembled in roughly the same manner. Your shop manual will provide the particulars. I'll provide you with the rest.

Normally the cylinder head is the first item to go. Different engine designs require different procedures. If the engine in question is a two-stroke, it's a simple matter of unbolting the head and removing it. If it's an overhead cam design you'll have to deal with both the cam and cam chain. Depending on the make and model, you might have to remove the engine from the frame before removing the head.

Here's the drill for removing generic four-stroke heads. Start by backing off all of the valve adjustments. If the pushrods and rocker arms or rocker boxes require removal, do so. Some rocker arms are located in rocker boxes, à la Triumph, in which case the rocker box requires removal. Remove the rocker box nuts and bolts by loosening each one a half-turn at a time in a diagonal pattern to prevent warping. On some engines—BMW air-cooled

engines, for example—the cylinder studs might also secure the rocker arms. Occasionally—Norton twins, for instance—the pushrods are removed and replaced with the head. In any case remove them, mark their original locations, and set them aside for further inspection. Make careful note of any shims that go with the rocker arms and their locations and keep them together.

Overhead Cams

If your intended victim is an overhead cam design, you'll still have to relieve tension on the valves before removing the cam(s). The only real exception is any motor that uses a bucket and shim system—like the Kawasaki KZs—with the shims located under the bucket. A few manufacturers that utilize over-the-bucket shims also have a procedure for cam removal that won't require you to remove every shim—again, when in doubt consult your manual.

Start by releasing the cam chain tension. In a few cases you might have to break (as in separate) the cam chain to remove it. Special tools are required to stake it, although a die grinder can be used to cut it. Make sure to look for a master link before you do any slicing. Even if the chain doesn't have a clip type of master link, it'll still have a staked master link, and that's the link you'll want to cut. If you don't have the proper chain breaker, grind the staked ends of the master link off with a die grinder. Thread a piece of wire through each end of the cam chain. Tie the wire off until you either remove the chain from the engine (in the case of a complete rebuild) or

The only problem with this stand is that engines with vertically split crankcases must be removed from the fixture when it's time to split the cases, a fault that will be remedied in the next version.

A simple wooden box makes a handy engine stand, and it works on engines with vertically split cases, too! This one is made from 2x3s; the inside opening measursg 12 inches in both directions.

When removing a cam chain, always identify the master link (dark link in illustration) before you do any slicing. And remember that many cam chains come off in one piece. If the cam chain must be separated, be sure to secure the ends with wire.

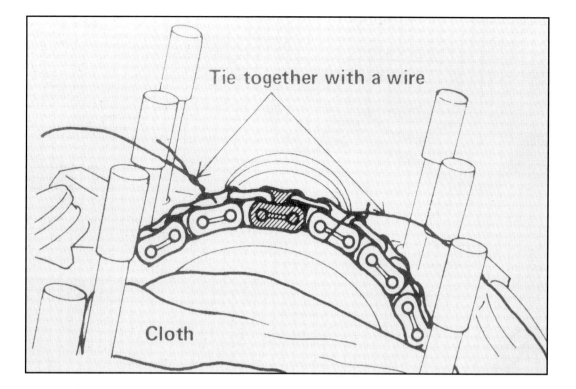

Tie together with a wire

Cloth

Heads are unbolted using the same pattern you use to torque the head down. Slacken the bolts a turn at a time until all tension on the head is released.

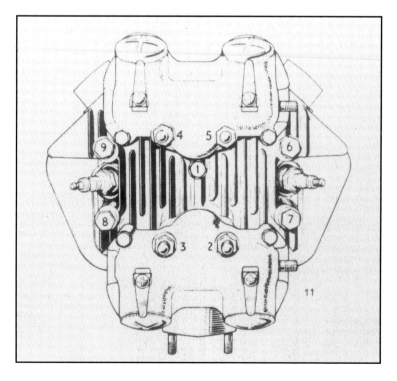

reinstall the head. Resist the temptation to simply drop the chain into the bowels of the engine. Chances are you'll be turning the crank at some point and the last thing you need is a cam chain wadded up in the bottom end.

Before removing the cam sprocket—if it's removable, that is; some are, some aren't—be sure to mark or familiarize yourself with its location. Some sprockets might be slotted to facilitate adjusting the cam timing. Adjustable sprockets are usually seen in old race bikes or high-performance engines. If you stumble across a nonstandard sprocket or one that's obviously been altered, stop and measure both the cam lift and duration; there's a good chance you have a set of aftermarket cams in there.

Multi-cylinder engines generally incorporate some sort of camshaft holder and bearing. Loosen them in steps, mark and inspect each one for galling and wear, and place it aside. Normally the manufacturer marks these caps during assembly, but you can never be too careful.

Inspect the cam or cams for signs of undue wear—anything you can feel with a fingernail will require attention. Tag each cam, spray it down with a little WD-40, and put it in a safe place.

Unbolt the head using the same pattern you'd use to torque it down. It should lift straight off—it probably won't, but it should. A sharp blow to the side of the head with a plastic mallet should loosen it. Make sure you hit it dead square, parallel to the fins, to avoid bending or breaking them. Occasionally you can remove a stuck head by installing the sparkplug(s) and turning the engine over, letting compression, in theory, perform the hard part. In all honesty I've never had much success using that method. Resist the temptation to pry the head off. Chances are you'll only ruin the gasket surface or break a fin.

If the head really won't come off, check your head bolt inventory against the shop and parts manuals; chances are you've forgotten one or two. Nortons, in particular, have a few hidden nuts and bolts that always stymie the first-time rebuilder, and occasionally the experienced one.

Once the head has been removed the cylinder(s) can be lifted from the block. Two considerations here: First, we don't want any dirt to fall into the crankcase. The best way to prevent that is to stuff clean rags around the opening as you lift the cylinder.

Normal practice is to lift the cylinder base clear of the crankcase, stuff plenty of clean rags into the opening, and then continue lifting the cylinder until it's cleared the piston(s). This way if any of the rings are broken, the rags will stop the pieces from entering the crankcase. Obviously this procedure takes on considerable importance if you're not planning to split the cases. Remember to support the rod and piston as the cylinder is lifted clear (see sidebar).

A rag stuffed into the case as the cylinder is pulled free will prevent any dirt or broken bits from falling into the cylinder.

The second consideration is this: How do you remove a cylinder that doesn't want to be removed? I'll deal with seized cylinders separately. For the moment let's assume the piston(s) are free to move in the bore; the bloody cylinder just won't budge from the crankcase. Again, resist the temptation to pry; chances are, all you'll do is damage it.

Check the cylinder base bolts. Are they all loose? In some instances—Triumph and Norton,

To pull the cylinder barrel from the crankcase, all cylinder bolts must be removed.

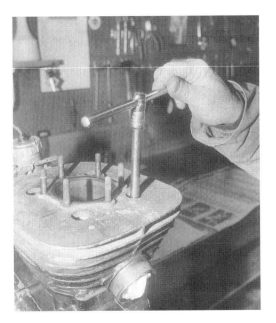

These Yamaha cylinder bolts are accessed through holes in the barrel. This method of bolting down the cylinder is fairly common. Anytime you see large holes like these, look for a nut or bolt at the bottom.

Fetch the barrel a
stout blow with a
mallet—at least
that's what my
1950 Triumph
shop manual says.
Since this is an
early 1970s
Yamaha, we'll
whack it with a
plastic hammer.
Never use anything
but a plastic,
rubber, or hide
mallet to hit a
cylinder, and
always hit it
dead square.

to name two—the cylinder block must be lifted slightly before the retaining nuts can be completely unthreaded. If the block moves a quarter-inch or so and then stops, see if the long outer nuts are still threaded onto the studs. Occasionally a cylinder will have a hidden nut or bolt holding down the block. For example, the H-D/Aermacchi 2-strokes have four base nuts located inside the cylinder. These are easily overlooked.

OK, you've checked all the hardware against your parts and shop manuals and the cylinder still won't budge. Now what? Chances are that the gasket and cylinder dowel pins are conspiring to hold the block down. A few sharp blows with a plastic or rawhide mallet should shock the block loose. Again, hit dead-on to avoid any fin damage. You might need to repeat the bang-wiggle-bang a few times, but eventually the block should free itself.

The major source of anguish occurs when the piston and cylinder have become one. Normally, seizure is caused by the ring(s) rusting to the bore or by a mechanical catastrophe. If it's a

simple case of rust or corrosion-induced seizure, begin by flooding the bore with penetrating oil. Next, set a block of wood on the piston crown; apply a heavy hammer, repeat. If the piston starts to move, great, if not, apply more oil and let the damn thing sit for a day or two.

If it's really stuck, fire up the "smoke wrench," and use your torch to heat up the cylinder liner. Expansion will help the oil work its way down and around the rings and eventually break the bond. It might take several tries and what seems like an inordinate amount of time, but eventually it should come free.

Suppose the piston is already at bottom dead center? You might ask, what then? Have faith, grasshopper, all isn't lost. Try rotating the engine to lift the entire assembly—block and piston. Place a spacer or two under the cylinder base and apply the hammer again, driving the piston down and around. The idea here is to keep applying oil, heat, and force; at some point the piston will break free.

But what if it won't? Well, pilgrim, at that point you've got limited options. You might

Most pistons have an arrow or some other mark indicating the front. It's always a good idea to check the piston position before disassembly.

be able to split the cases, remove the crankshaft, rod, piston, and barrel as a unit, and then proceed to a machine shop where you can press the piston out of the bore. In a worst-case scenario the piston might have to be destroyed; it isn't pretty, but unfortunately it's sometimes necessary.

Pistons frozen in place by mechanical damage such as a broken ring, a valve punched through the piston crown, or lack of lubrication (i.e., seizure) can also be a bear to remove. Since the damage is already done, it's hard to make it much worse. As a rule of thumb I'd have to say that whatever works in a particular case is acceptable, with increasing levels of aggression. That includes cold chisels, large hammers, and hacksaws.

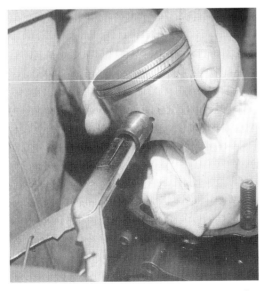

External snap ring pliers can be pressed into service as piston pin pullers.

Once the cylinder has been lifted clear you can remove the pistons, pins, and bearings (if so equipped) in the prescribed manner. Mark them even if you don't intend to reuse them. Normally, pistons are marked with an arrow indicating which way they face. Usually they are interchangeable from side to side, although occasionally they are "handed"—that is to say, left or right. Pay particular attention to piston location in all two-strokes. Getting them wrong way 'round is quite easy, and it will drastically alter the port timing—and reduce horsepower just as drastically.

GENTLE PERSUASION: PISTON PIN REMOVAL

Piston pins come in a variety of fits and with a variety of retaining clips. Removing the clips is straightforward and requires little explanation. I don't even need to tell you not to reuse them, do I?

Removing the pin, however, is another kettle of fish. Here's my method. First, be sure the piston and rod are adequately supported. If it takes more than a light tap or push, warm that sucker up. Much easier to heat the piston and s-l-i-d-e the pin out than to belt away with a big hammer and risk bending the rod! A heat gun or propane torch will do. If the pin puts up a fight, you might have to resort to a piston-pin puller. Usually, though, just heating the piston crown should be enough.

Spare the Rod

Once the cylinders come off, you'll need to protect the connecting rods from nicks, scratches, and gouges, especially if they're

This wrist pin is shot, as is its bearing, and both should be replaced.

Support the
connecting rod to
keep it from
getting nicked or
dented against the
case. Plastic tie-
wraps do a good
job of this.

made of alloy. Presumably you've got a fistful of rags stuffed in there, which helps provide some sort of support for the pistons until you remove them. Triumph recommends covering the cylinder studs with pieces of fuel line or old shift rubbers to prevent them from damaging the rods.

Some builders use rubber bands placed diagonally across the studs to support the rods. Me? I like to wrap a few inches of electrical or duct tape around the rod.

Once the top end is off, continue dismantling the rest of the engine. Common pitfalls encountered in bottom-end work include—but certainly are not limited to—stripped screws, left-hand threads, odd timing gears, hidden fasteners, and parts that go "sproing" in the night.

Outer cover screws—clutch covers, timing covers, primary covers, and so on—generally seem to be made of some sort of processed cheese, especially the infamous Phillips head. Japanese bikes, particularly older ones, are notorious in this respect. The heads seem to strip at the mere mention of the word "screwdriver."

British bikes are somewhat better; German and Italian bikes, with their copious use of Allen-head fasteners, are best of all.

Like the old saw goes, an "ounce of prevention is worth a pound of cure." Using the wrong tool causes most fastener damage. Of course, that's one of the reasons the bike now has to be restored. If the head of the screw still resembles something like its maker intended, start by using an impact driver and the correct bit. Try not to confuse a #3 Phillips with a Pozi-Drive; that's probably what the last guy did to get us into this predicament.

Stripped case screws can be removed in a variety of ways. The easiest is to take a center punch or small chisel, rest the tip or point on the outer circumference of the screw and give it a good whack. Angle the tool slightly so that the hammer blow rotates the offending fastener counterclockwise; 9 times out of 10, that's all you'll need to loosen it.

Next choice is a left-handed drill bit (and reversible drill), which, if you're lucky will spin the broken fastener out as it cuts into it, or a

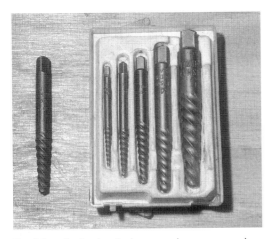

Traditionally, broken bolts or studs are removed with an easy-out. Start by drilling a hole as close to the center of the broken bolt as humanly possible. Make your hole as large as possible without cutting into the original threads. Drive the correct size easy-out into the hole. Twist the easy-out counterclockwise, and in theory it should remove the broken bolt. If the broken piece resists, use lots of penetrating oil and heat to help it along.

combined drill bit/bolt remover (sold under a variety of names, Drill-Out being the one I've used with some success). These tools use torque and shock to loosen the fastener. Otherwise, a good old drill bit and EZ-Out might work.

There's one other quick dodge that might work on really stubborn case screws. Try grinding or drilling the head off the screw so the case can be removed with the shank in place. Once the case is out of the way, grip the remaining stub with a pair of Vise-Grips and try turning it out.

Once the covers are off you'll be faced with a variety of parts that may or may not be secured with left-hand threads. Ordinarily the service manual should point these out, but take nothing for granted. I once wound the end off a very expensive BMW /2 oil pump because I assumed it had a right-hand thread. Much to my surprise, the 6mm shaft snapped before I could say "Holy expensive part, Batman." Assume nothing. If the nut resists turning, check the manual. In fact, as I've tried to point out, prudence dictates a thorough reading of the manual before you apply the first wrench!

Many bikes, particularly those from Great Britain, will require special pullers to remove the ignition advance units, timing gears, and clutch hubs. In some cases, Norton Commandos, for instance, or early-1970s Harley-Davidson

Sportsters, the clutch springs must be compressed with a special tool as well. In most instances these tools can be bought reasonably from suppliers, or they can be homemade.

Take caution when using "universal" gear pullers. While suitable for many applications they can ruin thin timing and idler gears by bending or even breaking them.

Always remove timing gears with the appropriate puller to avoid any damage. While the clever restorer might be able to improvise, consider the consequences of bending or warping the gear even slightly. Chances are the bike will be completely assembled before the offending gear gives itself away. Usually the first clue is a clatter or rattle from the timing chest. Everything comes apart, and parts reinspected, replaced, and reassembled again. Better to spring for the correct puller and avoid the entire hassle.

It's also an excellent idea to mark the timing gears before disturbing them. Yes, as a rule they are marked at the factory. But, they might use different marks for different engine applications—as in the case of Triumph. Trying to decipher which combination of dots, dashes, and keyways are correct for your particular application can turn into a real headache. Cut down on the aspirin and use a punch or dash of paint to mark the gears.

Keep an eye open for items not normally "timed" as well. H-D Sprints, for example, time the clutch assembly to the timing gears.

Before disassembly, check the cam timing marks. Some engines—Triumphs, for example—have multiple marks and may have more than one keyway. Some timing marks—again, Triumph is the perfect example—use an odd number of teeth on the cam idler gear. This prevents the timing marks from lining up after the engine has been rotated something like 98 times.

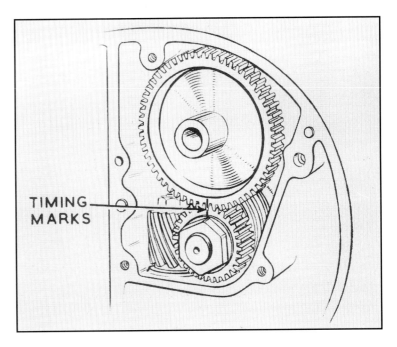

TIMING MARKS

At some point in your teardown you're going to remove a stud or two. Here's the easiest way I know to do it: Run two nuts down on the stud.

Lock them together and then turn the stud out using the bottom nut.

Stud removers work just as well, if not better. They use an offset cam device to grip the stud's shaft.

(The clutch is balanced, and timing it to the crank reduces vibration somewhat—at least in theory.)

Hidden fasteners and things that go "sproing" are always a surprise, even to the experienced mechanic. If the cases refuse to separate, start looking for hidden bolts or screws. Some Triumph twins, for example, have two small screws inside the crankcase/cylinder spigots that are often overlooked.

Pre-1970 Triumphs also have a timed crankcase breather located in the end of the intake camshaft. The spring-loaded tin plate tends to fall out as the cases are split; easy to overlook if it hits the floor, but leaving it out upon reassembly is guaranteed to ruin your day. BSAs have a small spring and check ball behind the oil pump. Remove the pump—sproing.

Japanese bikes are somewhat better in this respect but even they have their hidden foibles. Many have a small ball interposed between the clutch pressure plate and pushrod, or small shims located in out-of-the-way places. Disassembly is like crossing railroad tracks. You know: Stop, look, listen, then proceed slowly.

Continue stripping the engine until there's nothing left to remove. If the engine cases are going to be glass-beaded, leave the old bearings in place to protect their seats. Again, take plenty of notes. Identify parts with either tags or labels, and take your time. Once the engine is completely asunder, the individual parts should be thoroughly cleaned and inspected. Those slated for replacement should be culled out and new ones ordered. Those bound for the machine shop or platers, or those requiring special attention, should be made ready.

The Hot Ticket

Some engines come apart like they have zippers. Others require varying degrees of persuasion. Persuasion comes in various forms: large hammers, pry-bars, jacks, presses, and heat. Of the five, heat is usually the "hot tip" (sorry, I couldn't resist).

Motorcycle designers like to use lots of close tolerances and snug fits. They also like to use lots of aluminum and steel. Since it's usually a steel bearing or sleeve set into an aluminum case, there are two ways of separating most parts: No heat and lots of pressure, or fair amounts of heat and little pressure. Since the former tends to turn big intact parts into small broken ones, I prefer the latter.

Some engines—BMW twins and many two-strokes, for instance—are difficult at best to disassemble or reassemble without heat. In fact, anytime a bearing is removed or installed from a case, the case should be heated to sizzle—if you drip a drop of water on the case it should sputter and hop. Or do as I do. Spit on it—if it spits back it's hot enough.

ENGINE ASSESSMENT—TOP END

Making an accurate assessment of a running engine's condition can frustrate even the best mechanics. There are ways to determine gross condition; smoke pouring from the exhaust, for instance, is usually a sign that something's amiss in the top end. The sound of rocks being crushed in the crankcase is likewise a symptom that all's not well in main bearing land.

Once the engine has been reduced to its component parts, problems are relatively easy to pinpoint. While there is no substitute for experience, the novice restorer can certainly make an accurate assessment of the engine's internal parts by using his five senses and a few simple measuring tools.

Common sense tells you something needs to be done when parts display signs of extreme wear, mistreatment, or abuse. If upon removing the head of a non-runner you notice that one of the intake valves is hung out in the breeze, the other is bent like a pretzel, and the combustion chamber looks like it was retrieved from the deck of the Titanic, it shouldn't take a rocket scientist to realize that a little valve work is in order. If, on the other hand, the engine was a runner, then it's time for a little investigative work.

I like to start at the top and work my way down—no jokes, please. I should also mention that while the assessment process can be performed after the engine is stripped, most experienced mechanics and restorers find it just as easy to do as the individual parts are removed. That way there's less clutter and you're less likely to overlook some small bits (like the main bearings) while they're buried in a box.

Small parts such as rocker arm shafts and the rocker arms themselves should be cleaned and inspected for damage. Look for the obvious first. Deep scores, cracks, and burnishing are all indications that things are not right. The fingernail test works again here; if you can feel any wear with your fingernail, it'll probably need attention. If it all looks good, use a micrometer to measure the diameter in the middle and both ends of the rocker shafts.

Carefully examine the rocker arms for worn bushings, cracks, and stripped threads at the adjuster. With overhead-cam rockers, check for worn flats where they contact the camshaft. Broken bearing cages are a common problem on older BMWs with needle-bearing rocker arms. Check the pushrods for true by rolling them on a piece of glass or known straight surface, or placing them side by side. Check the ends for signs of damage. On Triumph twins you might notice a polished area near the valve end of the pushrod. This is perfectly normal and occurs where the pushrod passes through the rocker-box gasket.

If you're not sure about a particular part, remember that there's an old adage in racing that goes something like this: "Anyone can build a bottom end, the cylinder head's the trick." Horsepower is created largely in the cylinder head. By the same token a smooth running, steady idling, and powerful motor is only possible if the engine's top end is in good condition. Valves and rings must seal properly to create a gas-tight motor, so remember that before you OK any questionable parts.

Cylinder Head, Valves, Guides, Seats, Springs

It's a safe bet that your project is going to require a complete valve job—valves and seats re-cut or replaced, new guides, and probably new valve springs. Resist the temptation to just grind or lap the valves in and let it go. While it might work for a few miles, the end result will be a poorly sealed top end that wheezes like an old pump organ.

If you feel the need to, by all means pour a little gas or solvent into the ports and look for leaky valves; I'm confident you'll find a few. The next step is a thorough degreasing of the head. You don't have to go nuts here; at this point it's only inspection time. Once the head is stripped, we can go back and give it a real polishing.

After the loose oil and munge have been washed from the head, inspect it for any combustion chamber damage or cracks. Look for cracks around the sparkplug hole, the valve

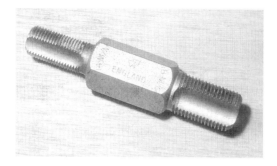

This handy gadget is an old-fashioned spark plug thread chaser. It doesn't cut threads, it just cleans them up a bit. First pack the flutes with grease, then run the tap through the plug holes to clean up the thread. The grease should catch and hold any loose chips.

seats, and the area between adjacent cylinders. You might encounter some damage to the combustion chamber itself, usually in the form of small pits or craters.

Since any sharp edges in a combustion chamber can cause pre-ignition, they should be polished out, if possible. Don't go crazy here. Just smooth down any rough edges with fine sandpaper and let them go. Generally these are caused by either detonation or debris from some past incident. While extremely deep or jagged ones may require filling, in the main they are relatively harmless.

Any cracks call for a trip to the machine shop. Normally the crack is drilled, welded, and then the head machined back to its original contour. Most cracks can be repaired—in fact, most types of cylinder head damage are repairable. I've seen heads that were broken in half put back together, for that matter—the only question is expense. If a cylinder head is fairly easy to come by, repairing it might not be economically feasible, but that's a question to address at the time.

Remove the valves from the head. Don't be overly concerned about the condition of the valve; if it's bent it's done for anyway. If not, it's going to be refaced. If it can't be refaced it's going to be replaced. Usually, valves are relatively cheap and available. Even if your specific valve isn't listed, chances are excellent that a generic replacement is. If you are restoring something exotic and a valve just isn't obtainable, pick up a manufacturers catalog, find one close, and let your machinist's lathe (or your own) do the rest.

Likewise, guides are either shot or they're not. The easiest way to check a guide is to insert a new valve and see how much play exists. This is a judgment call, of course, but in general, if the new valve wobbles around like a Saturday night drunk, then the guide's whipped. Gouges, deep scoring, or any other

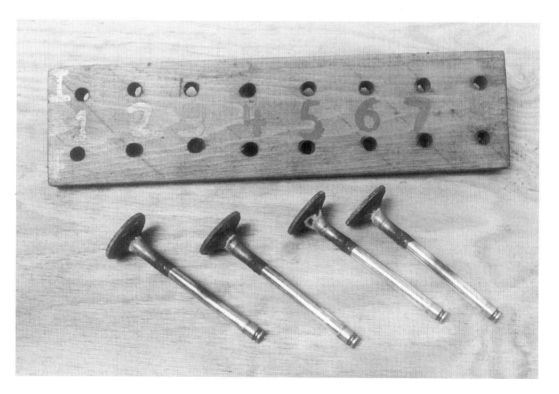

This homemade tool helps avoid confusion. The upper row holds the intake valves, the lower the exhaust.

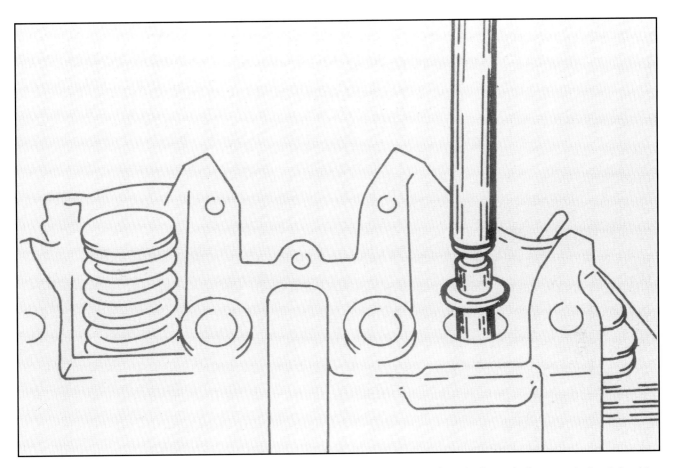

signs of physical damage mean replacement time is nigh as well.

Small hole gauges can also be used to measure the guides' inside diameter more accurately, but again, replacement is more or less mandatory during restoration. Like valves, OEM guides are easily replaced through the aftermarket. In fact, guides can be turned up on the lathe from stock with little trouble.

A GUIDE TO GUIDES

If you decide to remove the guides yourself, a few simple precautions will make the job much easier. In some cases the guide must be pushed through the head and into the combustion chamber. The easiest way to accomplish that is to machine off the top of the guide flush with the head. Then heat the head to about 180 degrees F and drift or preferably press the guide through.

The other tack is to push from the combustion chamber out. If you use this method, remove every bit of carbon from the bottom of the guide before you attempt to drift the guide through the head. The guide must be spotless. If it isn't, the carbon effectively makes the guide oversize, and as you drive it through the head, it will ream the hole out.

Valve seats should be re-cut. In some cases the seat might have to be replaced—a simple enough task, but one that's best left to a specialist. The question at this point would be, "Should I replace my original valve seats with ones for use with unleaded fuel?" Good question. My feeling is this: If the valve seats look good and show no sign of recession or sinking, then cut them, fit new valves, and be on your way. None of the bikes I owned at the time of this writing had ever been fitted with hardened seats, and honestly, none were needed.

On the other side of the argument, some bikes are known for the poor quality of their valves and valve seats—mid-1980s BMWs and some Harleys, for example. If the seats need replacing, by all means use the best Stellite steel seat you can find. To the same extent if hardened seats are important to your peace of mind install them. (See sidebar.)

As far as the work itself goes, unless you're building a hot-rod, I'd stick with a simple three-angle valve job. It offers a good compromise between longevity, performance, and cost.

The head should be heated prior to driving the new valve guide in. Use only the proper drift. After the guide is in place, the valve seat will have to be recut and the valve itself refaced or replaced.

HARDENED VALVE SEATS

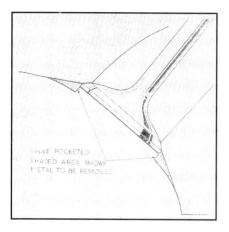

VALVE POCKETED
SHADED AREA SHOWS
METAL TO BE REMOVED

With the demise of leaded fuel, riders became concerned that their valve seats were "too soft." In fact, the problem arose because the lead in the fuel acts as a lubricant between the valve head and its seat. Without it, the exhaust valves can momentarily weld themselves to the seat when they close. As the valve opens again, it breaks the bond, taking a minuscule piece of the seat with it. After prolonged running, the valve seat eventually wears away and the valve seats deeper into the head.

Hardened steel seats resist this kind of welding, and as a result are compatible with low-lead fuels. How can you tell if you need to install hardened seats? If your bike's valves need continual adjustment because they lose their running clearance, the engine is probably a good candidate for new seats.

Japanese motorcycles are normally equipped with hardened Stellite valve seats, so they should have no problem. In my own experience the British valve seats are also more than up to the task of running on low- or no-lead fuel. Some BMWs, particularly those made between 1979 and 1981—hardly vintage bikes—do need hardened seats, however, and the stock ones should be replaced.

Valve springs have a tendency to collapse and lose tension after prolonged use. Most service manuals list a "free" length for springs—that's the length of the spring as it sits on your workbench. Measure your spring and compare; if it comes up short, replace it. If that's not good enough, most machine shops that perform cylinder-head work (I just couldn't bring myself to say "head shops"), have spring-pressure gauges that measure the spring's strength in pounds. Avail yourself of their services if you feel the need. Again, valve springs are both cheap and available, so don't scrimp on questionable parts.

CAMSHAFT INSPECTION

Since the cam(s) control the valve action we'll examine them with the rest of the top end, although I suppose if you're working on a flathead or pushrod engine, you could argue that they rightly go with the bottom end. But hey, it's my book.

In general a cam is either shot or it isn't. If deep ridges are worn into the lobes, it'll have to be replaced or reground. Pre-1970s Triumph 650s are particularly prone to exhaust-cam wear. On some Hondas the cam runs directly in the head—early XLs are notorious for ruining both the head and cam. Fortunately, MEGACYCLE has a repair. The head,

cam, and cam cover are all machined to accept a ball bearing. It works, and that's gospel.

Also gospel is this: If the cam is shot it's a safe bet that anything that rubs against it—cam follower, tappet, or rocker arm—is history as well. Extraneous cam damage, like a ruined tach drive, broken auto advance, or oil pump drive, might require cam replacement as well. Since these last three are usually owner-induced injuries, you should look out for other ham-fisted damage, both in the engine and on the bike overall. Forewarned is forearmed.

GLASS BEADING

After the head is stripped but before any work commences is the time to glass bead, if that's the way you want to go. Mask off any threads or oil passages before you let fly. Once the head has been cleaned to your satisfaction, give it a thorough cleaning with compressed air and warm water, then put it aside until it's time to rebuild it.

Removing the leftover grit from glass beading is imperative. One acquaintance recommends boiling the parts in water for 20 minutes or so to ensure that all the beads are washed out of the head. I tried it once and was amazed to find a tablespoon or so of crud in the bottom of the pot. My wife wasn't too thrilled, but it does work.

How To Anneal a Gasket

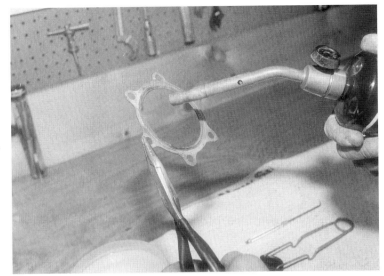

Use your torch to heat the gasket to a dull red.

While I don't recommend doing so unless a replacement isn't available, in a pinch a copper head gasket can be annealed and reused. All you need is a torch, some cold water, and pliers to hold the gasket.

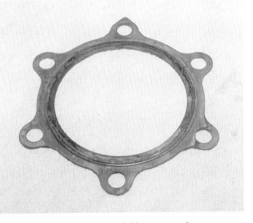

The annealed gasket should be as good as new . . . or at least good enough to reuse.

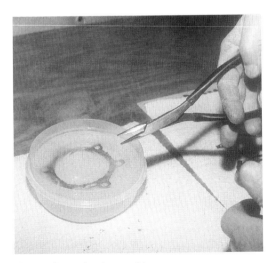

Plunge the gasket into cold water.

CYLINDERS, PISTONS, RINGS, AND BROKEN FINS

If the piston is in good shape, free from scuffs, scores, cracks (check the skirt just below the pin bosses both inside and out), and big gouges, mike it up and compare it to new. OK? Then set it aside for the time being and measure the barrel.

The cylinder should be checked for taper, out-of-round, and overall diameter. If any of these are out of spec, the cylinder(s) should be bored and oversize piston(s) fitted. If everything is within spec, hone the cylinder and recheck it. If everything is still within tolerance,

Remember that YZ 250 in the introduction that was rough but running? Upon first inspection, the piston and bore don't look too bad.

When we removed the barrel we found a real nightmare: The intake side of the cylinder liner was broken completely.

This Bultaco cylinder has been turned into a doorstop by some bonehead with a hammer.

Fortunately, a replacement can usually be found.

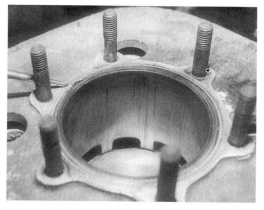

Under the head gasket we found a chunk missing from the cylinder—puzzling, but not a disaster.

refit the piston. In all cases the rings should be replaced without consideration. Insert new rings into the barrel and measure the end gap. File the ends to fit.

Before performing any machine work, glass bead the cylinder. Paint it after the machine work is finished.

Broken fins on the head or barrel are an annoyance, not the end of the world. There are several ways of replacing and repairing broken fins. If you have the original fin, the best solution is to have it welded back in place. Once the weld is dressed and the head or barrel glass beaded and painted, you'll never know the difference. The fin might also be epoxied back into place with any number of different glues, but don't expect this to be as permanent a fix. Personally, I prefer to weld.

There are also a few outfits that actually re-create missing fins from scratch. They are listed in the appendix. One dodge some restorers employ is to pirate fins from donor barrels and heads that are too badly damaged to use on an engine.

FINISH (PAINTING)

Most cylinders are painted, most heads left in their natural condition. Of course there are always exceptions, and there is certainly no rule that says you can't color any part of the bike you'd like in any manner you like. Normally glass-beaded parts that are left uncoated tend to attract dirt; however, a quick shot of WD-40, brake cleaner, or plain old soap and water is enough to clean them up. Several products, Cast-Blast and Alumi-Blast to name two, are available to protect freshly blasted iron and aluminum. And of course clear, high-temp lacquer is always popular.

If the parts are to be colored, I'd give serious consideration to powder coating them. Powder coating will be dealt with in detail in chapter 18. I won't discuss it much here except to say that because a fair amount of heat is involved in the process, some machinists prefer to bore the cylinder after it's been coated. I've done it both ways. Frankly, the cylinder that was powder coated after being bored stayed just as straight as the one that was coated first and then bored. Just to be on the safe side, however, I'd still recommend powder coating before boring.

THE BOTTOM END

Crankshafts fall into one of two very broad categories: built up (i.e., pressed together) or one piece. Built-up cranks include most two-strokes, Harley-Davidsons, Ducati singles and early V-twins, and many Japanese engines. These require special techniques and large hydraulic presses to dismantle and rebuild.

As the name implies, these crankshafts are built up of several components: normally two or more flywheels; a connecting rod or possibly two, three or four; an equal number of crank pins plus assorted bearings. Multiple-cylinder two-strokes also have seals between adjacent cylinders. Built cranks generally use one-piece connecting rods and needle or roller bearings in the big ends.

If you have access to a 5-ton or better press, the rebuild process is simple. Press one side of the crankshaft off the crank pin. Remove the rod and bearing. Press the pin out of the other side. To assemble, reverse the process and then true.

It sounds easy, doesn't it? With practice and the proper tools, it is. If you don't have access to the tools, though, forget it and farm the job out. I'd also recommend farming out any machine work on multiple-cylinder crankshafts. Crank-throw phasing is critical. If it's out of true by any appreciable amount, your engine will vibrate like a jackhammer until it eventually shakes itself apart.

One-piece or forged cranks are your garden-variety automotive, plain-bearing crankshafts. These feature two-piece connecting rods. They are most commonly found in British and European motorcycles, occasionally in some early Japanese models.

This nine-stud Bonneville head is ready to go. It's been sprayed with Alumi-blast™, which really makes it shine.

Crank bearings are inspected like any other: check roller, needle, and ball bearings for normal wear, binding, and physical damage such as broken bearing cages. Plain bearing damage is easy to spot; worn bearings will show copper where they've worn through. Physical damage in most other cases shows as small pieces flaking off, or metal particles embedded in the bearing material. Plain bearings should be replaced as a matter of course, but check the corresponding crank journals of any damaged bearings for scoring or other damage.

CRANKSHAFT INSPECTION

The easiest way to check a roller-bearing crank is simply by giving the connecting rod a good yank; if there is any appreciable up and down play, it's due for a rebuild. As a matter of fact, you don't even need to remove the rod from the crankcase. Once the top end is off, give the rod a tug. If it's got enough up and down play to be felt, it's going to come apart, one way or another.

Plain-bearing cranks are checked in the traditional manner. Remove the rods and bearings, look for signs of distress—scoring or heat discoloration—and then measure everything

The rod shouldn't have any up-and-down play, although some slight side-to-side movement is permissible.

Believe it or not, this one made its way into the shop under its own power. It was also repaired!

If there is no discernible play at the crankshaft end, chances are the main bearings are OK. If there is noticeable up-and-down movement, a complete bottom-end rebuild will be needed.

with your micrometer. Normally a crankshaft or main bearing on the way out gives plenty of advance notice. Metal chunks in the oil, loud noises emanating from the crankcase, and increased vibration are all signals of the bottom end's imminent demise.

Quick tip: Triumph engines route oil through their crankshaft ends. Always replace the case seal with the original-equipment type featuring a metal support, and always measure the end to make sure it hasn't worn down. If it has, don't panic; undersize seals are available.

QUICK CRANK CHECK

You suspect the crank may be about to grenade, but of course it could be something else. How can you tell without pulling down half the motor?

First check the oil—no metal scraps? Good. Next, pull one side cover, preferably the alternator or primary drive. Grab the end of the crank and give it a shake. If it moves—uh-oh—the crank is on the way out, if it doesn't, start looking elsewhere.

A loose clutch hub, worn primary gears or a bad cush drive—not to mention an out-of-synch carb on a multi—can mimic a bad big-end bearing. Of course you may still have a rod bearing on the way out, but you'll generally see signs of that showing up as metal flakes in the oil.

SLUDGE TRAP REMOVAL

Some British bikes—BSA and Triumph in particular—incorporate sludge traps in their crankshafts. Anytime the crank is removed, these should be removed, the wire trap replaced or cleaned, and the passages themselves cleaned out thoroughly. The problem is that the access screw can be difficult to remove—as a matter of fact, it can be damn difficult.

These screws were tightened and then staked with a prick punch at the factory. The punch point must first be relieved and then the screw removed. Usually an impact driver and the correct-size bit will remove the screw. If it doesn't, try this method recommended by the Triumph Owners Club.

Sludge Trap Removal

Before the retaining screw on this crank can be removed, the staking point will have to be drilled out.

Heat is a great persuader; without it, removing the retaining screw for the crank sludge trap is next to impossible.

Use an impact driver to loosen the retaining screw; don't be afraid to really belt it, either.

Once the plug is loose you can use a large screwdriver, helped by an even larger adjustable wrench, to spin the plug out the rest of the way.

Drill a series of 1/8-inch holes along the length of the original slot. Connect the holes with a sharp chisel or die grinder to form a new slot. Make it large enough to accept a Snap-On #SW-405A 1/2-inch-drive screwdriver blade. Attach the longest 1/2-inch-drive ratchet you can find to the bit and remove the plug. Replace it with an Alloy Tech Allen-head plug. Send John Healy at the Triumph Owners Club a nice thank-you note.

OIL PUMPS

If oil is the engine's blood, then it stands to reason that the oil pump is the heart. I know

Sludge Trap Removal (continued)

The crankshaft's center bolt must also be removed before the sludge trap will come out.

Next, tap a large easy-out into the sludge trap.

Use the adjustable wrench to turn the sludge trap out of the crank.

Once the trap has broken loose, it should come out fairly easily.

This particular crank was a time bomb waiting to go off.

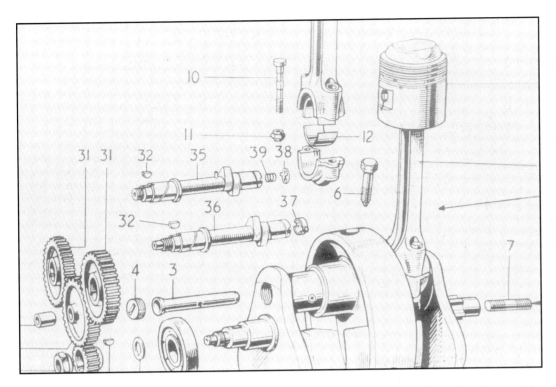

Triumph Twins prior to 1970, and many other bikes, use a breather disc located in the end of the camshaft (disc no. 38, spring no. 39). Make certain it's in place and stays there during reassembly. If it falls out and you force the case halves together, you'll ruin the disc and cam bushings.

that's a vastly overused metaphor but it works for me. Give the oil pump a thorough cleaning and inspection. Because the pump is always immersed in oil (or should be), wear should be negligible. Problems are usually centered on sticking check valves or balls in American and British motorcycles that employ dry sump systems with return side scavenge pumps. Check valves can generally be reseated or replaced. Older Hondas employed a centrifugal filter that should be cleaned periodically.

It might be worth considering updating your oil pump when the motor's apart. Many aftermarket pumps are available for British and American machines, including a very effective rotary pump for Triumphs available from Morgo.

BREATHERS

Crankcase breathers might be timed, vacuum controlled, or simply holes drilled in some convenient spot on the engine. While the latter are seldom a problem—which is why most manufacturers prefer them—timed breathers can sometimes be a headache, especially when they aren't timed correctly. Oil leaks, smoking, and sluggish performance can be a direct result of an improperly timed breather.

Pay particular attention to breather valves that might be located in the end of the camshaft à la BSA and Triumph. It's easy to lose the breather disc and spring during disassembly, and just as easy to pinch it during reassembly.

BASIC MACHINE SHOP PRACTICES

At some point during the course of any restoration you're likely to require some machining services, especially if it's your first foray into engine rebuilding. Even the most experienced hobbyist restorer is unlikely to have all of the equipment needed to return an engine to like-new conditions.

Machine shops handle cylinder boring, valve-guide replacement, valve-seat replacement, crankshaft truing, and a wide variety of other repairs that require specialized equipment. This isn't to say that these jobs can't be performed at home—they can and many times are. But unless you're willing to invest heavily in boring bars, valve refacers, lathes, and milling machines, I'd recommend leaving them to the pros, at least the first time out.

Some, or perchance all, of the above might be available through your local motorcycle shop, particularly if they're involved in any type of racing. In the last 10 years or so quite a few shops specializing strictly in motorcycle machine work have sprung up. Falicon Performance Engineering Inc. of Clearwater, Florida, a shop dedicated to rebuilding crankshafts and clutches, is a perfect example. I once sent

Your basic boring bar, used to bore cylinders.

them a BMW R69S crankshaft with a bent and, at the time, unavailable connecting rod. Ten days later they handed me a crank with new bearings and a straight rod. They also handed me a bill that was far less than the cost of a new crankshaft. Most areas of the country have a local tuning or machining guru. If not, UPS delivers daily.

In the meantime, let's look at a few of the common machine shop procedures and how they're performed.

I'd venture a guess that the most common job is cylinder boring. A boring bar is nothing more than a precision-milled surface (the table) that holds the cylinder securely while a cutting tool mounted in a tool post or bar is fed through the cylinder. The table holds the cylinder at a perfect right angle to the cutting tool. The cutter then bores a perfectly round, oversize hole in the block.

The boring bar leaves a smooth, almost polished, finish. It looks nice but doesn't do much for ring seating. Once the boring is finished the cylinder needs to be honed. Honing leaves the cylinder with a series of microscopic ridges or plateaus. These act like tiny files to help seat the rings.

Not all engine overhauls require cylinder boring. Cylinders must be honed anytime the rings are replaced, although they only need boring if they're worn out and require an oversize piston. If the piston-to-cylinder wall clearance is within specs and the bore is straight, then it's likely that a quick pass with the hone to deglaze the cylinder is all you'll need.

This rod honing machine repairs damage caused by a spun plain bearing; it can also be used to hone small cylinders.

Hones are available in a variety of sizes and shapes. At the top of the heap is the precision cylinder hone. Prices start in the $200 range, so unless you plan on a fair amount of honing, these are best left to the pros. Precision hones generally use four cutting stones, and feature micrometer-style adjustment. A 1/2-inch drill turning the hone through a solid drive shaft usually drives them, although some of the nice commercial models incorporate self-contained motors. These "big gun" hones are occasionally used for boring cylinders.

Surfacing or glaze-breaking hones normally use three spring-loaded stones and have a flexible—either rubber or spring steel—drive shaft. They are somewhat less precise than the precision models but considerably cheaper. Prices start in the $30 to $40 range. These can be spun with almost any variable-speed drill and work fine for home use.

Flex hones, sometimes called "bottle washers" or "ball hones" have dozens of abrasive balls set on stalks around a central shaft. Ball hones are terrific for breaking glazes. They remove virtually no material, but do impart a beautiful crosshatch. Prices are very reasonable, from about $10 on up depending on the size. Flex hones are perfect for the home restorer. You can't do any real damage with them, and they're cheap and easy to use.

Hone stones range from a coarse 60 grit up to 400, which imparts a finish so fine that it's virtually a polish. Normally the ring manufacturer specifies a cylinder finish, but for most vintage bikes a finish of 180 to 220 is right in the ballpark.

HEADWORK

Starting at the top and working our way down, valve guides are replaced by heating the head up and then using the appropriate drift and a large hammer to drive the guide out. More progressive shops use a hydraulic press to remove the guides, but either method works fine.

Once the guide is removed and the head cools, the guide passage is inspected and a new guide test fitted. If the passage is galled or worn too badly to accept a new standard guide, an oversize guide is installed. Some shops might suggest knurling oversize valve guides, which takes up excess clearance by forming ridges in the inside diameter. You might be tempted to knurl a worn guide.

Frankly, I see no point to it. Guides are inexpensive and, as we discussed in the previous section, easily obtained.

Once the new guide is in place the valve seat can be cut. The reason the guide is replaced before the seat is cut is to ensure that the seat is cut concentric to the guide—but you knew that. In theory, all valve seat cutters work on the same principle. First the pilot is inserted into the guide. The cutting tool is then placed over the guide. The tool is then turned either by hand or mechanical means.

In my opinion, the best tool on the market for seatwork is the Serdi. The Serdi tool uses a carbide bit to cut all three-seat angles at once. It is expensive, though, and not every shop has one. Close behind is the Neway. The Neway cutter cuts each angle individually, using a different cutting tool.

If the valves are reusable, they should be refaced using a valve refacer. Valve refacers can be either hand or machine operated. The valve is placed into the chuck, and then either a cutting bit or stone contacts the valve face and renews the face. The valve head angle might be cut from 0 to 46 degrees depending on the type of engine it's to be used in, although the norm is generally either 30 or 45 degrees.

When valve seats are replaced, the standard operating procedure is to remove the old one by cutting it away. The head is then heated and the new seat pressed or pulled into place. It is then cut like any other valve seat.

A finished cylinder head is a thing of beauty. This one is ready to bolt back in place (after the valves are installed).

BOTTOM END

Most bottom end work revolves around the crank (cheap pun intended). Machine work might include turning down the journals to accept an undersize bearing, building up worn-out journals with weld and refacing, or resizing connecting rods. Rebuilding roller bearing cranks and truing them or straightening bent rods and so on are also common.

All of these jobs should be farmed out, as they require a sizable investment in machinery, time, and knowledge. If you've got access to a press, and you're overhauling a single or twin cylinder with a built-up crank, by all means have at it. Likewise, bolted-up cranks à la Harley V-twin; if you're willing to invest in the tools, they can be done at home quite successfully.

Other common machine work includes, but is by no means limited to, reclaiming worn parts, truing gasket and case surfaces, Helicoiling, and just about anything else you can imagine, including manufacturing new and custom parts.

A good relationship with the machine shop of your choice is almost a prerequisite to restoration. Once you find a good one, stick with it. If you like their work, pay their price, and treat them with affection.

Over the years I've worked with no more than five or six different machine shops on a regular basis. The guy I use now I've known for at least 10 years. In all that time he's never let me down; in fact, several times he's bailed me out of some very tough situations. I accept his opinion, don't haggle about price, and try not to rush him.

The cylinder liner of this modern two-stroke has been worn beyond repair; however, a new liner (at left) can be installed without a lot of drama.

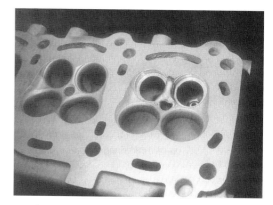

Harder to repair, but not impossible for a good machine shop: This modern sport bike cracked the head in the area between the valves. It was welded up, and will now be remachined, and have new valve seats installed.

I suggest that if you are serious about restoring motorcycles you cultivate the same type of relationship with your local guy. Treat him to lunch once in a while, pay his price gracefully, and smile and say "thank you" when he hands you that trick piece of unobtainum he whittled up for your project.

STRIPPED THREADS

One thing you are sure to encounter during your rebuild is the ubiquitous stripped thread. We all know the feeling, just as the bolt should be nipping up tight, it suddenly goes slack. Damn. Or as the bolt is withdrawn, a long curlicue of aluminum comes with it. Now what?

There are several methods of repairing stripped threads. From the tiniest tank-badge screw to a stripped sparkplug hole, you can redrill the hole and tap it to the next oversize—acceptable perhaps, but not the preferred method. You can jam a self-tapping screw in the hole, which definitely heads the unacceptable list. Or you can install a new thread, which is the correct way to repair a stripped thread.

There are several acceptable ways to replace threads. All involve opening up the original hole and installing either a solid insert or a piece of spring steel to form a new thread. My favorite, and probably the best-known method, is the Helicoil. I like them because they're available almost anywhere, they're inexpensive, come in a wide variety of lengths and sizes, and are easy to install. I've no doubt other repair methods are just as durable, but

in my experience they fall short in one or more of the above areas.

TYPICAL HELICOIL INSTALLATION

Uh-oh now you've done it—stripped the case screw, badge screw, sparkplug, or drain plug. Oddly enough, it's an 8x1.25 thread. Gee whiz (or words to that effect), the local auto parts store stocks 8x1.25 Helicoil kits. Inside you find a dozen little coils of spring steel, an installation tool, and a special tap. The outside of the package tells you what size drill to use.

If the hole is small, I use a tap handle to turn the drill bit by hand. If the hole opens up into the engine internals and I don't want to take the engine apart, I pack the flutes of the drill with grease to catch most of the chips. Once the hole is opened up, I use the tap the same way. Helicoil might be installed with the stripped thread in situ, using the greasy bit trick, or a vacuum cleaner to suck up the loose chips. I've seen both in action and both work well. Then degrease the area with solvent.

Follow the instructions for installing the coil. Bingo, all fixed. If the coil is too short,

Helicoils are used to replace damaged threads. The Helicoil kit contains a special tap, the inserting tool, and a dozen or so coils; all you have to supply is the right size drill bit. New coils are available separately. Helicoils come in every size and thread pitch I can think of. The kit shown here retails for under $40.

you can either order longer ones—the coils are sold separately—or stack two or more of them together. If the coil is too long, just cut it down to size. Damaged coils can be removed by prying one end out of the thread and pulling the coil out with a needle-nose pliers.

REPAIRING STRIPPED THREADS WITH HELICOILS

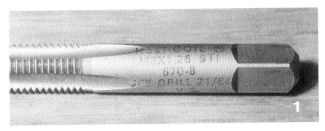

The Helicoil kit includes a special tap; all of the necessary information, including the drill size, is listed directly on the tap. Note: sparkplug Helicoil kits use a tapered tap and do not require a drill.

Since I didn't have anything in the shop with stripped threads (at least nothing I knew about), I used this piece of aluminum bar stock to demonstrate. First, the correct size hole was bored, in this case 21/64 inch.

The kit includes the installation mandrel and a half-dozen or so inserts. The steel tang on the insert engages the drive slot of the mandrel. The tang is removed before the bit is inserted.

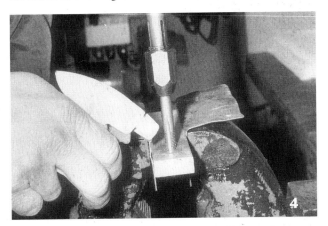

Next, using plenty of lubricant, the tap is used to cut the new threads. Run the tap in only until it bottoms.

The tapped hole will look something like this.

Place the insert on the mandrel, making sure the tang is engaged.

Thread the insert into the hole . . .

. . . until the top thread of the insert lies flush or slightly beneath the surface of the hole.

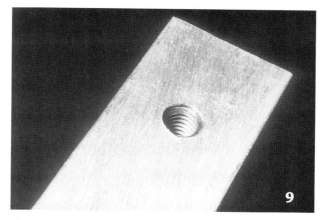

The installed Helicoil should look something like this.

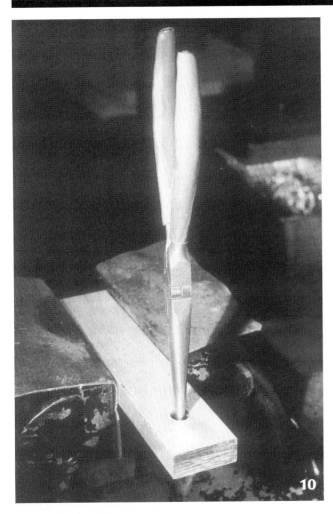

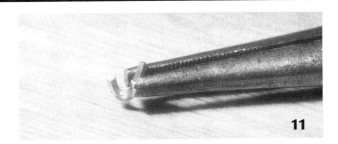

Push down to break the tab off. It may help to give the pliers a sharp whack with the flat of your palm. If the hole is a short one with a bottom to hit, or if you can't reach the tang with pliers, you can knock the tang off with a short punch. Just make sure you'll be able to get the tang out of the hole, or that it won't fall down into the bowels of the engine or tranny.

Reach into the hole with a pair of long needle-nose pliers and get a good grip on the drive tang.

Finally, install the correct fastener in the Helicoil. The repair is actually stronger than the original threads.

ENGINE REASSEMBLY

The parts are back from the machine shop, all the sub-unit repairs have been made, and the new parts are on the shelf. Gentlemen, assemble your motors. It's easy, like the manual states. "Assemble in the reverse order of disassembly." Sorry, I just couldn't resist a little joke.

As I said in the beginning, this book isn't intended to teach anyone basic mechanics. I'm not going to walk you through engine-building by the numbers. Here's how I do it. Use all of my ideas or pick and choose, whatever you feel comfortable with. Just remember there's nothing worse than installing your freshly rebuilt engine into your just as freshly restored bike and having it go BANG!

I start by covering the top of my bench with clean cardboard. I then place a spotless teardown tray on top of the bench and a clean wooden assembly box in it so I have some place to place the first part, which is usually a crankcase half.

Next I lay out all of the parts, tools, and supplies I think I'll need for that portion of the job. If you plan to use a gasket sealer or case sealer, make sure you've got enough of it to do the job. Make sure you've got whatever lubricants you think you'll need, as well as a supply of clean rags and some spray solvent for a quick, spot clean. Finally, make certain you've got all of the tools you'll need to do the job, including enough fuel for your torch.

I then make a trial run, placing the various parts in their respective locations. I don't actually install them. I just arrange them loosely in the order of assembly. Then I double-check the parts on the bench against the parts book to ensure that I actually have everything I need and it's in the right place. There's nothing worse than assembling the cases only to find that you've overlooked a shim, clip, or plug and must do it all over again.

Before you start assembling the engine, make sure it's actually ready to assemble. Run a tap through any threads. Make certain there's no grit or polish trapped in there. Blow out all the nooks and crannies one last time to remove any dust and dirt. Do the same with the oil passages. Double-check any hardware that's inaccessible once the engine is assembled.

I hate to sound like a broken record but "haste definitely makes waste." Proceed slowly, take your time, and make sure everything is the way you want it before moving on to the next step. In fact, don't ever assemble an engine "because you have to." Only work on your engine, or any portion of your motorcycle for that matter, because you "want to." Of

course that caveat falls by the wayside when you're stranded on the side of the road, but that's an exception.

One other chunk of advice: I generally assemble an engine in spurts. I'll do the bottom end, for instance, and then take a break. Or maybe I'll take one between installing the cylinders and bolting on the head. I find a little break helps keep your head on straight, if you catch my drift.

Gasket Sealers

Modern gasket sealers are just about the best thing since sliced bread when it comes to rebuilding any engine, vintage or modern. Available in a wide variety of styles and application methods, sealers definitely make life easier. The principal concerns are which one to use, where to use it, and how much of it to use.

Gasket or silicone sealers, like thread-locking compounds, are anaerobic, meaning they cure in the absence of air. Gasket sealers are either hardening or semi-hardening. Which one you use depends on the application and the manufacturer's recommendation. The sealant might come in a squeeze tube, or it

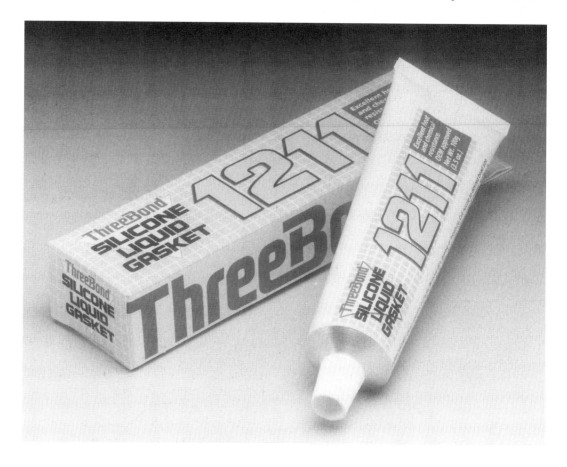

Modern silicone sealers will keep the oil on the inside of the engine. Follow the manufacturer's recommendations when applying the stuff, and try to keep it out of your hair. *Photo courtesy of Three Bond Corporation*

might be a liquid brush-on, or an aerosol. Some are used to dress a gasket, some in lieu of a gasket.

The one thing sealers have in common is that everyone, perhaps subscribing to the theory "if more is better, than too much must be almost enough" tends to overuse the stuff. Most of us have seen some "mechanic" lather the stuff all over a gasket or side cover. When the cover is tightened down a bead of sealer as thick as your little finger oozes out. "No problem," as Joe Wrench wipes the goo off with his bandanna.

Well there is a problem. Whatever squeezed out also squeezed in. Now there are little snakes of silicone frolicking away inside your freshly rebuilt engine just waiting for a chance to plug up oil galleys and lodge in bearings. Believe me, it's a real problem. I bought a very nice Saab once because some mullethead used half a tube or more of blue silicone seal to glue a transmission cover on. After a week or two the silicone worked its way into the carrier bearings, ruined them, and in disgust the owner sold me the car at well below market value.

Most sealers have instructions printed right on the container—most of us don't bother to read them, but they are there. In the meantime, this is the method I use to apply sealant that comes in a tube—YamaBond-3, for example. In most cases, forget about using the handy-dandy applicator tip. Those are fine for gooping up Chevy valve covers, but in general, even the smallest opening is way too large for motorcycle applications.

Instead, cut down an acid brush to about one-third its original length. That makes the brush nice and stiff. Squeeze a little sealer onto a piece of cardboard, dip the brush into it, and paint the sealer onto the surface of whatever it is you want to seal. The sealer coat should be so thin that it's almost transparent.

If the sealer comes in an aerosol can, as many gasket dressings do, then follow the instructions on the can. Most recommend giving both sides of the gasket a light coating and then letting it "tack up." Liquid sealant usually comes with a built-in applicator brush in the can or bottle. Again follow the directions—a little goes a long way. When the parts are bolted home, all you should see is a little bit of "sweat" on the outer surface. Clean up any excess with lacquer thinner or some other solvent.

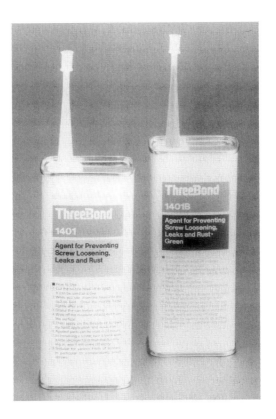

Thread-locking compound should always be used on crucial fasteners. Different grades are required for different-size fasteners and different applications.

Thread-Locking Compounds

Thread-locking compounds are in the same boat as gasket sealers, and by and large suffer the same abuses. Since Loctite is the best-known thread-locking compound, I'll use it as an example. There are lots of good locking compounds on the market. I mentioned Loctite only because it's almost become a generic term for liquid locking compounds.

Loctite is graded by fastener size and degree of security needed. For example, the blue stuff works well on fasteners up to about 3/8-inch diameter. You can also use it on larger nuts and bolts that tend to vibrate loose, but aren't crucial fasteners.

For big bolts that need to be kept really tight—studs or bearings that are a little loose in the case—use the next grade up, which is red. While the bolts secured with blue can usually be broken loose with hand tools, parts glued on with the red might require a little heat, or a whacking big wrench.

Next on the list is the green. This stuff is the devil's own glue. Its primary use is to retain cylinder liners, sleeves, and bushings. Figure on using a press and lots of heat to break a green Loctite bond.

Before you lather the stuff all over the place, the threads must be absolutely clean and dry. Locking compounds work by filling the open spaces between the threads. If there is oil or dirt in there the compounds won't harden. Make sure the compound grade is appropriate to its task. Locking a badge screw to a gas tank with stud-and-bearing mount is foolish, to say the least. Oh, it'll stay on, all right; it'll just be impossible to remove.

Of course locking down a crankshaft pinion nut with a light grade compound is just as silly—in fact you'll be reminded just how silly it is when you pull the timing cover off to retorque the nut. Most shop manuals will tell you when, where, and what grade of compound to use. Believe them. Also, follow the directions regarding the amount. Locking compounds are sold in small tubes. Why? Because it doesn't take much to be effective—when they say "only a drop," they mean it.

NOTES ON GENERAL ENGINE ASSEMBLY

Always assemble the bottom end "wet," that is, with plenty of oil. Bearings, gears, and shafts—especially the cam lobes and tappets—should be well drenched with either the recommended engine oil or a dedicated assembly lubricant. Always prime the oil pump.

My normal practice is to lubricate everything in the top end except the cylinder. While it was once common practice to drench the piston and rings with oil before assembling the top end, today's oils are so good they won't allow break-in. The accepted practice now is to install the rings dry, facilitating break-in. Put just a dab of oil on the piston skirt to prevent scuffing on start-up. Use a petroleum-based oil; synthetics can prevent the rings from fully seating, leading to problems down the road.

Some manufacturers recommend a light break-in oil for the first 100 miles or so; BMW used to spec a straight 20 weight for the break-in period of the /5-/7-series bikes, mainly because the bikes had a tough time seating the rings.

It's worth mentioning that there might be some advantage to leaving the engine partially disassembled. They are certainly lighter in this state—no small consideration when you're working alone. The missing covers sometimes allow access to better handholds, though it's easier to pinch fingers in an open gear train. Engines are often much easier to shoehorn back into the frame if they're minus the head, rocker boxes, or side covers. Besides, you can't scratch a cover that's not on it.

Before you decide, make sure that the missing parts can be installed once the engine's back in the frame. On many Japanese bikes, for example, the engine comes out in one piece and goes back in the same way.

If the engine is going to be stored while you work on the rest of the bike, make sure it's protected from the elements, otherwise you may find yourself restoring it a second time! I'd place it in a garbage bag, spritz a little WD-40 in there and seal the whole thing up. In fact, I'd do that if it's stored for any appreciable time. I'd recommend turning it over every few weeks and re-spritzing it.

7

Chapter
S e v e n

Fuel Systems

CARBURETOR OVERHAUL

Carburetors get blamed for far more problems than they actually cause—95 percent of the carb problems I see are caused by nothing more than a little dirt or (owner-inflicted) maladjustment.

The first step to restoring a carburetor is to give it a thorough cleaning and identification. Since carbs are easily swapped from bike to bike and are usually one of the first items replaced by "speed merchants," what you have may not be what you need.

For example, with few exceptions the Amal Monobloc was the standard carburetor for British motorcycles from 1954 to 1966. In 1967 the Amal introduced the Concentric. When Monoblocs wore out—or mechanics assumed they had—a lot of them were replaced with Concentrics. In fact some restorers will hang Concentrics on an older engine because they're relatively cheap, they work well, and they can be construed as being "correct"—although that takes quite a leap of faith if the motor in question is an early Vincent or pre-unit Triumph. If you plan to make it original, you'll need to know which carbs were originally spec'd for your bike versus which ones are on it.

Carburetor Types

For the most part British, European, and Japanese motorcycles are equipped with variable-venturi style or "slide" carburetors. American designers favored the fixed throat or "butterfly" carburetor.

British motorcycles are normally equipped with Amal carbs, with the occasion-

al S.U. or Zenith thrown in to keep things interesting. You might also find Solex carburetors, particularly on Ariel motorcycles. Villiers carbs were used, appropriately enough, on Villiers engines. Go back far enough and you might run into a variety of lesser-known carburetors, including Binks.

As a general rule, Japanese bikes will use some variation of either the Mikuni or the Keihin. Honda favors the Keihin; after all it owns a controlling interest in the company. The rest, particularly the older models, tend to wear Mikunis.

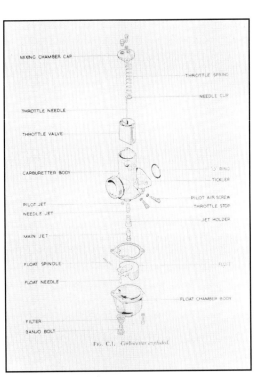

FIG. C.I. *Carburetor explained.*

The Amal Concentric was in use from 1967 until 1978. Mainly used on British and Spanish bikes, they were also found on early Ducati GT 750s.

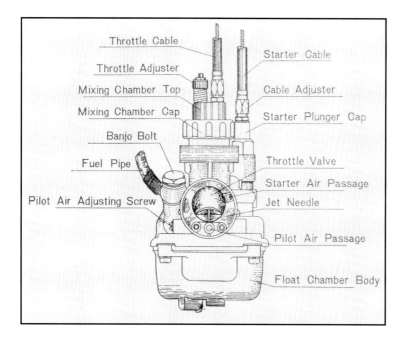

Throttle Cable
Starter Cable
Throttle Adjuster
Mixing Chamber Top
Cable Adjuster
Mixing Chamber Cap
Starter Plunger Cap
Banjo Bolt
Throttle Valve
Fuel Pipe
Starter Air Passage
Jet Needle
Pilot Air Adjusting Screw
Pilot Air Passage
Float Chamber Body

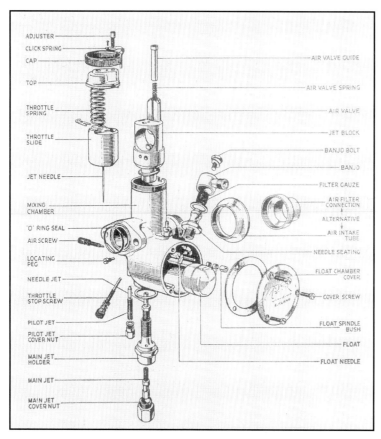

ADJUSTER
CLICK SPRING
CAP
AIR VALVE GUIDE
TOP
AIR VALVE SPRING
THROTTLE SPRING
AIR VALVE
THROTTLE SLIDE
JET BLOCK
BANJO BOLT
BANJO
JET NEEDLE
FILTER GAUZE
AIR FILTER CONNECTION
MIXING CHAMBER
ALTERNATIVE AIR INTAKE TUBE
'O' RING SEAL
AIR SCREW
NEEDLE SEATING
LOCATING PEG
NEEDLE JET
FLOAT CHAMBER COVER
THROTTLE STOP SCREW
COVER SCREW
PILOT JET
PILOT JET COVER NUT
FLOAT SPINDLE BUSH
MAIN JET HOLDER
FLOAT
MAIN JET
FLOAT NEEDLE
MAIN JET COVER NUT

The Amal Monoblock was the standard carburetor used on most British bikes from 1954 to 1966–1967, when it was superceded by the Concentric. They are easy to rebuild and parts are widely available. Worn bodies can be resleeved. Used ones can be found at most swap meets, and some new ones are also available.

You don't see too many of these anymore. Some Mikuni carburetors—often those used on rotary valve engines—had their idle speed adjusters mounted vertically. In all other respects, they were identical to standard Mikuni carbs.

Euro models tend to carry either Bing or Dell'Orto. Expect to see some crossover. Late Triumph Bonnevilles, T140ES's, LEs and EXs came equipped with 32mm Bing CV carbs. BMW's R90S wore a pair of Dell'Orto "pumpers"—with accelerator pumps. If you're restoring a race bike, expect to see almost anything—Lectrons, E.I.s, you name it.

Variable Venturi Carburetors

The variable venturi carb comes in two basic designs and a host of variations. The no-frills, good old-fashioned carburetor is called, simply enough, a slide carburetor. A cable pulls the slide up against spring tension. Releasing the throttle allows the spring to return the slide to the idle position.

The other type is the CV or CD, constant-vacuum or constant-depression carburetor. Both CV and CD use the same basic theory and design. A butterfly in the throat is controlled by the cable. As the butterfly opens, the air rushing past creates a vacuum in the sealed chamber above the slide. Air pressure in the throat lifts the slide dependent on the vacuum above it.

CVs have several advantages over the basic slide carb. They are altitude compensating in that they maintain the correct air/fuel mixture even at higher altitudes. In addition, since the slide can only rise as fast as the air in the throat and the vacuum above the slide allow it to, they tend to eliminate off-idle stumbles. They also tend to run cleaner, which is why virtually all new carbureted motorcycles feature CV carbs. On the other hand, the basic slide carb still enjoys an overall performance advantage. Both types are restored in essentially the same manner.

Fixed Throat

Known by a variety of names—fixed jet, fixed venturi, or fixed throat—this is your basic, garden-variety automotive-style carburetor. Rather than have a slide move up and down to vary the carburetor venturi (as in the slide carb), the venturi in a fixed jet remains constant. A pivoting plate (the butterfly valve) in the ven-

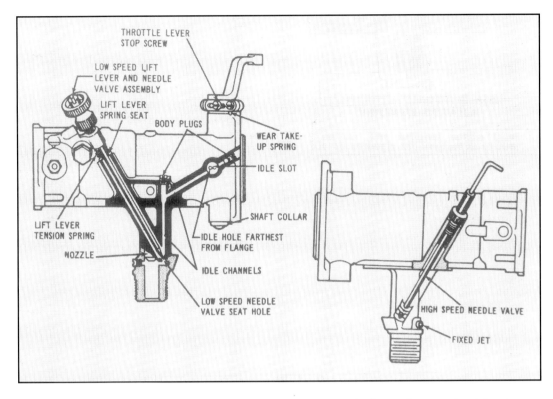

THROTTLE LEVER STOP SCREW

LOW SPEED LIFT LEVER AND NEEDLE VALVE ASSEMBLY

LIFT LEVER SPRING SEAT

BODY PLUGS

WEAR TAKE-UP SPRING

IDLE SLOT

SHAFT COLLAR

LIFT LEVER TENSION SPRING

NOZZLE

IDLE HOLE FARTHEST FROM FLANGE

IDLE CHANNELS

LOW SPEED NEEDLE VALVE SEAT HOLE

HIGH SPEED NEEDLE VALVE

FIXED JET

There's not much to the Linkert: check for excess wear at the throttle shaft, make sure the jets and air passages are clean, and it should work fine. If everything mechanical checks out in the carb but you still can't get it to idle properly or run well, check for air leaks at the mounting flange and cylinder-manifold joints. Both H-D and Indian used these mixers for almost 40 years, so they must have been doing something right.

turi varies the airflow through the instrument.

Typically, American manufacturers used fixed venturi carbs almost exclusively, at least where their big twins were concerned. The most prominent exception—and in fact the only one I'm aware of—is the post-World War II Indians. From 1951 to 1953, Indian 80" Models were equipped with 1-3/16 Amals. Likewise, 1948-1949 Arrows were equipped with domestic slide carbs, usually replaced by the owner with 7/8-inch Amals at the first opportunity.

Common fixed-venturi carbs include Bendix, Linkert, and Schebler as original-equipment carburetors. The S&S has been a popular aftermarket replacement.

Overhaul and Repair

Rebuilding kits are available for most, if not all, carburetors through a wide variety of aftermarket suppliers. In general, they are fairly inexpensive and contain most of the bits needed to revitalize your mixer. For the most part, all carburetors are inspected and repaired in the same manner; only the details differ.

A thorough disassembly and cleaning is the first step. The pieces and body should be thoroughly soaked in solvent and blown dry with compressed air. Resist the temptation to run a bit of wire through the various pas-

sages. Hard wire such as mechanic's wire can enlarge or burr the passageways, creating problems down the road. Better to clean them with a blast of aerosol solvent or air. If you need to remove any obstructions lodged in the passageways, use a strand of soft copper wire as a last resort.

Be sure to remove and check each jet against your parts manual. It also goes without saying that you should familiarize yourself with your particular instrument before you dismantle it. For example, early Amal Concentrics used a run-of-the-mill pilot jet; after 1969 this was discarded and replaced by a simple drilled passage. Look all you want; you won't find a pilot jet hanging around in the float bowl of a post-1969 Amal.

The most common trouble areas are a damaged pilot screw seat, leaky needle and seat, and a worn slide/carb body. Amal mixers are particularly susceptible to slide-throttle bore damage. Fortunately, they are inexpensive to replace and widely available.

There are also a few firms that specialize in resleeving them, a process in which the body is bored straight and an oversize slide installed. Different shops use different repair methods. One process does away with the choke, for instance, so make sure that if you decide to resleeve you understand exactly

Always keep an eye out for cracked rubber intake manifolds. Not only won't the bike run right, but an air leak and the resultant lean mixture can cause overheating and a holed piston.

what's going to be done. Check the appendix for a list of specialists and their addresses.

Other chronic problem areas are the manifold-joint "O" rings on H-D V-twins. Check for dry rotted or cracked rubber cylinder head intake sleeves on anything that uses them. Also look for cracked heat insulators between the head and carb. Dell'Orto carbs use tiny idle jets, which are susceptible to blockage.

Flange-mounted carburetors should always have the flange face checked for true. If it's only a wee bit warped you might be able to resurface it by lapping it in on a glass plate. Fold a sheet of 600 wet-and-dry sandpaper across the glass, and make a few passes using a circular motion. I keep the paper saturated with WD-40 to prevent it from "loading" with aluminum. High spots will show up instantly. It shouldn't take a lot of work to flatten out the surface; if it does, a trip to the milling machine might be in order.

Floats should always be checked for leaks. Brass ones can often be repaired by draining them and soldering up the hole, but it's a good idea to weigh the float prior to applying the solder. You'll want the repaired one to weigh the same. It won't matter whether the float's overweight from solder or fuel—it'll still cause the bike to run rich. Damaged cork or plastic floats must be replaced.

Carburetors are fairly delicate instruments. They use lots of tiny screws, brass fittings, and die-cast parts, all of which are easily damaged. Work slowly and carefully. Cleanliness is paramount; a little bit of dirt in a carb can cause anything from poor idling to holed pistons.

In a similar vein, use caution when removing and installing the jets and adjusting screws. Use a screwdriver that fits the slots correctly. When it says "seat the pilot screw lightly" it means just that, lightly—the taper should just kiss the seat. Ham-fisted mechanics ruin more than their share of carburetors by overtightening everything from the main jet to the pilot screw. When it comes to alloy and brass, snug is fine.

A simple inline fuel filter will prevent errant bits of dirt from clogging up the works. In addition, the gauzelike sock over the air filter prevents it from clogging up with mud and dirt—a worthwhile addition on an off-road racer.

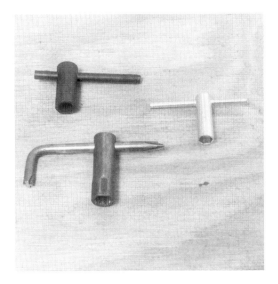

Carburetor jet wrenches can make life a lot easier. The one in the center has a small Phillips head screwdriver that's perfect for unscrewing AMAL float bowls.

This Mikuni conversion on an H-D Sprint looks great in black. I'm not crazy about the sharp bend in the throttle cable, though. Steel elbows are available for just such a situation.

Special Tools

Some aspects of carb repair can drive you nuts. Removing the parallel Amals on Norton twins, for example. Synchronizing a rack of four-cylinder carbs. Replacing main jets with the carbs in place. It all sounds simple, and with the right tool it can be.

Some tools you'll need to make yourself. To remove the carbs from the Norton, cut down a 5/16 Allen wrench to squeeze between the manifold. Entire slews of tools are available from the various manufacturers to help rebuild Mikuni carbs, including some peculiar-looking screwdrivers to help sync them.

If the subject of your ministrations wears multiple carbs, a vacuum-gauge set is definitely in order. I prefer mercury-filled carb sticks over gauges. I find them a lot easier to use, but gauges work well, too.

There's a whole raft of jet wrenches out there, including a very nice one for Amals that incorporates two Phillips head screwdrivers that are perfect for removing float bowl screws. Last, but not least, is the good old "stubby" screwdriver. Find one that fits between the float bowls so you can remove the bowls without pulling the carbs off the bike.

Refinishing

Original equipment carburetors were rarely polished—who had the time? If you want to buff one to a mirrorlike finish, don't let me stop you. Carbs can be painted of course—mask off any ports and have at it. Eventually fuel will stain them just like the originals. Specialty metal cleaners can also blast them clean, using walnut shells, plastic beads, or baking soda—not sand or glass beads.

Personally, I like to clean them up, give them a light polish with Simichrome, and then let them dull off a bit. This seems to be the best compromise between overrestoring and leaving them cruddy-looking.

The carburetor on this immaculately restored Harley-Davidson "peashooter" speedway bike from the 1920s is almost as big as the cylinder!

BOUND UP

So you've rebuilt your carb. It works perfectly on the bench. You install it on the bike and the throttle sticks tighter than a clam at low tide. What happened? First, check the obvious, cable routing being the most likely culprit. Also make sure the throttle isn't binding against the handlebar and so forth.

Then check the not so obvious. If the carb bolts directly to the head, loosen the nuts slightly. If the carb(s) work freely, chances are you overtightened the mounting nuts slightly. When mounting bolt-on carburetors, torque the fasteners down evenly and just enough to secure the carb—any more is overkill and may well warp the carb body. By the same token never use anything other than hand pressure to tighten a screw-on carb top. Clamping the delicate casting with your favorite pair of pliers is one way to warp the body and cause the slide to stick.

Conversely, if the slide is sticking and it looks terminal, as a last resort you can sometimes relieve the sticking by grasping the carb body just below the cap with a pair of water pump pliers and applying some torque—try clockwise first, if that doesn't do it, counterclockwise. Remember—this is the court of last resort and is not recommended procedure. Also bear in mind that a sticking throttle is a potentially life-threatening condition and not something to treat lightly.

G.P.S, T.T.S, S&SS, AND SMOOTH BORES

As every dyed-in-the-wool Anglophile knows, the Amal GP and TT carburetors are the ultimate performance accessories—at least as far as bolt-on eye candy goes. The TT was primarily intended for racing and high-performance street use, the GP for pure race engines. They are somewhat different in their construction from a plain Jane Monobloc or Concentric, mostly by way of their remote float bowls.

The problem is that both the GP and TT can be a pain in the butt to live with on the street, even more so if you plan on using your bike on a daily basis. As an alternative you may want to consider using something else—perhaps an Amal Concentric or MKII—for day-to-day riding, and saving the exotic and somewhat finicky race carb for show use.

On the other hand, the S&S fixed venturi carb is considered to be superior in every way to the carburetors it replaces. There are several varieties available, all aimed, of course, at the Harley-Davidson market. In fact, unless you're planning a catalog restoration, you may well consider just dropping the appropriate one in place rather than rebuilding that old stock piece.

At one time the Mikuni smoothbore was the performance carburetor of choice for the superbike aficionado. Unlike many high-performance carbs, smoothbores are an all-around improvement over the stock units. If you're restoring some version of the Universal Japanese Motorcycle and come across a rack of smoothbores, by all means use them. If you're

building or restoring a period hot-rod, even better—nothing looks better on a late-1970s Japanese four than a rack of gleaming smoothbores and a four-into-one pipe.

One last word on carburetors. Over the years many of us have come to realize that some carburetors work better than others. Amal MKIIs, Mikunis, and Dell'Ortos all come to mind as particularly well-designed and workable slide carbs. For a fixed venturi you'd have to go a long way to beat an S&S. The point is that these carbs—and a few others like them—can go a long way toward civilizing some motorcycles.

If your intent is to restore to ride, don't be afraid to replace that cantankerous lump with something better and easier to live with. Sudco, in fact, makes adapter kits to mount various Mikunis on just about anything. Sudco's Norton single-carb conversion kit, for instance, works wonders on civilizing late-model Commandos.

FUEL TANKS AND PETCOCKS

While overhaul and repair of the fuel tank is covered in chapter 17, some mention of the inside of the tank is appropriate here. For starters, while you might not need or want to repaint your tank, you might be forced to clean it internally. In chapter 17 we'll go through the more aggressive methods; for now, we'll assume that the tank has only the normal loose scale and dirt in it.

The first step is to drain the tank completely, remove the petcocks, and set them

This old steel CZ "coffin" tank has been welded and patched a dozen times, but it still looks presentable!

This early H-D tank carries fuel and oil. It's been cleaned and glass beaded. The next step is repair and refinish. The small holes in the top are where screws from a "slide hammer" (dent puller) were inserted to pop out small dents.

aside. Seal the petcock openings: You can use pipe plugs, plates or tape, and rags. Dump a quart of kerosene, WD-40, or some other light, non-flammable solvent into the tank. Diesel fuel, parts washer solution, or even brake clean will also work well. Throw in a handful of 1/4-inch nuts, old steering-head bearings—balls only, please—or even some loose change. If you really want to get fancy, buy a tube of BBs.

Replace the cap, put on a pair of headphones, set the stereo to loud, and select some tunes that rock. Hold that tank out in front of you and boogie till you puke—I mean shake that thing like you got no brain! (Which you won't if you keep doing it too long.) After a few minutes of this nonsense—actually, do it as long as you can stand it—drain the tank, rinse it once with fresh gas, and take a look inside. Still grungy? Then repeat.

Chances are all of the loose stuff will be washed away, as will any stale gas, water, or errant spiders that might have turned it into the arachnid version of Trump Towers. This method works well if the tank is essentially sound to begin with. If it's not—well, more drastic measures are called for, and we'll get to them in the appropriate chapter. As a side note, this method works just as well on an oil tank: Just remove any internal filters, plug any openings, and rock on!

Petcocks

As we all know, petcocks come in every size and shape imaginable. Some are rebuildable; just as many aren't. British ones tend to

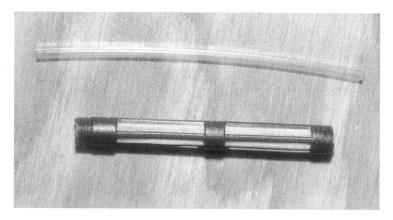

Standpipes may have a filter in them or they may be just a straight piece of pipe. Resist the temptation to shorten them or leave them out. The standpipe is your first line of defense in keeping crud out of your carb.

be both readily available and cheap. German versions, while generally available, are usually pretty pricey. Japanese petcocks are expensive, but rarely fail. Italian ones clog but are easily cleaned.

Maintenance is fairly straightforward. Remove the valve from the tank. It should have a

Fuel petcocks like this Ideal unit are rebuildable, if you can get the parts.

standpipe sticking up into the tank; if it has two, the shorter one is for reserve. The pipes might or might not incorporate a filter, depending on the maker's whim. If it does utilize a filter, clean it or replace it as required. Some petcocks also incorporate a sediment trap, usually in the form of a removable bowl below the fuel lever. These should be serviced anytime the carburetor float bowls are drained, or at least twice a year.

Resist the temptation to remove or shorten the standpipes in an effort to squeeze out a few more ounces of fuel between fill-ups. The standpipes are there so water—which is heavier than gas and tends to lie at the bottom of the tank—can't flow into your freshly refurbished carburetors. Remove the standpipes and the petcock inlet may now be so low that any dirt or water floating in the dark recesses of your tank has a straight shot at your main jet.

If you've got a leaker and a rebuild kit is available, by all means rebuild it. If not, it's a case for straight replacement. Trying to bodge something together is more often than not an exercise in frustration. You'll install your petcock, fill the tank with gas, and watch it run right out through the petcock you so proudly rebuilt from used parts. Bummer: been there, done it.

When reinstalling the petcock, use a little Teflon tape or paste on the threads to keep them from weeping. Remember that the fuel system is potentially the most dangerous subsystem on your motorcycle. When treated carelessly, gasoline develops a real mean streak.

I once watched a brand-new Norton go up in smoke because of a leaking float bowl. By the grace of God we put the fire out before it consumed the bike, the building, and all of the profit in the sale. It still cost the shop a paint job and a seat. Imagine how it feels to lose a bike after you've spent a year or two restoring it.

8

Chapter
Eight

Exhaust Systems

Depending on the circumstances, it's quite possible that your motorcycle will be missing the original exhaust system entirely, missing a substantial portion of its exhaust, or have a complete exhaust system that's completely shot. On the other hand, you might find yourself with a perfect exhaust that's wrong for your bike. Or simply a perfect exhaust.

TWO-STROKES

If you're restoring a two-stroke of any stripe, finding the correct exhaust can be a major concern. Without it, the bike just won't run

Dinged and dirty but still serviceable. Sometimes your only alternative is replacement, even if it means finding and repairing a used pipe.

properly. Swap meets, dealers, and pleading ads in the magazines are the obvious routes. If you're restoring a race bike or cafe racer, the task becomes a little less daunting. There are several pipe builders out there who either have blueprints on hand for a large assortment of pipes, or can build one to your specifications. Gemco, Circle F, and Bill's are the first ones I can think of that specialize in building two-stroke expansion chambers to order.

Two-stroke pipes that are on the bike present less of a problem. The inherent nature of a two-stroke, which causes it to burn oil with its fuel, tends to keep the pipe from rusting from the inside out. If the surface rust is only that—on the surface—then the best bet is a deep cleaning and possible re-plate. If the rust has eaten holes in the pipe, it might be possible to patch it, but only as a last resort. The best bet for a rusted-out pipe is always replacement.

Servicing Two-Stroke Pipes

If the pipe and muffler are sound, you're 75 percent of the way home. Most two-stroke mufflers are going to be equipped with a re-movable—and quite likely plugged—baffle. Getting the baffle out can be a real struggle; rust and carbon make a helluva glue.

Every manual I've seen shows some joker removing the baffle by pulling it out with a pair of pliers—after the retaining bolts have been removed, of course. About half the time they actually will pop right out, and 25 percent of the time they put up an argument. The remainder of the time they hold on like a barnacle on the Titanic. When a baffle is stuck, man, it's stuck. I've used heat, soaked them in carburetor cleaner, and used brute force. Honestly, brute force is the worst solution—the last thing you need is a damaged baffle.

Start by removing the retaining screw, but you already knew that. Fasten a Vise-Grip to the bar in the back of the baffle and pull. If it comes out, fine; if not, tap on the Vise-Grip with a plastic or brass mallet, and it should come out. If it doesn't, don't keep beating until the bar bends or even breaks. Stop.

If the baffle refuses to budge, try a little heat. Shoot the flame from a propane torch right down the center of the baffle. The heat should loosen up any burnt-on carbon, freeing it up. It'll also smoke like blue blazes, so this is a job best performed outdoors.

If the heat doesn't work, try soaking the baffle in WD-40 or penetrating oil overnight. Plug up both ends of the pipe, fill it with WD, and let 'er sit for a day or two. If you have access to a radiator shop, you can have the pipe "tanked"—soaked in a mild caustic solution to remove the carbon.

Finally, if you've run out of patience, you might be able to remove the baffle by inserting a long wooden dowel—a broomstick works well—into the muffler's open end and doing the predictable thing. Make sure the dowel is driving the baffle out, though, and not merely hammering the muffler apart.

Once the baffle has been removed a torch and wire brush should remove all of the carbon deposits. Many baffles were initially wrapped with a few layers of fiberglass "packing." Fresh packing is available at most motorcycle shops. A few wraps are all you need to take the edge off the exhaust crackle.

FOUR-STROKE EXHAUST SYSTEMS

Restorers of four-strokes (that's likely the majority of you) have it a lot easier in the exhaust department. In the first place, four-stroke engines aren't so finicky about their exhaust systems. In the second place, there are literally dozens of manufacturers reproducing mufflers and pipes for four-stroke motorcycles. As a last resort you can even fabricate, or have a specialist fabricate, an entire exhaust system from photos and patterns.

The head pipe is the portion of the system that probably causes the most grief. Original equipment pipes might have odd kinks and jogs to clear frame obstructions. Unfortunately, some aftermarket suppliers shortcut the design process. Their pipes fit, after a fashion. The only solution is to keep hunting until the right pipe shows up. The other fault I've run into more often than not is poor chrome plating, this holds true for many other aftermarket parts as well, however. If need be, you can have the new pipes rechromed before installation.

Stripped Threads

We touched on this a bit in the teardown section and perhaps I should have addressed it in the cylinder head section. I didn't. Some motorcycles—older Japanese bikes, Ducatis, BMWs, and Nortons, to pick the most troublesome—have their exhaust headers held on with a threaded ring nut. The threads might

EXHAUSTING POSSIBILITIES

Exhaust collars on /5, /6, and /7 BMWs have always had a tendency to weld themselves to their exhaust spigots. Removal—specifically removing the collars without removing the threads from the spigots—can prove difficult, to say the least. In fact it is such a common problem that a thriving business has developed in replacing those threads. While I'd hate to think I was responsible for anyone going hungry, there is a simple way to remove those collars—which are inexpensive—and save the spigots—which aren't.

1. Obtain a single-sided hacksaw or wrap a hacksaw blade in tape.

2. Saw through the collar. Make your cut parallel to the exhaust pipe. This puts the cut at 90 degrees to the threads.

3. Cut almost all the way through the collar. Check the depth of the cut frequently to be sure you're not cutting into the threads.

4. When you've cut three-quarters of the way through the collar, insert a wide chisel into the cut, and "fetch it a good blow," as the English say. The collar should split, or at least spread itself apart enough for you either to snap it off or spin it off without damaging the spigot threads. Clean up the threads as required and install new collars.

You may run into a situation where the collar will unthread a few turns and then stop. Don't force it; if moderate pressure won't do the trick, split it.

BMW Exhaust Collar Replacement

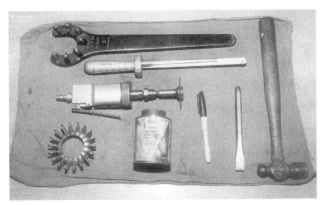

Everything needed to remove and reinstall a frozen BMW exhaust collar. From the top, BMW exhaust collar wrench, single-sided hacksaw, a replacement collar, anti-seize, a chisel, and a man-size hammer. The felt pen and air-powered cutoff wheel are optional.

A line is marked on the collar to provide a guide.

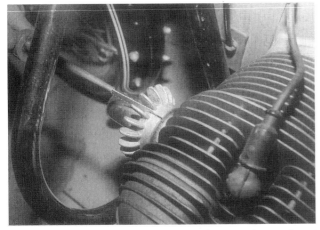

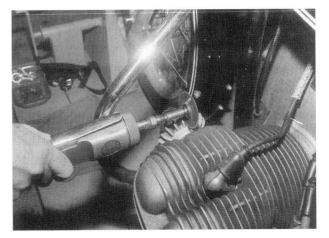

The collar is sawn through, either by hand or grinder, to about 3/4 of its thickness.

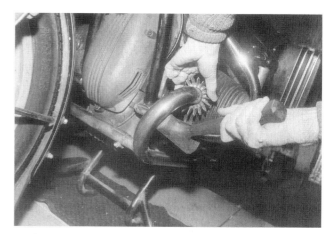
Remove the pipe.

Apply plenty of anti-seize compound.

The chisel is inserted and given a good blow, which should split the collar. At that point it can be spun off using the wrench or simply broken off.

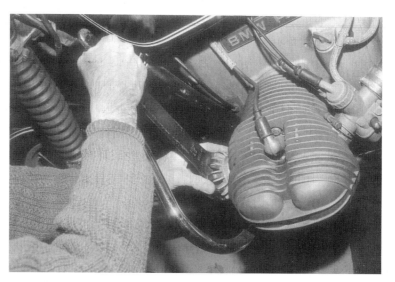
Reinstall in the normal manner.

be internal or external. You might also encounter a design similar to some Triumphs, where a stub threads into the exhaust port and the head pipe clamps to it.

The internal-thread system usually causes the most trouble. Over the miles the securing collar tends to loosen up slightly and vibration does the rest. In short order the threads are worn away. There are two solutions: The first is to rethread the port. That's the preferred way and the most practical, but it's not something you can do at home; you'll find the shops that perform this service listed in the appendix.

The second method, which really applies only to bikes that use a stub, is to have a new stub turned out of aluminum. This stub is then pressed into the head and secured either by a hidden set screw between the fins, or by Loctite or welding. Installing a stub is also the hot tip for replacing the push-in head pipes on late Triumphs with the clamp-on pipes designed for the earlier bikes.

Stripped external threads present a different problem. In most cases they'll have to be built up with weld, and then turned down and rethread-ed—a daunting task—or simply rethreaded to a smaller size with new collars made to suit.

INSTALLING THE EXHAUST

Install any new gaskets that are required. Place the head pipe in position and bolt it loosely in place. If the bike uses a crossover pipe, install it over the head pipe that's in place and then install the head pipe on the opposite side.

Let me digress for a moment. I generally coat all interlocking surfaces, including exhaust pipe connections, with anti-seize compound. Some restorers don't agree. They claim that push-in joints like those used on late-model Triumphs tend to leak and vibrate out of the head if installed with any type of lubricant. While I understand their point of view, I don't subscribe to it. If you prefer not to use anti-seize, then don't. But the next time you try to separate an exhaust connection that appears to have been welded together, you'll have no one to blame save yourself.

Back to business. Leave the head pipes loose and hang the mufflers and any attendant brackets. Once the entire system is in

At the bottom of this display of special BMW tools is the one you'll need to remove and install the exhaust retaining nut. It's aluminum so it won't ruin the nut. It's also designed to fit the fins snugly. If you're working on BMWs, do yourself a favor and get one.

101

place start at the front and snug everything up, making certain that there's no strain placed on any one part of the system. Wiggle the head pipes slightly as you bolt them up to make sure they're seated. If you're working on a twin with dual mufflers, make sure they're both aligned and hanging in the same plane.

Finally go back and secure all the connections. If the system is rubber-mounted—many two-strokes are—make sure it's free to move. If not, make sure the pipes and hangers are tight. Also make certain the system itself is. Stress and vibration will destroy any exhaust system in a matter of miles. You might need to shim the exhaust hangers to avoid undue strains.

Triumph Push-in Pipes

The pipes used on most 1971 and later models can be a real headache to install. At the factory they were literally driven into the head with a huge rubber mallet. The major aggravation with these pipes is probably leaking at the head joint. Minor aggravations range from falling out of the head to denting upon installation. The best solution I've come up with is to install stubs and use a pair of clamp-on pipes—which is what the factory eventually did.

The next best solution is to install them with shim stock if need be. Shim them to the point where they will slide into the head about a third of the way. Then drive them in the rest of the way until they seat. Position the lower mounting tabs in front of the exhaust pipe tabs. That way an inward force is exerted on the pipe, which helps hold them in.

Peripherals

While in most cases the exhaust system itself will be readily available—or at least easily duplicated—some of the peripheral stuff may be a little hard to come by. For instance, a few

For a few years some Triumphs used pipes that were just shoved into the head. It's not really the best way to mount an exhaust system. The clamps are just on there for show; their worth as a heat sink is debatable. A better solution is to install mounting spigots and clamp-on pipes from an older, pre-1971 model or newer, post-1981 model.

Someday someone is going to restore one of these behemoths. Hopefully the pipes will still be there.

years ago the "chip basket" exhaust guards that were standard equipment on T100C and TR6C Triumphs were nearly unobtainable; likewise the similar fitting on the BSA Firebird. Heat shields for Japanese Street Scramblers were also in short supply. The situation has improved slightly, at least as far as the British stuff goes.

This brings up another topic. In most cases American and British exhausts are so easy to find that unless you're dead set on restoring the bike with the original equipment, you're

This 1957 Ducati 175 Sport is exceptionally rare. It employs an equally rare exhaust system.

going to find it easier and cheaper to replace everything with new replacement or new old stock. European machines are also fairly easy to find exhausts for—especially the sports and competition models. For some reason Japanese exhausts are rather difficult to come by and expensive as hell to boot.

Finally, a recent look through the Domi Racer/Accessory Mart catalog yielded head pipes for everything from Ariel to Zundapp, and the same in mufflers. It includes pipes and mufflers to fit Rudge, Douglas, Sachs, and Panther models. Believe me; if you need it, it's out there somewhere.

Chapter
Nine

Ignition Systems

If there was a weak point on older machines, it was definitely the ignition system—in fact, the electrics as a whole often left something to be desired. For the most part, the ignition systems on older bikes can be broken down into magneto fired or battery and coil.

Magnetos can also be broken down into flywheel types—common on many small displacement machines—and the traditional, external engine-driven high-tension magnetos commonly found on British and European machines prior to 1962. The battery-and-coil system employed by most motorcycles is identical—in theory at least—to most of those used in general automotive service until a short time ago.

With few exceptions, most vintage singles, twins, and triples with battery/coil ignitions use one set of points and one coil per cylinder. The exceptions include a few bikes that use an automotive-type distributor. Some twins may use a single set of points to fire either dual coils or a single coil with twin towers. Although the coils fire simultaneously, one cylinder is on the exhaust stroke when the adjacent one is on the compression and no harm is done. (These are sometimes known as "wasted spark" ignitions.) These systems may use two coils wired in series so watch the connections.

In general, four-cylinder bikes simply double this system, with dual point setups firing through a pair of dual-tower coils. Most Harley-Davidson twins use a single set of points to fire a dual tower coil. However, there were some versions of the 74-inch motor that used dual points and dual coils.

MAGNETOS

For the most part magnetos were phased out in the late 1950s with the almost universal adoption of the AC charging system and battery-and-coil ignition. Over the majority of its active life, the magneto changed very little—if you understand how a 1911 Bosch works, you'll be able to figure out a Lucas or Fairbanks-Morse magneto. Most magneto maintenance revolves around cleaning the mag and adjusting the point gap and timing. If your mag, regardless of make, turns out to be kaput, I'd be the first one to send you to a specialist. There are, however, a few dodges to resuscitate one that's yet to slip over the edge.

Construction

There are two basic types of magnetos: the high-tension, engine-driven magneto and the flywheel magneto. High-tension mags are usually found on vintage British motorcycles, pre-1970 BMWs, pre-1970 XLCH Harley-Davidsons, and a variety of older European bikes. Flywheel magnetos are used primarily on small, older displacement motorcycles and current model off-road bikes.

The high-tension magneto is usually driven from the engine by a chain or gear set. Some aftermarket mags are driven directly from the cam or crankshaft, as are some of the rotating magnet versions.

Basically the H-T magneto consists of a permanent magnet and a series of electrical windings known as the armature. Some magnetos rotate the windings past the poles of the magnet, while others—such as the Bosch unit fitted to BMWs and the Dixie installed on

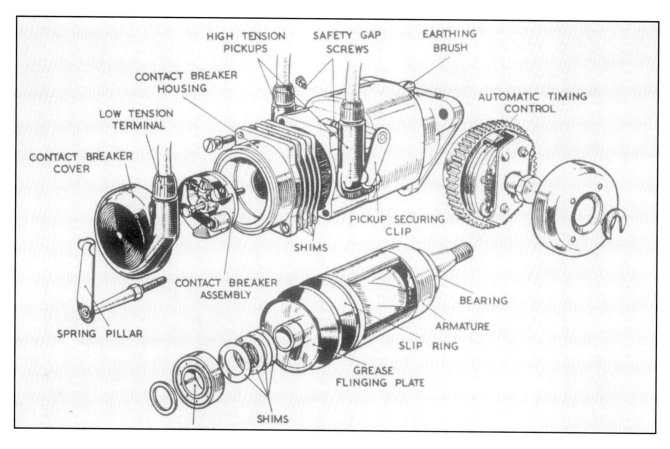

HIGH TENSION PICKUPS

SAFETY GAP SCREWS

EARTHING BRUSH

CONTACT BREAKER HOUSING

LOW TENSION TERMINAL

AUTOMATIC TIMING CONTROL

CONTACT BREAKER COVER

PICKUP SECURING CLIP

SHIMS

CONTACT BREAKER ASSEMBLY

BEARING

ARMATURE

SLIP RING

GREASE FLINGING PLATE

SPRING PILLAR

SHIMS

Breakdown (no pun intended) of the Lucas twin-cylinder magneto with automatic advance. The Lucas magneto is arguably the most widely used mag in the world. Parts are widely available and most rebuilders are familiar with them. Note the shims between the bearing at the contact breaker (points) end and the contact breaker housing used to adjust armature free play.

older American and British models—rotate the magnet past the windings. Most aftermarket magnetos intended for high-performance work are the rotating-magnet type.

As the lines of magnetic flux are broken by rotating either the armature or the magnetic rotor, a current is induced in the windings. By stepping up the current through two separate windings, a primary and a secondary, the magneto creates enough voltage to fire the sparkplug. A set of points breaks the circuit at the crucial moment for ignition. Essentially all high-tension magnetos work in the same fashion; everything else is just a detail.

Magneto Maintenance

Aa rule of thumb that says most magnetos are relatively trouble-free. There isn't a whole lot that can go wrong, mainly because there isn't a whole lot in there. If the bike came in a box, the first step is to make sure that the magneto is actually the correct one for the bike.

British bikes in particular might prove problematic, in that magneto rotation and engine rotation have to coincide. More than one purchaser of a basket case has found himself

with an engine that rotates clockwise and a magneto designed to run counterclockwise. Drive direction is taken from the drive end and normally there is either an arrow or some other mark indicating direction of rotation.

Older magnetos might suffer from a variety of problems, most of which can be repaired relatively simply, although some problems require the services of a magneto specialist. Probably the two biggest problems—and the ones most likely to require outside assistance—are "Shellactitis" and loss of magnetism.

In the old days magneto armatures were coated with shellac. The coating has a tendency to absorb water from the air, which softens it. Eventually the heat from the engine causes the softened shellac to fly off the armature. When the engine is shut off and allowed to cool down, the shellac solidifies and seizes the armature in its housing. Fortunately, modern epoxy coatings have eliminated this problem.

The other problem is simply a product of age. Despite their name, "permanent" magnets don't last forever; their strength weakens with age. As the magnets weaken, the magneto's voltage output drops accordingly. Loss of magnetism can be rectified by specialized equipment that "recharges" the field or rotor magnets, as the case might be.

As you can see from the diagram, the basic construction of a magneto is simple and straightforward. Most other repairs can easily be done at home with a shop manual and parts list to guide you. Worn bearings are probably the next most-serious problem, and in all likelihood fairly rare unless the mag was abused in some way. Lucas mags can tolerate up to 0.002–0.003 inch of up-and-down play, and 0.006–0.007 of end play. When up-and-down play exceeds 0.005 inch, it's time to replace the bearings.

Magneto advance units might be automatic or manual, depending on the bike. Make sure they work smoothly without binding. You might have to disassemble them and grease the pivots for the advance weights, but that's about all they'll require. Occasionally you'll run into a situation where the threaded portion of the shaft has been wrung off by overzealous tightening on the lock nut securing the advance unit. Normally the solution is to drill the shaft and install a bolt to replace the lock nut.

The rest of the maintenance program is a matter of cleaning or replacing the points and condensers. A note of caution here, however. The Lucas magneto's condenser is located inside the armature. Replacing the armature, or at least rebuilding it, is usually the best solution if the condenser is shot.

Aftermarket bolt-on magnetos were moderately popular additions during the chopper craze of the mid-1960s and early 1970s. Units by Joe Hunt and ARD were the most popular. They were also extremely popular with dirt track racers of the day. Parts (and in some cases the magnetos themselves) are still available through a variety of sources, as are some highly compact replacement units. The M.A.P. Cycle Enterprises Inc., Undercover Mag is one of my favorites. Several companies will also fit a modern electronic ignition into standard magneto housings. (See appendix.)

Flywheel Magnetos

As you may have guessed from the name, the flywheel magneto, sometimes called an AC magneto, uses the rotor as the engine's flywheel—or vice-versa, depending on your perspective. Flywheel mags are normally used on small-displacement motorcycles, and often incorporate the charging system as well as the ignition. Today, flywheel magnetos are used primarily on very small machines and off-road or dual-sport bikes.

All flywheel magnetos utilize rotating magnets and stationary coils. Most mount the secondary coil externally, like a battery-and-coil ignition. Most add some sort of "lighting" coil, which is used to power the headlight if the bike is so equipped. Many two-strokes mount their ignition points behind the flywheel, opened by a cam ground into the hub of the flywheel itself. Others, such as Japanese

The flywheel magneto as used on a variety of different motorcycles. This one is from a Yamaha trail bike.

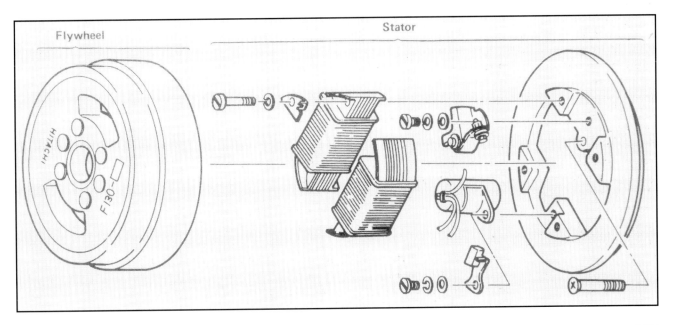

Note how the flywheel portion of the magneto fits on the crankshaft taper. Removal requires a dedicated puller if damage is to be avoided. Loose securing nuts allow the flywheel to slip on the crankshaft, shearing the woodruff key and possibly scoring the crank.

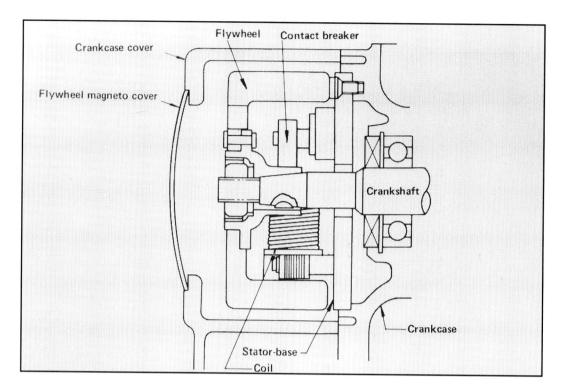

Older machines using flywheel magnetos generally have the points and condenser located inside of the flywheel, as shown on this Bultaco Matador. Note the vertically mounted condenser. Due to the mounting location, which subjects the condenser to a fair amount of heat and vibration, the condensers tend to go south. My solution has been to mount an automotive condenser under the tank. You can hang it from the coil bracket or any other convenient spot.

dual-sport bikes or early Ducati singles, feature conventional, remote-mounted points.

With any flywheel mag the first order of business will be to remove the flywheel—in fact, you probably had to deal with it before now if you've done any motor work. Many of these require a special puller, and in most cases it's not something you can jury rig. Bite the bullet and buy the correct tool; chances are it's a lot less than a new flywheel.

Once the flywheel's off, inspect the coils for signs of damage. Remove any rust from the flywheel itself with a wire brush or fine sandpaper. In most cases there is no advance unit. If there is—and some bikes do have them—make certain that it moves freely in both directions. Replace the points and condensers, or at least clean the points, and reinstall the flywheel.

BATTERY-AND-COIL SYSTEMS

Battery-and-coil ignitions consist of a high-tension coil, points, and condenser and the wiring to make it all work. There should be an advance unit somewhere in there as well. All battery-and-coil ignitions are serviced the same way. Points and condensers should be inspected, and replaced as necessary, the wiring inspected and the advance units inspected and replaced or rebuilt as required.

It's worth mentioning that new points may have a protective film on them; always clean them with contact cleaner prior to installation. I shouldn't have to mention it, but the condensers should be replaced whenever

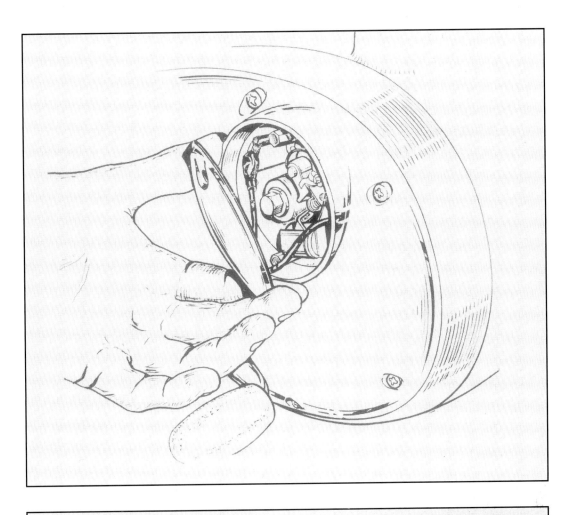

Lucas points can sometimes be a pain in the butt to adjust, but they are generally easy to get to. Later, they moved the condenser to the coil bracket or up under the tank, depending on the year and model.

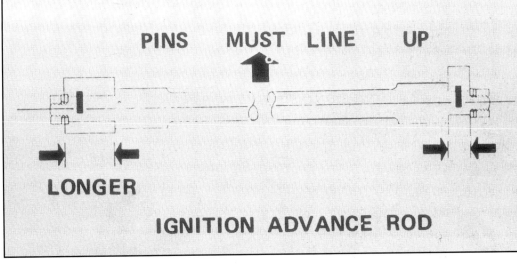

PINS MUST LINE UP

LONGER

IGNITION ADVANCE ROD

This diagram is in here because I've seen this one done a dozen times. The advance unit on the Yamaha XS 650 is spun by a long rod that goes through the head. The points are located on the left side, the advance unit on the right. It's easy to get the rod turned the wrong way around. No big deal normally, but why do it twice!

the points are. Auto advance units should always be checked for slop in their mechanism. Make sure that the movement is free and the cam surface isn't pitted or corroded.

You might find it advantageous to install heavier advance springs (available through knowledgeable dealers) to delay total ignition advance, especially if you're restoring a sports model and "pinging" (or "pinking" as our British cousins call it) may be, or has been, a problem.

Most advance units are positively located in some fashion, usually via a notch or peg in the drive end. Some, like those used on many

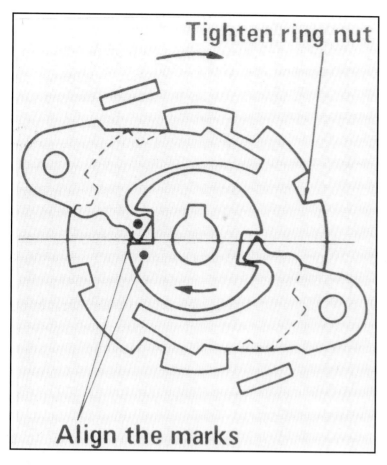

Some advance units are keyed to prevent them from being assembled 180 degrees out of phase. This unit (from a Yamaha 650) uses two punch marks to ensure correct assembly.

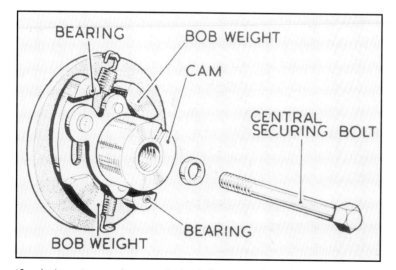

If replacing a Lucas advance unit check that the total advance is the same as the one you're replacing. If you plan to reuse the old advance unit, check the pivot points for wear and replace the springs.

BSAs, are simply set on a taper. Yamaha 650 advance units can be installed 180 degrees out of time. The moral? Pay attention, and mark the parts if you must before disassembly.

If the advance unit requires replacing, make sure that the replacement is the correct one for the bike. British bikes in particular can get a little confusing. While the advance units might look the same, they aren't. Triumphs, for instance, use one advance unit for battery and coil ignitions and another one for the infamous Energy Transfer system.

Though they look identical, substituting one of these units for the other will cause ignition problems you won't believe. Since the advance unit determines not only the advance curve but the overall total advance, confusing them can cause severe engine damage—burned valves or detonated pistons. Since the units are all stamped with a degree figure on the back, confusing them shouldn't be a problem, but it still happens occasionally.

TIMING

Timing procedures are almost as varied as engine designs. Because most vintage motorcycle engines are air-cooled, and can be somewhat high strung, ignition timing assumes a greater significance than it does in your family grocery-getter.

Modern motorcycles are generally timed dynamically using a strobe or timing light. Today's bikes are also basically the "set and forget" variety. Once the timing has been correctly set, usually at the factory, you can forget about doing it again unless it's disturbed. Older motorcycles weren't so painless. Frequent—and in some cases painstaking—adjustments were required to keep the bike running at its best.

There are two methods you can use to set your engine's ignition timing: static or dynamic. Of the two, the dynamic method—with the engine running—is preferable. Dynamic timing shows you exactly when the timing occurs, allowing you to precisely adjust it. It also allows you to check the timing at both full advance and in the fully retarded position. The timing light will pick up any inconstancies in the advance curve as well.

Normally, any good automotive timing light will work with a motorcycle engine. If your bike has a 6-volt electrical system or runs no battery at all, the light might need an

SPARKING IMPROVEMENTS

Ya say you want good starting, improved performance, low maintenance, and a whiter smile, Bunkie? Why not trash those points or ditch that worn-out magneto in favor of an electronic ignition? Seriously, replacing the OEM stuff with an electronic system is probably one of the single biggest improvements you can make to a vintage bike.

Consider the points and advance unit commonly found on British bikes: In most cases you'll need to gap and time a set of points for each cylinder—every few thousand miles, in fact. You'll also need to maintain and occasionally rebuild the auto advance unit and you'll need to replace the points and condensers periodically. Or you can replace the whole shooting match with a Dyna, Lucas Rita, or Boyer-Bransden electronic system.

The beauty of each system is that in one fell swoop you eliminate all the mechanical pieces—points, condensers, and advance unit. And since there are no longer any moving parts to wear out (OK, so the condensers aren't moving parts), maintenance is greatly reduced. Likewise timing is a one-shot, set-and-forget deal. Side benefits include more accurate and consistent timing, which helps starting, enhances power, and prolongs engine life.

There are kits made for just about any bike I can think of, including systems designed to fit inside a Lucas or BTH magneto housing. In all cases outward appearance remains stock. If the bike is to be used on a regular basis, the electronic conversion is the only way to go.

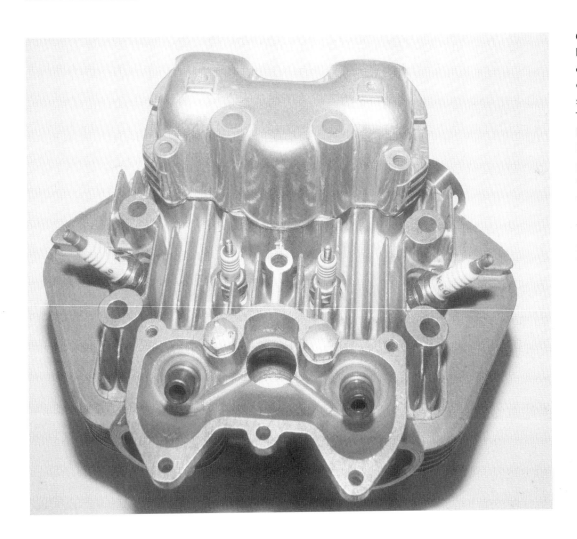

OK, so a cylinder head isn't normally considered a part of the ignition system. This Triumph head has been modified by Britech to use four plugs. The two extra plugs prevent detonation and increase power. When used in conjunction with the proper ignition, they really wake the motor up.

external power supply—a small 12-volt battery will suffice. I might be dating myself when I mention it, but only purchase one with an inductive pick-up.

The alternative to dynamic timing is static timing, but I'll wager you've already figured that out. Static timing usually involves the use of either a degree wheel or a dial indicator. Some bikes give static timing in degrees before top dead center, others provide it in millimeters before TDC. You turn the crankshaft to top dead center, set the degree wheel or dial indicator to zero, then back the engine off until it reaches the correct specification.

The first hurdle facing the novice restorer is likely to be the absence of timing marks. Many older machines simply don't have them. The mechanic was expected to remove the primary cover, install a degree wheel, and adjust the timing statically. In fact, it was quite a leap forward when makers began to install access plates in their primary cases to eliminate at least one step in the process.

Both BSA and Triumph eventually equipped their bikes with flywheels slotted at both TDC and 38 degrees before TDC. After removing a plug in the crankcase, you could drop either a special tool or the correct size drift into the corresponding slot. To adjust the valves you locked the engine in the TDC position; to set the timing, you found the 38-degree slot. At the time it seemed like the best thing since sliced bread.

Among the general motorcycle population these days, static timing a motorcycle is more or less a forgotten art. Some miscreants, myself included, will occasionally static time a bike that can be dynamically timed—especially ones like Triumphs, BSAs, and some Hondas that have a tendency to spray oil all over when you attempt to set the timing dynamically.

Dynamic Timing

Since most of us are familiar with the dynamic method of adjusting timing, I'll try to hit only the high points peculiar to motorcycles. To begin with, it's a good idea to set up some sort of cooling fan—an old window fan works fine—to keep some air blowing over your freshly restored engine. Otherwise you might find yourself restoring it again.

If your bike's timing marks are positioned where oil spray might be a problem—Honda CB350 and 450 models, Triumph and BSA

unit twins or Sportsters, for example—a little forethought might prevent a huge mess. H-D sells a little clear plastic timing plug. Some guys claim the plug makes it difficult to see the timing marks, but at least it prevents oil from flying all over the place. If you're timing a Honda, you might find it worthwhile to bore a hole in an old rotor cover—positioned so you can see the timing marks, of course. Said hole will keep the majority of the oil out of your face and in the engine where it can do the most good.

Normal procedure is to run the engine and adjust the point backing plate by levering it about with a screwdriver or turning a small, easily stripped eccentric screw. Naturally, when you tighten down the hold-down screws the timing changes slightly, so you leave them tight and whack the backing plate with a hammer and punch or screwdriver to shift it. Isn't that what ruined it in the first place? Do it right and adjust it with the screws loose.

Next on the agenda: BMWs. On the /5- through /7-series bikes the points sit behind the advance unit, where they're nearly inaccessible. When dynamically timing the engine it's tempting to use a long screwdriver and hammer to shift the plate—careful, Bunkie, one wrong move and you've shifted the advance unit as well. Since it sits on the end of a long, thin, and very much unsupported (and expensive) camshaft, it's easy to ruin A) the advance unit, B) the camshaft, and C) your day, all in short order. I'm not saying don't do it; I am saying be careful. And by the way, never, ever try to turn the engine over with that 6mm nut that secures the advance unit to the cam. I promise it'll shear off flush before you can say, "holy big repair job."

Once upon a time I watched a mechanic who should have known better check the timing on a brand-new XS-1B Yamaha. As he'd rev the bike to check the advance it would walk backwards on the lift. "The Gargoyle," as we affectionately called him, seemed to be having some trouble setting the timing exactly where he wanted it. As the rest of the shop watched in awe and ill-concealed delight, he revved the bike up time and time again. Every time he whacked the throttle the bike walked another 6 inches or so. Eventually the predictable happened and it walked itself right off the bench. The point of this story, I hope, is obvious.

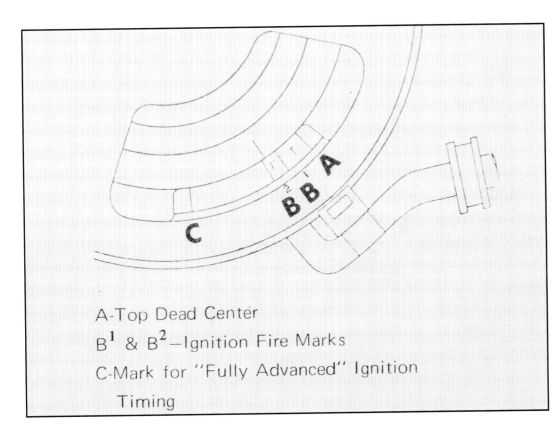

A-Top Dead Center

B¹ & B²—Ignition Fire Marks

C-Mark for "Fully Advanced" Ignition

Timing

Some bikes, mainly Japanese, will have datum marks on the rotor indicating top dead center, initial timing, and full advance. Others, particularly British bikes, will have only a timing mark for full advance.

Static Timing

Static timing is usually done with either the factory marks, or in some cases, slots cut into the flywheel, or with the aid of a degree wheel or dial indicator. In most cases the use of a dial indicator is reserved for two-strokes—after all, they don't have those pesky valves to get in the way and for the most part their sparkplug holes are set vertically.

One of the problems in static timing a bike is knowing exactly when and where the points actually break. The dial indicator or degree wheel should show you where. But how do you know when? The best way—in fact, the only way—to determine when the points break is by using some sort of audio or visual signal. There are several options available.

The "Buzz Box" is probably the oldest; buzz boxes look like small transistor radios. When the points break, the box gives off a loud buzz. It's simple and you can watch the indicator to synchronize the when and where.

Point checkers are nothing more than highly sensitive ohmmeters. They are probably the most accurate means of watching the points break. A good one will actually start to jiggle the needle as the points start to lift. When the points break it will swing the point-

er instantly to open. On the downside they are easily damaged, especially if you do like I've done and kick the bike over with the meter hooked up. The resulting voltage and amperage surge fried the meter instantly.

At the bottom of the food chain are continuity lights—you know, those self-powered circuit checkers. They work in a pinch but by and large are not sensitive enough to work really well.

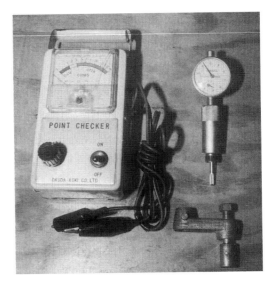

The best tools to use when static timing an engine. On the left, a very sensitive ohm meter sold by Yamaha specifically for ignition system work. At right is a standard dial indicator with spark plug adapter, and on the bottom, a fixture for use when the heads have been removed.

Statically Timing a Two-Stroke

Statically timing a two-stroke is as easy as it gets. Start by removing the spark plug and inserting the dial indicator adapter.

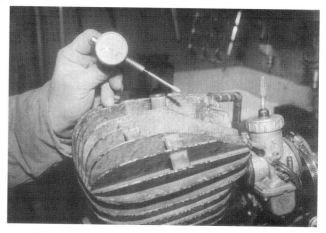

Install the dial indicator . . .

. . . and find top dead center.

Rotate the engine backwards the prescribed amount . . .

. . . line up the timing marks or adjust the points, depending on your ignition system.

Since there aren't a lot of two-strokes running around the streets these days, adjusting the timing has become something of a lost art. Because I'm a big fan of two-stroke engines, that's where we'll start. You'll need to obtain a dial indicator and either a "Buzz Box," a sensitive ohmmeter, or point checker, all of which are available through most motorcycle shops. If the sparkplug hole angle is greater than 8 degrees—Yamaha DT and RT 360s and 400s come to mind—then you'll also have to use a gauge stand and remove the head to get an accurate reading.

Begin by removing the sparkplug(s) and installing the dial indicator. Rotate the engine in its normal direction of travel until you reach TDC. The dial indicator's needle will stop moving. Zero the gauge by turning the outer dial. Connect your point checker and then turn the engine backward, stopping at the specified point before TDC. If the buzz box buzzes, the test lamp lights, or the ohmmeter shows the points are opened at exactly that point, then you're all set. If not, adjust the backing plate until the points are just opening.

Some engines incorporate automatic advances. In these cases you'll have to determine whether the timing should be adjusted at full advance or full retard. Most manufacturers give static timing specs at full retard, and many give both specifications. If it's to be adjusted at full advance, you'll need to wedge the advance open in some fashion.

Degree wheels are used in a similar fashion. They are usually mounted to the end of the crankshaft with an adapter. The rest of the procedure follows that of the preceding paragraph. Triumph used to sell a small degree wheel that could be mounted directly to the advance unit. It had holes cut in it so you could adjust the points and backing plate without removing the degree wheel. Used in conjunction with a strobe light to dynamically check timing, it was for a short time the neatest thing since pockets on shirts.

In some circumstances your ohmmeter might be affected by the resistance from the coil(s) and respond slowly or not at all to the points' movement. The solution is to disconnect the points from the coil, set the timing, and reconnect.

By the way, I'd avoid using a digital meter to measure point break; they simply respond too slowly. With an analog meter the needle will swing the instant the points start to break.

Transmissions

TEARDOWN AND ASSESSMENT

While there are several basic transmission designs, as a whole, motorcycle gearboxes break down into two broad categories. The first is unit construction, where the tranny and engine are contained in a single housing: post-1963 BSAs and Triumphs, H-D Sportsters, and most Japanese and Italian bikes. As you might guess, the opposite is non-unit construction, where the engine and gearbox are kept separate. BMW, Moto-Guzzi, and Indian fall into this category, as well as Harley big twins and older British, European, and American motorcycles.

It really doesn't matter if you're working on a unit or non-unit box. The internal workings and theory are more or less the same. For the most part, motorcycle transmissions are said to be constant mesh, meaning all the gears and shafts are always engaged with one another and turning at the same speed. This design does away with the need for the synchronizers and other hardware found in the common automotive manual transmission. It's also why most motorcycles allow you to run through the gears without clutching.

Although it's possible to perform a cursory examination of the transmission with everything in situ—particularly on a unit construction engine with horizontally split cases—I don't recommend doing so. Start by removing the clutch, the gears, bearings, and shafts from the cases and give them a thorough cleaning.

This part might seem redundant—particularly if you've already stripped the box down as part of your engine overhaul. Sorry, but that's the problem with how-to books as opposed to service manuals. In the meantime, we'll go through each of the components that make up the transmission.

Clutch

Since the clutch is usually disassembled before any transmission work commences, let's bow to logic and begin there. If the bike had any kind of shifting problems, pay particular attention to the clutch. Many shifting problems—grinding gears, hard shifts, or difficult-to-find neutral—are due to a worn or binding clutch.

Remove the pressure plate in the prescribed manner. Normal procedure is to reduce tension slowly by backing off the bolts a turn or two at a time to prevent the pressure plate from warping. Some designs, Triumph, for instance, use a little tang under the bolt head to keep it from backing out in use. Use a pocketknife or small screwdriver to release the tang. Some designs use a spring and pin design, older Suzuki MX'ers, for instance. Obviously, getting them apart involves a slightly different technique, but the same concept.

Norton Commandos and any other clutches that use a diaphragm spring must have the spring compressed before the clutch can be dismantled. Other bikes requiring a spring/clutch compressor include some Harley two-strokes and post-1970 Sportsters.

Once you've removed the pressure plate, withdraw the clutch plates themselves. There are basically two types, drive and driven. Drive plates are splined into the outer basket, and driven plates are splined to the clutch hub. The plates should alternate: drive, driven,

On the left, a worn-out fiber clutch drive plate. On the right, its new replacement. In most cases the fiber plates should be replaced as a matter of course.

drive, etc. If not, check what you've got against the parts manual, particularly on older models. It's pretty common to have mismatched or out-of-order clutch plates. Also note the location of any extra thick or thin plates. Usually these plates will be either the first plate or the last plate in the stack. Often you'll find an extra steel plate adjoining an aluminum pressure plate.

As an aside, every once in a while you'll run into a balanced clutch—the plates in these will have punch marks that correspond with a similar mark on the face of the clutch basket. These should be reinstalled in the correct order.

Once the plates, springs, and hardware are out and degreased, they may be inspected. The service manual should give you a free length measurement for your springs as well as dimension for the clutch plates. If they come up short or there is any doubt, replace them.

Check the steel plates for true by laying them down on a known flat surface—a thick piece of plate glass, for instance, or a surface table. In a pinch a piece of window glass will do, or you can check them against one another. If there is any sign of warping, replace them. If the steel plates show any sign of overheating, likewise bin them and acquire new ones. How do you know if they've been over-

heated? They'll be blue along the edges, as if they'd been heated with a torch.

The fiber plates should be measured for thickness. If worn beyond their service limit, or close to it, replace them. In fact, if the clutch has been known to slip don't even bother measuring them—replace or reline them. Occasionally you'll run into an all-steel clutch—these are common on Bultacos and a few other competition models. If they measure up, reinstall them. By and large these

The clutch hub on the right has had a long and stressful life. The grooves worn in the hub will prevent the clutch from ever releasing and engaging properly. This hub must be replaced or repaired.

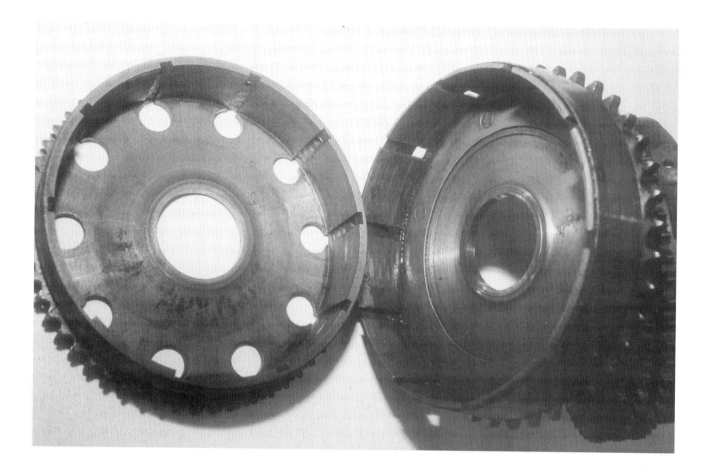

The same holds true for the clutch basket. In reality, it will be far cheaper to replace them both.

To separate the cushion drive from the clutch hub, the three screws holding the hub together must first be removed. This Triumph hub is typical of many British designs. When the hub is reassembled, apply locking compound to the screws and stake the screw heads in place.

clutches tend to drag when cold, but are incredibly long-lived and robust.

Check both the clutch hub and the clutch drum for notches worn into their splines. The notches will cause the plates to hang up and drag, and make clutch operation a real chore.

While we're looking at the clutch assembly take a good look at the clutch shock absorber

or "cush" (for cushion) drive. The cush drive might be located in the clutch hub or in the clutch basket, dependent on the maker's whim. Look for loose hardware, sheared rivets, or excess play between the drive and driven members.

While we're at it, inspect the clutch pushrod and all parts of the release mechanism. Pay particular attention to the order of the bearings and thrust washers that make up the release mechanism. Japanese enduro bikes, particularly Yamaha DT-RT models, use a cheap plastic worm gear in the case that has a propensity for self-destruction. Some bikes use a steel pushrod with hardened ends or a small steel ball to actuate the clutch. Try not to lose the ball and make sure the ends of the release rod or pushrod aren't mushroomed.

During reassembly it goes without saying that any lock tabs, lock washers, and circlips should be replaced. By the way, the transmission is no place for thread-locking compounds; use new stock lock tabs or washers.

When reassembling multiplate clutches pay particular attention to the way the clutch plates are installed. Since the steel

118

This clutch is typical of the designs found in many Japanese and some European motorcycles. It is unlike the British counterpart in that it doesn't require truing after it's installed.

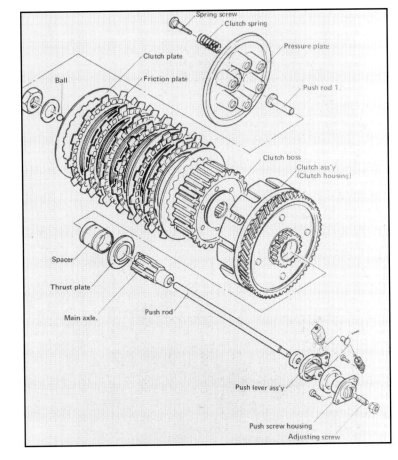

plates are stamped they will have a sharp edge on one side and a dull edge on the other. To prevent the plates from binding install the plates with all of the sharp edges facing in the same direction.

Some clutches—British-built in most cases—will need to be trued after the springs are installed. Hold the clutch in and kick the engine over while watching the pressure plate. Any wobble should be obvious. Turn the adjusting screws until the pressure plate spins true. If for some reason you can't get the clutch to even out, remove the springs and recheck them; a worn spring can keep the clutch from truing up.

Chances are the clutch will be left to stew in its own juices for a bit while you look at the rest of the gearbox.

Trident Clutches: A Cush Job

The Trident clutch is one of the strongest clutches in motorcycling. Unfortunately, the

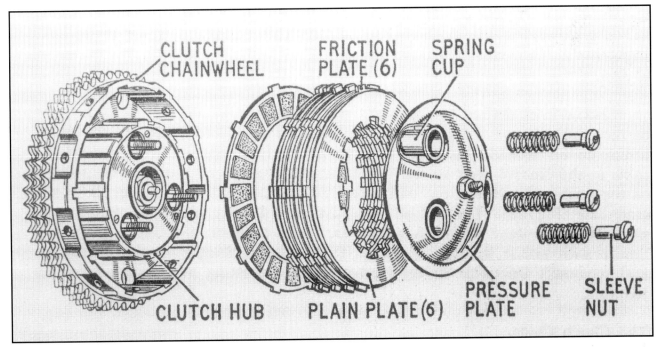

While some details may differ, this BSA clutch is a typical wet clutch as used by most British and European manufacturers. This style clutch needs truing after installation. With the clutch disengaged, operate the kick starter while watching the pressure plate. If it doesn't spin true all the way around, you'll need to adjust the sleeve nuts until it does.

BMW INPUT SHAFT SPLINES

The transmission input shaft splines on /5/6/7 BMWs require particular attention. The delicate spline shafts need to be lubricated every so often; if they aren't, they soon strip.

The first indication of trouble is usually a chattering noise at idle, caused by play between the shaft and the inner clutch hub. Phase two is rapid and difficult-to-control clutch engagement as the clutch plate tends to bind on the shaft rather than release cleanly. Phase three? You push. The splines go away and the bike can't be ridden.

My advice: Once a year or so loosen the mounting bolts and pull back the tranny—you don't have to remove it. Dab a little—a little—molypaste or anti-seize on a toothbrush or screwdriver and lube the splines.

This is as good a way to store the tranny as any. After a thorough cleaning and inspection, the transmission gears, shims, forks, and kick starter pawl are assembled onto their respective shafts. The shift forks and rod can be held together with wire to prevent them from coming apart.

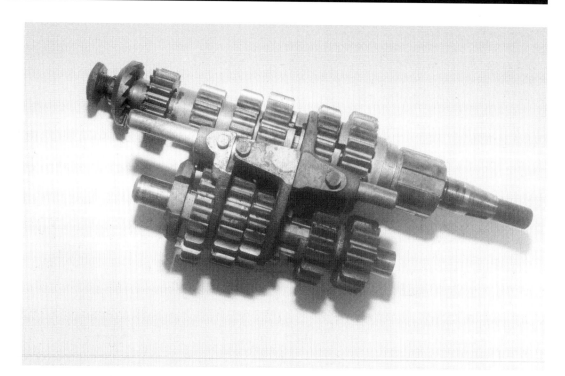

center seal that's installed to keep oil from finding its way into the hub center leaves a lot to be desired. When the inevitable occurs and oil contaminates the cush drive, the Trident's prodigious torque soon makes short work of the oil-soaked rubber biscuits that compose the cush drive. At idle, the now cushless cush drive sounds for all the world like a bad main bearing. Never assume a Trident or Rocket 3 has a bad main bearing without investigating the clutch hub first.

TRANSMISSION

As the transmission parts are removed, be particularly alert for any shims or thrust washers that might adhere to the various pieces. Many bikes will have a thrust washer behind the clutch basket, for instance. Oil vis-cosity will tend to stick the pieces together, making the small shim or washer easy to overlook. Some thrust washers will have oil sluice-ways milled into them to help lube the bearings they butt up against; make sure these face the correct way upon installation. As you remove the shafts, it's not a bad idea to place everything that came off the shaft back on it until you have time to dismantle and inspect it. A piece of wire secured at both ends should hold everything in place.

Regardless of the make of transmission, inspection procedures are always the same. Start by thoroughly cleaning everything in solvent. Do not use compressed air to blow dry the bearings. Rinse them in solvent and let them dry on a sheet of newspaper, cardboard, or whatever. Place one shaft on the workbench, preferably

This gear has seen better days—it's now a paperweight.

Since you already have a paperweight, you can toss this one out.

one that's clean and uncluttered. Dismantle the shaft following your manual's recommended procedure. I find it easier to inspect each piece as it comes off the shaft.

You'll probably start by removing a snap-ring, though not always. Snap-rings, or circlips, as they might be called, should be replaced as a matter of course, but don't trash them until you have the replacement in hand. Check gear teeth for chips, cracks, and signs of over-heating. Inspect the tip of each tooth as well as the base. Look for cracks or flaking of the hardened outer surface. As a rule of thumb, if you find a gear with bad teeth on one shaft, chances are its mate on the opposite shaft is

bad as well. Check the area around the spline hole for any sign of a crack.

The gear dogs also need a thorough examination. The dogs are the hardest-worked portion of the gear. If they're rounded off, chipped, or cracked replace the gear, unless you enjoy riding a bike that jumps out of gear a lot. Always check the adjacent gear's mating slots; they have a tendency to elongate and chip, making gear engagement sloppy. If you find a gear with dog or slot problems, its mating gear on the same shaft should be replaced as well.

Lots of times gear tooth problems don't reveal themselves without a physical inspection—that is unless they break and destroy

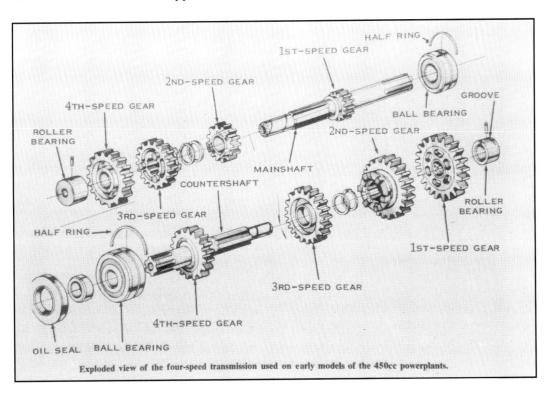

Exploded view of the four-speed transmission used on early models of the 450cc powerplants.

Note the location of all snap rings and shims. This gear cluster, from an older Honda 450, is indicative of early Japanese four-speed units.

your gearbox. Bad dog/slot problems usually manifest themselves externally—the bike misses gears, the gears won't stay engaged, etc.

KICKSTARTERS

As you'd expect, kickstarter gears and pawls take a real beating. Big singles—especially narrow-case Ducati singles—and magneto equipped XLCHs in particular should have everything examined twice. If you've been riding the bike at all prior to its restoration, you're probably painfully aware of any problems with the kicker gears.

SHIFT FORKS, DRUMS, AND CAM PLATES

Inspect the shift fork ends for bluing, which indicates overheating—but you knew that. Also check that the ends are parallel and that there are no deep scores in the face of the gear where the shift fork rides. If you have any doubt, replace the fork and its gear.

Shift cams need to be checked for flatness and nicks and chips in the racetrack area (the portion where the shift fork runs).

Shift forks should be checked for scoring. This is a perfect—actually an imperfect—example of a shift fork too scored to use.

This Triumph shift cam looks perfect and is ready to be reinstalled.

The shift fork on the left is typical of one that's been in use for a while. It's not terrible and could be reused, assuming the ends are still parallel and the other side isn't damaged. The one on the right is new.

Check the shift drum itself for nicks, chips, worn spots, or grooves in the shift fork raceways. If your tranny uses a cam plate instead of a shift drum the process is identical, with the added step of making sure the plate itself isn't bent. While you're at it inspect the shift detent, which might be either a ball or plunger, and be sure its spring is straight without any wear or tear. An occasional case of hard shifting on late-model Triumphs can be attributed to a detent plunger that's become worn to a point. A few swipes with a file to re-profile the tip can ease shifting considerably.

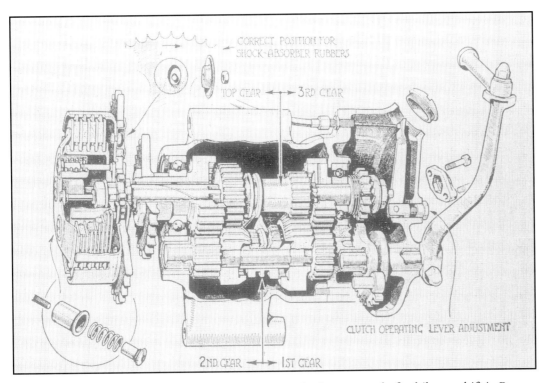

Correct position for shock-absorber rubbers

Top gear ← → 3rd gear

Clutch operating lever adjustment

2nd gear ← → 1st gear

The Burman C.P. and B.A. gearbox was used on a wide variety of British bikes through the 1950s. It was compact, robust, and easy to repair. Mainly used on Matchless and Ariel motorcycles, it is typical of a non-unit design.

ASSEMBLING THE TRANSMISSION

Replace all seals as a matter of course. Glue any loose ball bearings or needle rollers in place with stiff grease. As the case halves are drawn together, rotate the shafts slightly to ensure they aren't binding. If you need to force the cases together, something's wrong; stop and solve the problem before you proceed.

Once the cases are together, make sure the tranny shifts through the gears. You'll have to spin the countershaft while you shift it. Be sure the kickstart engages at the correct angle. Many gearboxes have timed selectors, which must be indexed correctly to pick up all the gears. If your five-speed has suddenly turned into a three- or four-speed, chances are it's only mistimed; remove the selector and try again.

If your gearbox suddenly has a reversed shift pattern—one-up/four-down, perhaps—you've installed the camplate upside down.

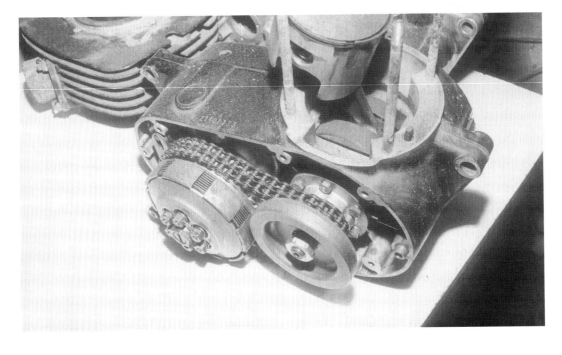

Most primary chains are either two-strand (duplex) or three-strand (triplex).

123

Occasionally you'll run into an older bike with a single-strand primary chain.

Some riders prefer the one-up pattern, which is commonly used on race bikes. If so leave it; just don't forget which way it shifts. Once the box is together, fill it with the correct grade of oil to prevent rusting.

Chains and Sprockets

Both primary and secondary chains and their sprockets are considered to be an integral portion of the transmission/drive line. Normally, primary chains don't give too many

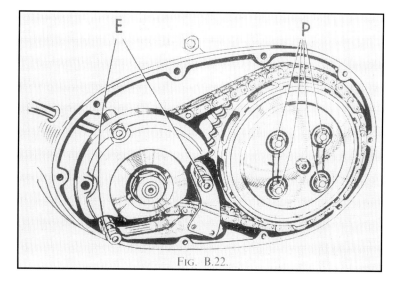

Fig. B.22.

problems. For the most part they run in an enclosed oil bath and are duplex or triplex (two- or three-strand) design. The oil keeps them cool, clean, and well lubricated, while the enclosed primary cover keeps road grit out and clean oil in. In most cases you'll find that unless the bike has astronomical mileage or some sort of mechanical damage the primary chain is probably OK. If the primary or clutch sprocket is hooked or worn, of course replace both sprockets and the chain.

If you're rebuilding a basket case, check the number of teeth on the sprockets you've got in hand against the ones listed for your make, model, and year. Every so often I run across a bike that revs and pulls like a freight train but has the top end of a golf cart. Usually someone's installed the wrong primary crankshaft sprocket or transmission countershaft sprocket.

If the crankshaft cush drive is built into the primary sprocket, à la Harley-Davidson

After the primary drive is assembled, the chain should be adjusted to 1/2 to 3/8 of an inch freeplay. If the adjusting screws are drilled for lock wire, wire them up as soon as you're done installing the clutch.

124

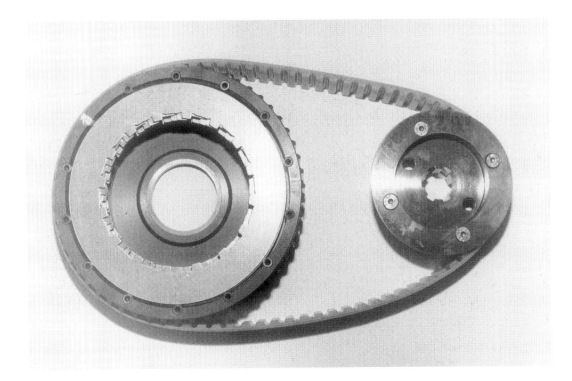

If the bike is going to be used in anger you may want to upgrade to a belt-driven primary.

"compensating" sprockets or various British bikes, now is the time to inspect it. These consist of a two-piece, ramped sprocket and a short, heavy spring. Check the spring for height and cracks and check the ramps or cams for chips and nicks. [compensating sprocket H-D/ Triumph.]

Check the primary and drive sprockets for wear and tear and replace as required. If the countershaft sprocket is a pain in the butt to get to—as it is on many British bikes—you may want to change it now as a safety precaution. If you do, bite the bullet and replace the drive sprocket and chain as well. Again, check the tooth count of your sprocket against the spec sheet. By the way, there's no crime against altering your gearing to suit your needs: Go up or down as you see fit.

O-Ring Chains

There's no doubt about it, in my book "O"-ring chains are one of the best things since sliced bread. Unfortunately, they may not fit your motorcycle.

Because chains of the same pitch may—and often do—vary in width, some bikes may run into clearance problems when substituting an O-ring or other modern chain for the OEM links. Those with close-fitting primary cases, for instance, may simply not have the lateral clearance.

My best advice is to "suck it and see," as the Brits say. Try to find one that fits. Most manufacturers can provide you with a chart that compares all of their chains' overall widths. If an O-ring Diamond or RKS won't fit a particular application, you might be able to turn up a Tsubaki or Reynolds that does.

SHAFT DRIVES

What can I say here? Shaft drives are about as bulletproof as you can get; that's why the touring bikes use them. Check the normal stuff—U-joints, constant velocity joints, and splines are subject to wear, although they rarely require replacement. Some models use a seal between the rear drive and shaft that might have to be replaced. One thing you should look at on a shaft-driven bike are the splines that drive the rear wheel. BMWs, particularly ones that have recorded high miles (and what BMW hasn't?) or have had spotty maintenance, are prone to wearing out the drive splines on the rear end. The wheel should be a tight fit on the splines, with very slight play. If there is appreciable play, if the splines are worn to a knife-edge, or if the splines are gone entirely, you've problems. The only right way to repair worn-out drive splines is to replace all of the worn parts. The largest part of the problem is that the drive splines are part of the ring gear.

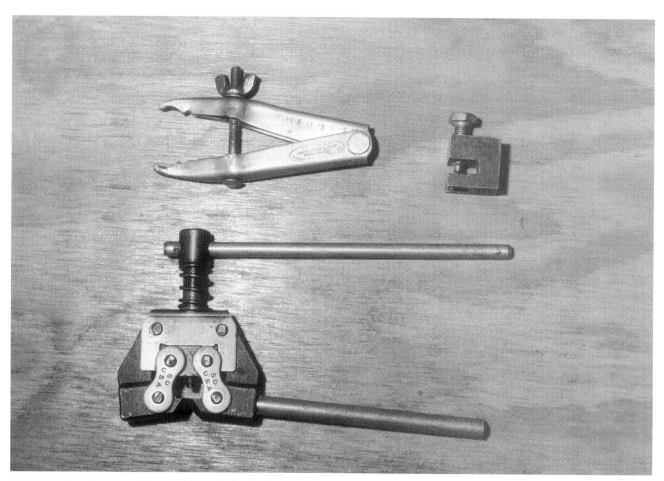

Chain repair can be messy, but the right tools make the job a lot easier. The top left tool is a small clamp for holding the ends of the chain together while you insert the master link. The small tool on the right is a small chain breaker. The tool is clamped in a vise or held with a wrench. The bolt is spun with another wrench to force the pin out of the link. On the bottom is a large, industrial-strength chain breaker. If you plan on doing a lot of chain work, get one; they make cutting a chain a whole lot easier.

Since new ring gears are only sold as a set with a matching pinion gear you're going to be in for a rear end rebuild. The drive spline, which is part of the rear wheel, is sold separately, as are the rivets. However, special tools will be needed to remove and install the splines in the hub. My advice would be to locate a used wheel or hub in good condition; they are usually available and the cost will be less than that of the spline and labor to install it. As for the rear end and drive spline, there is an easier solution than wholesale replacement. A few BMW dealers have come up with a procedure for replacing only the splines. The rear end is disassembled, the damaged spline machined off, a new one welded on and trued. If you run into this problem, which is fairly common, your local BMW dealer should be able to put you in touch with shops that can repair the splines. If he can't call one of the BMW specialists listed in the appendix.

11

Frames

While there are as many variations as there are manufacturers, when it comes to restoration all frames are more or less the same. It really won't matter if your project is a 1939 Indian Chief or a 1969 Honda Mini-Trail. As it says in the fine print, while details may vary, the base concept remains the same.

To put it in a nutshell, the frame should be stripped, inspected, repaired, and finally refinished. Basically, we'll take a look at three types of frames: rigid, sprung (both plunger and swingarm), and pressed steel. Pressed steel is typically used on lightweight bikes such as the Honda Cub or NSU MAX.

The Honda Benly utilized a stamped steel frame and bottom link forks. Despite its appearance and the stamped swingarm, the Benly handled extremely well.

STRIPPING

I'd love to tell you that the best way to begin is to just trot on down to your local sandblaster, hand him your frame and a $20 bill and retire to the nearest tavern until he's done. In fact, there are times when this is a perfectly acceptable practice; if your frame is a ball of rust have at it. Likewise, if you're restoring a bike that has a gloss-black frame (or did at one time) and no special decals, start blasting.

But what if you aren't sure what color the original frame was, or perchance there is some special emblem or decal that needs saving, then what?

In the first instance you can start by applying a little paint remover to the frame. Let it sit for a short while, and then scrape off some of the finish. Eventually you'll get down to the original finish, which you can then have matched. Traces of the old finish can usually be found where accessories have been clamped on or under frame lugs. Since some old frames were pinstriped, be on the lookout for any lining work.

Emblems and decals are another story. While most, if not all, of the common ones can be bought over the counter from specialists, some logos are unobtainable. That includes decals or stickers from old dealerships. Since they add a nice finishing touch I'm always tempted to save them. Of course they can be masked off and left in place—not the best solution, but often a workable one. They can also be copied by a sign painter or photographed and later reproduced by a shop specializing in decals. That might be a little expensive but is probably worth it in the end.

Once you've satisfied yourself that nothing more can be divined from studying the old frame, it's time to make the old finish disappear. The question is, how? You can hand sand the frame—a tedious procedure if ever there was one. You can use chemical strippers—better but just barely.

Or you can burn the old finish off using a torch or gasoline—don't laugh. In the old chopper days a lot of guys used to do a "burn-off." They'd set the frame in a vacant lot or alley, douse it with gas, and apply a little heat. Stupid and dangerous as it was, it worked, but personally I would hope that anyone shelling out hard-earned cash for this book would be a little smarter than that.

So what's my suggestion? Glad you asked. As I noted, I prefer bead- or sand-blasting. It removes all of the old paint, making it easier to inspect the frame, and it gives the new paint an excellent surface to adhere to. Before blasting you'll have to mask off all the threaded holes, or be prepared to give them a thorough cleaning. You should also mask off the steering-head races, although if you're going to replace them, just leave the old ones in place until you're done blasting. Likewise, the swingarm pivot should be protected.

If you're working on a stamped steel or sheet-metal frame, particularly one that's seen better days, pay attention to the grit and pressure used. You might well wind up with something that looks like it as made from a lace curtain.

Inspecting Rigid and Sprung Frames

Start your inspection with a check of the obvious. Are there any serious kinks in the frame—ones that aren't supposed to be there, that is? Are there any cracks in the frame? Were any of the engine-mount bolts—particularly long through-bolts—especially hard to pull out? Look closely around the steering-head stops, swingarm pivots, or any other point where frame tubes are joined together. Take a good look at the kickstand lug, a weak point on many models, particularly British Bikes and BMWs.

An often-overlooked point is the joint for the front down tube(s), which might become loose or crack, yet not pull away from the steering head. If you suspect crash damage, or anything looks amiss, you might want to have a complete frame alignment check performed. Most service manuals contain a set of frame drawings, complete with dimensions. Use these as a starting point.

If you run into a problem or something just nags at you, have the frame alignment checked by a pro. This is a specialist's job, not to be taken lightly. Likewise, straightening a bent or wracked frame is serious business and should only be entrusted to a shop with a demonstrable track record. I've listed a few of the better ones in the appendix.

Spotting a major tweak is pretty easy; flattened or kinked tubing is pretty obvious. Every so often, though, you'll run into a bike that's done duty as a sidecar tug. These frames might—and often do—acquire a subtle twist to

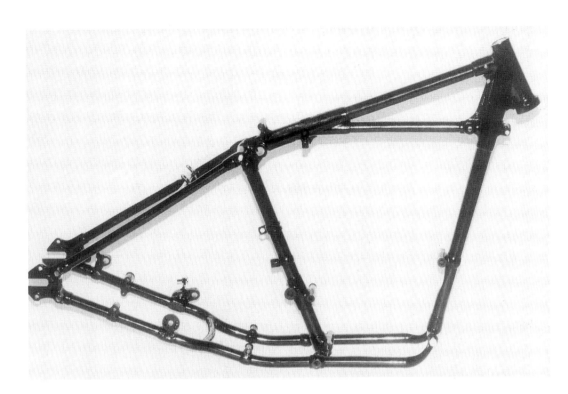

Rigid frames are as straightforward as they come. Your service manual should supply any needed dimensions. A bar inserted in the axle tabs will help check alignment. Make sure the steering head is straight and that any threaded holes are clean and in good condition.

them. If your bike is going to be restored sans hack, it's a good idea to have the frame looked at by a pro with an alignment table.

Minor cracks and small repairs can usually be handled by anyone who can handle a welding torch. New mounts can be brazed or welded into place, kickstand tabs reinstalled, and so on. Major repairs—frame straightening, tube replacement, steering-head repositioning—or any other out-of-the-ordinary work should always be left to the pros.

Rigid frames are pretty straightforward. If they're in-line and crack-free, any other damage is sure to be minor. Run a tap through the various threaded holes and chase the threads on any of the external mounts, especially after it's been sand-blasted. Make sure that any sand left over from stripping the frame is removed from all the little nooks and crannies.

Sprung frames are a little more complex, but not much. Some bikes—Ducati singles, for example—mount the rear shocks on threaded stubs welded to the swingarm and frame.

Swingarm frames also need the suspension mounting points and the swingarm mounting points checked. The swingarm itself needs checking and the swingarm bearings and bushings will need to be checked or replaced.

These tend to bend over the years, so be sure they are straight and parallel. In addition to the above, the swingarm pivot will need to be inspected. In many cases new bushings will need to be installed and reamed.

Swingarms must be checked in the same manner as the frame. Make sure there are no cracks, and that the swingarm legs are parallel to each other. Was the rear axle or swingarm pivot difficult to remove? If so, it might be tweaked. If there is any play in the swingarm pivot, replace the bushings.

One of the weirdest and worst rear suspension systems of all time is the infamous Triumph Sprung Hub—one of the first devices to carry a cast-in warning! These should only be taken apart if you're experienced, brave, and have the right tools.

Depending on the make, plunger frames can be as simple as a rigid frame or as complex as anything being built today. Most plungers will be relatively straightforward. Some, however—the Ariel Square Four with its Anstey-link plunger suspension—can be a bit weird. Inspect the links as you would any other mechanical device.

Stamped-Steel Frames

I've got to be perfectly honest here; I've never restored a bike with a stamped-steel frame. But I have serviced and repaired quite a few of them. Number one on your checklist should be a thorough inspection for rust and rot. Chances are if there is any serious rust the frame is a throwaway, and you might want to reevaluate the whole project. Likewise any serious crash damage.

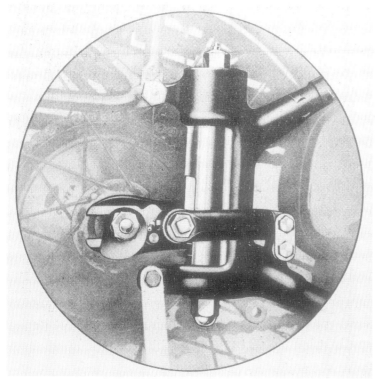

The Ariel "Anstey" link worked well but was high maintenance. Trouble spots that need inspection include the link pivot points and the shock sliders.

THE HOLE ENCHILADA

What's that? The engine mounting holes in your frame have become elongated from years of riding around with loose bolts? You think maybe they should be welded up and re-bored?

Years ago, builders of Superbikes used to ream out the engine-mount holes and install larger-diameter bolts. Doing so created a much tighter engine-to-frame fit and enhanced handling. Why not do the same during your restoration? My guess is that there's more than enough meat there to do it.

The exception would be something like an Ariel Leader or NSU Max, where the cost and time involved in replacing and repairing the sheet-metal would be well worth it. Honda 50s and other step-through designs are hardly worth the trouble and expense it would take to repair a rotted frame. That's my opinion, of course, and you are certainly welcome to your own.

Inspection is just like all the others, with the additional concern on older Japanese bikes of checking any spot welds joining the two halves together. Be sure they haven't cracked. The frame needs to be straight, sound, and roadworthy. Strip it, repair any damage, and get it ready for paint.

FINISH PREP

By now your frame should be ready to go to either the painter or the powder-coat booth. Either way, threads, bearing points, and machined surfaces should be protected. At the same time you might want to consider installing any bearings, bushes, or races that need replacing. If you wait until after the frame is painted you risk damaging the paint,

The Indian Warrior TT enjoyed limited success as an off-road racer, in part because it used a plunger rear suspension while everyone else was converting to a swingarm type frame.

131

This vintage cradle frame just needs the engine. Note the front support bracket used to steady the frame during reassembly.

should you get a little clumsy. Of course, if you opt for powder coat you'll have to wait, as the high heat involved might cause your new bearings to fall out.

If you decide to paint the frame, my advice is to install the new races and bushings before painting. That way a slip of the old punch and hammer won't send you into shock. Make sure that everything is well masked to prevent any errant spray from coating your bearing surfaces. Any overspray, however, should clean up easily. To prevent any overspray problems, though, I wouldn't recommend installing any bearings. Wiping out a race or bushing with a rag dipped in solvent is one thing; removing paint from the bearing itself is another thing altogether.

If powder coat is your thing, talk to the man in charge regarding masking procedures, particularly for threads, bushings, or races. Powder coating is thicker than paint—in some

cases, thick enough to obscure frame numbers or tags. If you're concerned about losing such details, ask the powder-coating shop how to deal with them. Everyone seems to have his own methods and requirement. For certain you'll have to mask any place where a bearing or bushing lives.

REAR SHOCKS

Let's keep this simple, shall we? The rear shocks are either shot or they aren't. If they are bent, busted, leaking like sieves, or just plain crusty, forget about them. OEM replacements that look like the originals but work ten times better are available just about anywhere.

If your shocks are unobtainable items—a genuine pair of Red Wing Hammer-Heads on a race bike, for instance—you have a few options. If they are serviceable, clean them up and use them. If they are rebuildable and you can obtain the parts you need, terrific. There

The old, worn out, and too short S&W shocks on the top were replaced with the new and correct length Koni shocks on the bottom. The Koni shocks look period correct and work much better the old S&W units.

are also enough shock rebuilders out there to populate a small town. I'm sure one would be only too happy to resurrect a pair of boingers for you.

If your shocks are spent and non-rebuildable but presentable, you can use them for show and install a modern pair for go. Or you can install a new pair and hang the antiques on the wall.

SPRINGS

Again, springs are available in a variety of weights, lengths, colors, and prices. If yours are rusty, sacked out, or just plain wrong—either too stiff or too soft—avail yourself of one of the aftermarket suppliers and install a set that looks or works better than what you've got.

Yamaha Monoshocks and Gas Shocks

This is strictly for the Yamaha crowd. Blown Monoshocks are expensive to rebuild and phenomenally expensive to replace—something to keep in mind when you're buying your bike. If you're restoring a vintage YZ, my advice is to contact one of the services listed in the appendix.

Likewise, a lot of European MXers featured Girling, Bilstein, or Ohlins gas shocks. These all take specialized equipment to rebuild, if they're rebuildable at all. Furthermore, the

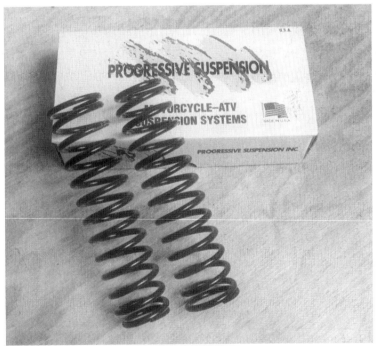

Springs haven't changed much over the years. These brand-new Progressive springs are a dead ringer for the clapped out original equipment they'll be replacing.

Removing and Replacing Shock Springs

So you don't have a fancy spring compressor. Here's the easy way to remove and replace the springs. Set the spring preload on its lowest setting and clamp the shock in a vise.

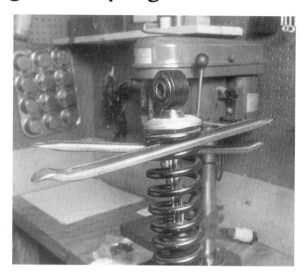

Insert two tire irons or pieces of flat stock in the upper spring coil.

Bear down until the retainer can be removed (an extra pair of hands may be helpful).

Before the new spring is installed push the bump stop as far down the shaft as you can, so it won't get in your way during reassembly.

It's hard to believe this swingarm came off a running bike—the Yamaha, in fact, shown in the introduction. Obviously this bushing died a long time ago.

high pressure some contain can be exceptionally dangerous. Leave them to the pros.

Restoring and Inspecting Shocks

Inspect the shocks by removing the springs and stroking them through a few compression-rebound cycles. They should move freely, yet demonstrate some resistance in both directions. If they have dead spots, bind, stick, or chatter, they'll need rebuilding or replacement. Shafts should be free from nicks, gouges, and rust. Obviously, they should be straight as the proverbial arrow.

If the bushings look less than perfect, replace them. If you're planning to strip the old finish off before painting, carefully mask off the shaft and seal before grit blasting. After painting, allow the shocks to air-dry for a day or two before installing the springs. I don't recommend powder coating shocks. The high temperatures involved will definitely ruin the seals and possibly boil the oil, blowing the shock apart.

Front Forks

Neither fish nor fowl, the Vincent "Girdraulic" fork combined the strength of a girder fork with the damping of a telescopic.

Forks are going to be broken down—no pun intended—into three very basic groups: mechanical, which includes girders and springers in most of their incarnations; hydraulic, which covers all telescopic forks; and others, which includes Earles, as used on /2 BMWs and one or two other leading- or trailing-link forks common to small Japanese, British, and European machines.

MECHANICAL

For want of a better term, I'll lump all spring-action types of forks into one big heap and call them mechanical forks. Prior to World War II, most motorcycles were equipped with some type of spring-action fork. After the war, telescopics became the norm for all but a few manufacturers.

Once the forks are removed from the frame, they should be bead-blasted and carefully examined for cracks. Although it's unlikely, forks have been known to snap in half. Clearly, if you find cracks, they should be repaired before proceeding.

After you've disassembled the forks, insert a pair of mandrels about 14 to 18 inches long into the spindle holes. It goes without saying that the mandrels should be an exact fit in the pivot holes and dead straight. Insert another mandrel into the axle lugs. Use threaded rod to make the mandrels; that way you can secure them in place with nuts and washers.

If your eyesight is better than mine, sighting along the mandrels should give you a good indication of the fork's alignment. If you haven't been eating your carrots, a measuring tape should suffice. Measure the distance from

rod to rod: with luck, they're the same. Any major discrepancy indicates a bend in the blade.

Perfectionists or restorers who plan to make this a long-term hobby can make up a jig that supports the fork assembly. Use two parallel straight edges that can support the fork. Rest the mandrels in the jig. If the fork is twisted to any appreciable degree, you'll see daylight under one or more of the mandrels.

Minor tweaks can be removed by cold-bending the blades. Insert long rods through the pivot holes and bend away. Because the blades have a "memory" you'll probably need to overbend the blades slightly. If the fork is really wadded up you'll have to send it to a pro. New blades or tubes might be required. These are repairs beyond the scope of the novice restorer.

Inspect the pivot bushings for signs of wear—any play you can feel is probably too much. New bushings can usually be found at a bearing supply house or turned on a lathe if you're ambitious. Indian and Harley restorers can generally just pick up a phone and order what they need. (See appendix.)

TELESCOPICS

Fitted to the majority of motorcycles since the 1950s, telescopics are the most common type of fork in the world. Telescopics come in a variety of styles: single damped, double damped, internal or external springs, adjustable or non. In theory, though, they all operate pretty much the same way. They are also disassembled and inspected in more or less the same way.

Removal

Normally the fork is removed from the bike about like you'd expect. Release the triple clamp pinch bolts and slide the tubes out. Some tubes, however, are held in the top clamp by a taper. There are special tools available to remove and install tapered forks. I've found that by loosening the top nut a few threads and whacking it with a plastic mallet you can usually pop them out of the taper.

Reinstalling the tapered tubes can be a bit tricky, especially with external fork springs. I've seen an old broom handle threaded into the tube used to pull the tube back in place.

The first step in fork disassembly is to remove the fork cap. Chances are you won't have a 1/2-inch drive air impact gun. My suggestion is to loosen the caps before the forks are removed from the motorcycle.

After the fork cap has been removed, the springs, any preload spacers, and a couple hundred cc's of goo should come out. Be prepared for a mess.

Some Japanese models—Suzuki in particular—used press-in fork caps that are secured by a snap ring. Careful—once you remove the snap ring, the cap can and might well pop out like a champagne cork. Wipe the springs down and check for any obvious problems; once in a while you'll find that one spring has collapsed. About the only other thing you can do to check your springs is to measure their free length. Your shop manual should provide the correct measurement.

Once the springs and oil have been removed you can separate the tube from the lower leg. Normally, the fork tube secures to the lower leg by one of three methods. British and older Japanese models feature an external threaded collar. Older lightweights, particularly Japanese small bores, often use a snap ring located above the seal. Ceriani-style forks, which most bikes built after 1970, feature an Allen bolt that passes through the lower leg and into the damper rod. Every so often you'll be thrown a curve ball and find a snap ring and a bolt through the damping rod. In these cases the snap ring is there to hold the fork seal in place.

Removing the threaded collar on forks so equipped usually requires a special tool—at least if you want to reuse the collar. As an alternative you might be able to use a strap wrench, but be careful; I've seen collars ruined by overzealous applications of torque. One method I've seen used with some success involves fastening a hose clamp to the bottom of the collar, fastening a Vise-Grip across the screw of the hose clamp, and spinning the whole shebang off. Of course a hammer and punch, pipe wrench, or chain wrench will always remove the collar, although the end result won't be very pretty.

Removing a snap-ring retainer is pretty straightforward. The rings tend to rust in place, though, so applying a little penetrating oil seems like a pretty good idea.

There are a couple of techniques you can use to remove the Allen bolt holding a Ceriani-style fork together. The problem you're most likely to encounter is that instead of the bolt coming loose, the whole assembly—bolt and damping rod—will simply spin like a top when you try to remove the bolt.

The best solution is an air gun. Torque will zip that little sucker out of there quicker than you can say, "Ted's yer uncle." Of course

I've also held the tube in place until I caught it with the nut and then used the nut to draw the tube into place. Be careful here, though, because it's very easy to cross thread the nut using this technique.

Inspection

Start by dismantling the forks—actually you should start by draining the fork oil, but you know that. If the fork has external springs they're probably already off at this point. If not, remove them.

If the forks use an internal spring you'll have to remove the fork caps, if you haven't already done so.

Occasionally you'll find the damper rod threads into the fork cap—Nortons, for instance.

The easy way to remove a damper rod bolt is by impact. If an air or electric impact wrench isn't available, you'll have to devise some method of preventing the damper rod from turning.

you might not have an air gun at your disposal. In that case you might be able to unscrew the bolt from the rod by collapsing the fork and securing the damping rod with a screwdriver, socket, or special tool made just for that purpose.

The least desirable solution—but one that's worked well for me—involves reinstalling the fork spring and top nut. The spring preloads the damping rod, which in theory keeps it from turning. Insert your Allen wrench, and "fetch it a whacking great blow,"

Once the bolt has been removed, you can separate the tube from the lower leg.

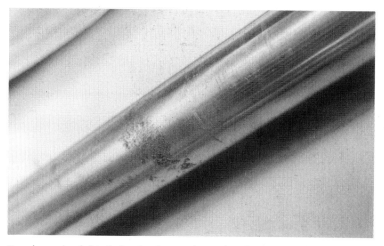

Rust has ruined this fork tube; it must be replaced.

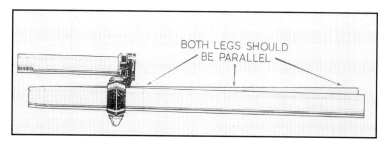

BOTH LEGS SHOULD
BE PARALLEL

Telescopics are easy to check. Insert the tubes back into the lower clamp and check the tubes with a straight edge. They must be parallel to each other.

Remove the damping rods, clean them, and give them the once-over. If the bike has high mileage, replace any bushings or wiper rings. In some cases alternative damper rods may be available. If so, they make a worthy upgrade and will provide a noticeable improvement in handling.

as the English magazines used to say. The shock and spring pressure should be enough to loosen the bolt.

By the way, you guys working on BMWs with U.S.-style forks, which includes /2 /5 /6 /7 models, have it a little easier. The damping rod extends through the leg and is secured by an 8mm nut. The rod itself is broached to accept an Allen wrench. You insert the wrench to keep the rod from turning, while a wrench or socket removes the nut.

Once the fork tubes are withdrawn from the lower legs they can be placed in V blocks and checked for true. Some forks use replaceable bushings pressed into the lower legs. The bushings might be fitted to the fork tubes. At the very least these should be measured and inspected for wear.

I'd also recommend removing the damping rod itself, and giving it the once-over. A few designs—BMW, for instance—use wiping rings on the damper. These should be removed and inspected if the bike has high mileage or if fork action is less than smooth. As a side note, BMW, Triumph, and a few other manufacturers offered alternative spring/damping rod combos for their bikes. BMWs, in particular, work a little better with a slightly stiffer front fork than what came stock.

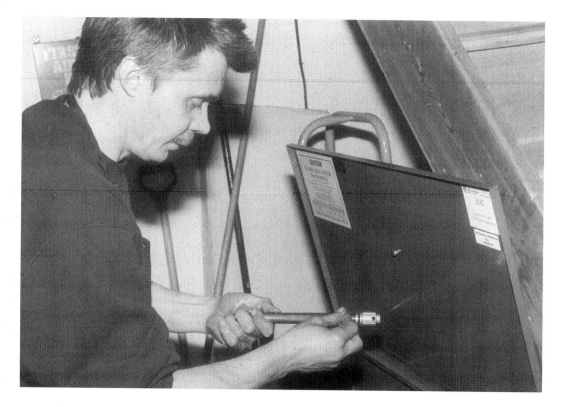

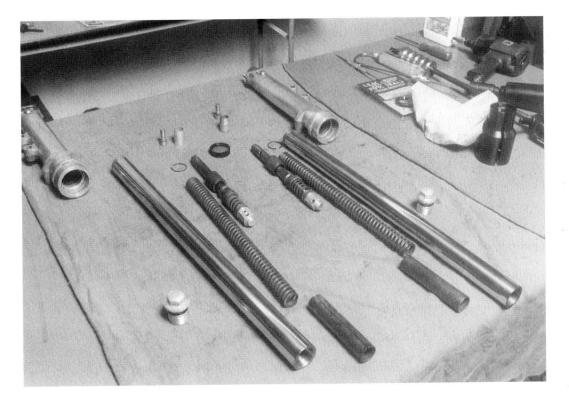

One item that's sometimes overlooked is the lower leg. Inspect the leg for any serious dents, especially on off-road competition bikes, cracks around the axle housing, and damage or cracks at the brake anchor. Pay particular attention to aluminum legs with axle pinch bolts; overtightening can crack the bolt holes. On some bikes the fender and its mount act as a fork brace; check these for cracks, breaks, or worn threads at the mounting boss.

Since wear patterns have been established, try to keep the legs with their original tubes. Clean everything twice and then reassemble it after replacing any worn parts. The seals should be replaced as a matter of course. Most seals are installed straight into the lower legs, although some designs carry them in the retainer.

Fill them with the correct weight and quantity of oil and set them aside until you're ready to reinstall them.

EARLES AND OTHERS

Earles forks, as found on /2 BMWs, Douglas, Greeves, and a few other makes, should be treated as front swingarms, which in reality

Carefully inspect the lower legs, especially around the fender mounting boss. If they're going to crack, it'll be here or at the axle mount.

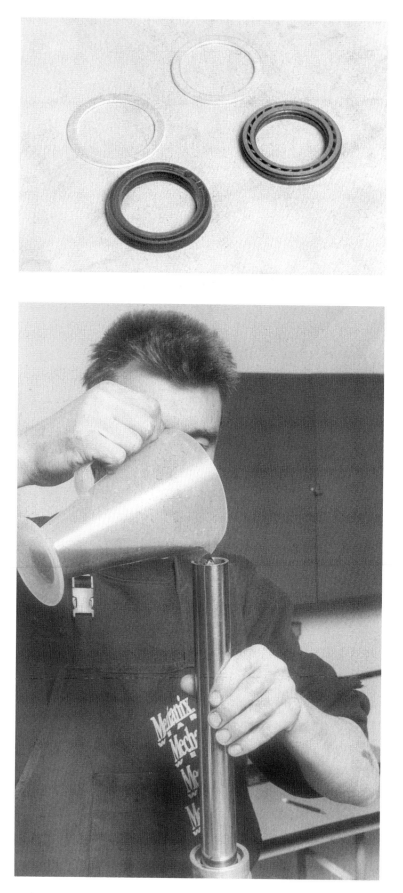

The factory seals may be long gone but generic replacements are available everywhere. These are made by Leak-pruff®.

is what they are. Reduce them to their component parts and inspect them as you would a swingarm. The shocks are removed and inspected as any other.

When reassembling the BMW fork, pay attention to the swingarm pivots. There are two pivot points. The forward pivot is for sidecar use, the rear for solo.

The sheet metal forks found on lightweight bikes—Honda, Yamaha, and Ariel, among others—present a few problems, the main one being that parts are a little scarce in the United States. If yours are badly damaged, the best solution might be to contact one of the shops that deal in that particular marque. The other major problem is that short of cutting out a damaged section and replacing it with new sheet metal, there is no practical way to repair the damaged fork. If they use an internal shock absorber, inspect and replace as you would any other.

Clamps, Crowns, and Bearings

Unless the bike's been seriously wadded at some point, it's unlikely that the triple clamp/fork crown assembly has suffered any damage. But since it's already apart, you might as well check it over. The easiest way to check the triple clamp is to place it on a known flat surface, bottom down. Any bends should reveal themselves instantly.

Another method is to reinstall the (straight) fork tubes. Are they parallel to each other and the steering stem? If so, the clamp is fine. If not, the clamp is bent. Unless the clamp is unobtainable I'd recommend replacement over straightening. Most clamps are cast, in either steel or aluminum, and don't take well to straightening once they've been bent. While they can be coaxed back into shape if they're only a little tweaked, any serious bends are cause for replacement. If you do opt to straighten, I'd recommend contacting a specialist.

When checking the lower clamp, give the steering stop a good look as well. Years of riding

After reassembly, fill with the correct weight and grade of oil.

Although the Earles fork was used by a few different manufacturers, it is most commonly associated with BMW.

tend to flatten out the stops. One sure sign is small dents or chips at the front of the fuel tank, where the fork has hit the leading edge. You might want to build the stops up with a spot of weld before installing your freshly painted fuel tank.

Fork crowns are checked the same way as the triple clamp. Place the clamp on a flat surface and see if it's warped in any way. If not, it's good to go; if it is, use it for a paperweight.

Pay particular attention to the flat steel top plate as used on U.S.-forked BMWs. These steel plates are somewhat flimsy and bend easily. They are fairly cheap, however, and easily straightened should you need to.

The Earles is really a front swingarm. Check for play at the pivot point and for distorted tubes. The shocks are replaced just like any other. Notice the alternative pivot point just forward of the swingarm bolt. The forward position is for sidecar use. Occasionally, a fork intended for solo use ends up with the pivot in the sidecar position. If the bike feels twitchy or handles oddly, check the lower pivot point first, and make sure a bike set up for solo use has the swingarm bolt positioned in the rearward hole.

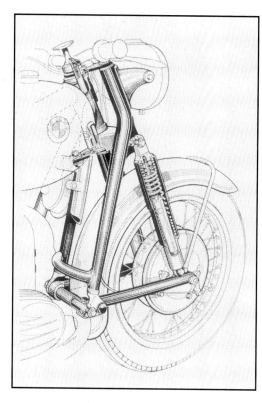

Steering Head Bearings

The steering head bearings will at very least need a thorough cleaning and repacking. During the initial disassembly of the motorcycle, the races and bearings should be inspected. If the races are dented, nicked, or notched, they'll require replacement. I'd leave the old races in place until the frame has been stripped of paint. In fact, if the races are good I'd leave them alone and in place; just tape them over during any glass beading and painting.

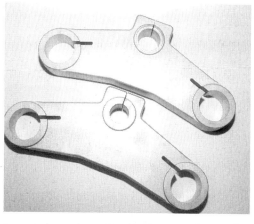

Inspect clamps by positioning them on a known flat surface, such as a flat piece of heavy glass. If they don't sit perfectly flat, they'll need straightening.

If replacement is called for you can either buy a special—and exorbitantly priced—extractor or a standard, over-the-counter bearing punch that can be used on a variety of other jobs. I'd go for the bearing punch. Likewise, you can install the new races with the gen-u-wine tool or make do with an old socket. I use the socket.

As an aside, this is one area where eye protection is mandatory. Bearing races are extremely hard, and occasionally throw sharp chips when they break.

Removing the old inner races can sometimes prove difficult. You might find that you need to wedge the punch in the steering head of the frame to catch the lip of the bearing enough to drive it out. The use of a regulation bearing drift or punch, with its oval face, will make it a little easier and give you a larger contact surface.

Normally, removing the outer race from the bottom of the steering stem can be accomplished by using a plain old bearing splitter to pry the bearing up. Chisels and tire irons also work. Every once in a while I'll run into an outer race that's stuck on the stem like chewing gum on a mohair sweater. If I've already got the new one in hand, I'll usually fire up the smoke wrench to remove it.

New races must be driven in squarely and firmly seated in the frame. If your bike uses loose ball bearings, fill the races with stiff grease—I'd recommend using grease rated for salt-water immersion—and insert the correct number of balls, top and bottom. If the balls don't go in easily or don't seat fully into the races, double-check both their number and size. Replace any that are the wrong size. If there's still a problem, you're better off leaving one out than you are having one extra. Pay attention to the lower bearing when reinstalling the lower clamp and steering stem. It's easy to knock a ball or two loose.

Tapered bearings must be packed with grease before installation. When installing the lower bearing over the steering stem you might need to give it a tap or three. Use a drift made from a steel pipe and ONLY drive against the inner race.

Once the complete triple tree is installed, tighten the centering nut by hand until it's as tight as you can make it. Use the appropriate tool to lightly tighten the nut until all the play is removed from the assembly. You don't have

Steering Head Race and Bearing Replacement

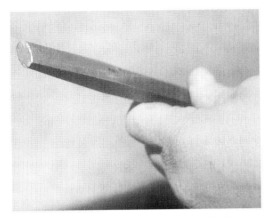

To remove bearing races, use a bearing. The head is formed with an oval tip that gives you a better purchase on the bearing race.

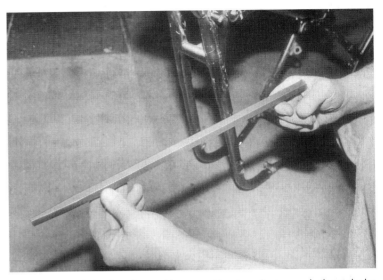

A bearing punch is also nice and long, making it easier to reach through the steering head.

Wedging the punch against the races will make it a little easier. Don't be afraid to use a man-sized hammer, either.

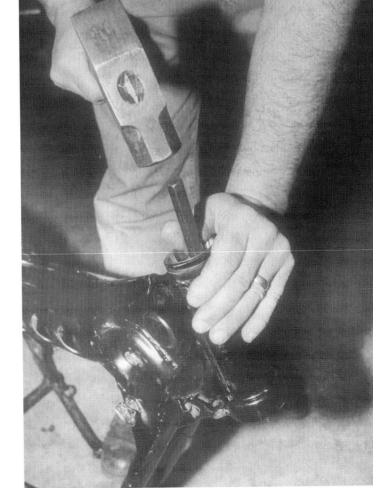

to go crazy here; you're only going to seat the bearings. While you're tightening the nut, rotate the clamp from side to side. If you feel it bind, stop and back it off a hair.

Some manuals might list an initial tightening torque. Torque the nut to the recommended setting. If there's no torque figure listed, snug the nut down, back it off a half turn, and then gently seat the nut again. The idea here is to simply remove any play between the triple clamp and the bearings. You don't want to preload the bearings in any way unless your shop manual specifically requires it. As a rule of thumb, tapered roller bearings as used in BMWs, Moto Guzzis, and late-model Triumphs need some preload. On the other hand, loose-ball steering head bearings can actually be damaged if preloaded.

Once the triple clamp has been installed and everything snugged up, the clamp might feel a little stiff from stop to stop. Don't worry; when the fork legs and wheel are installed, it'll probably be perfect. If you want to, you can install the fork legs at this point, or you can wait until you're ready to assemble the bike.

Steering Head Race and Bearing Replacement

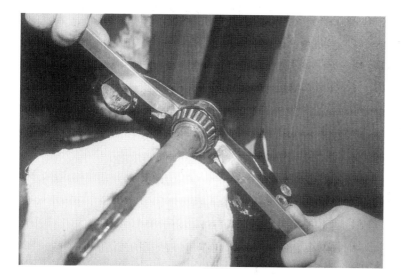

This is the right way to remove a lower bearing from a steering stem; sometimes it works.

If it doesn't, the bearing ends up looking like this.

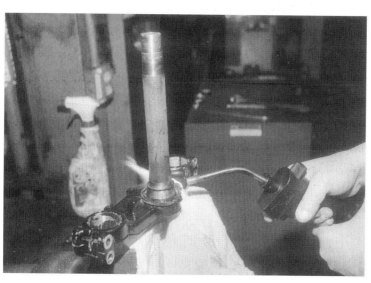

At that point all bets are off. Heat up the inner race . . .

Steering Head Race and Bearing Replacement

. . . and drive it off with a blunt chisel.

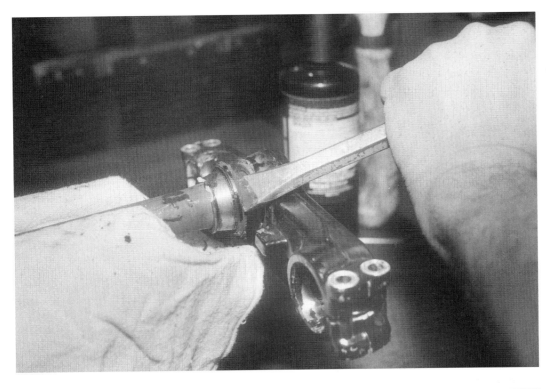

If replacement bearings are needed, it may be possible to save a considerable sum by sourcing them directly from a bearing house. All bearings carry a code number, the manufacturer's name, and the country of origin stamped into the outer race. Ninety percent of the time the bearing has a generic (and much cheaper) equivalent.

13

Chapter

T h i r t e e n

Wheels and Hubs

This is the simplest type of truing stand to build and use. Make the uprights out of 2x2s. Use a strip of leather or tin to hold the pointers in place and bolt it to your workbench.

'll be the first to admit it: I'm a terrible wheel builder. I'm just as bad at truing wheels. If it were up to me I'd send the wheels out to a professional wheel builder every time, but enough about me.

If you're lucky, the rims, hubs, and spokes of your project bike will be in perfect condition. A little polish, some elbow grease, and away you'll go. If you're unlucky, they'll be a rusted, twisted mess. Reality for most us will be a pair of wheels that lie somewhere in the middle.

If the wheels are serviceable, you'll still need to give everything the once-over. At the very least you'll want to remove and repack the wheel bearings and check the spoke tension. Obviously, a damaged or bent rim, spokes, or hub will require a complete dismantling and subsequent rebuild of the wheel. Let's assume the worst.

DISMANTLING

Before a single spoke is removed, you'll need to perform a few preliminary steps. To begin with, you'll either have to buy or build a wheel-truing stand. Commercial stands are relatively inexpensive, about $200. If you plan to lace and true a lot of wheels they are indispensable.

A perfectly serviceable stand can be built from an old pair of fork legs or an old bicycle fork. If you feel like a little carpentry, build your stand from a pair of 2x2s. Cut a notch in one end and screw or bolt them to your work-bench (see illustration).

The next step is to thoroughly document your wheels' spoke pattern and offset. The spoke pattern is usually called the "cross." Most wheels are laced to a cross-two or cross-three pattern, meaning that each spoke crosses over either two or three spokes on its way to the rim. The more spokes that are crossed, the stronger the wheel. Some off-road machines might employ a cross-four pattern, especially on the rear wheel. Still others might use a mix, with a cross-four on the rear wheel's drive side and a cross-three on the other.

Offset is the distance from the outside edge of the hub to the edge of the rim. It varies from bike to bike. Some wheels have considerable

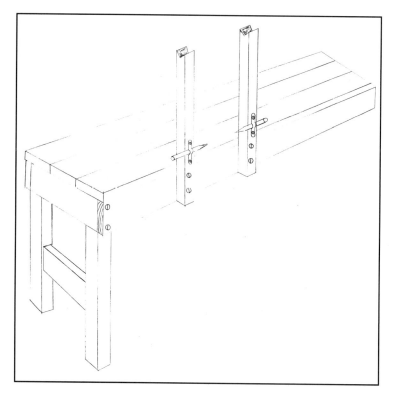

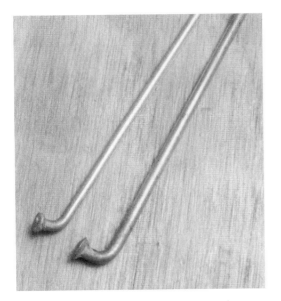

Be sure to identify the spokes as you remove them. These two were removed from the same wheel. Notice that they have different diameters and different bends at the butt. Someone at some time replaced a broken spoke with one "that worked."

offset; some have none. Lay a straightedge across the wheel and measure it on both sides. A photo or two at this point won't hurt either.

If the spokes are in good shape and you want to save them for reuse, you'll need to unscrew the nipples and remove the spokes. If you plan to renew all the spokes, use a bolt cutter to snip the spokes in the middle. A warning is in order here, though. If you decide to use the bolt cutters it's a good idea to remove at least one of each type of spoke used in the wheel to ensure that the new ones match up. Most rims employ at least "inner" and "outer" spokes. Some, particularly wheels with conical hubs, will also have three or possibly four different-length spokes. It's always a good idea to label the spokes as they are withdrawn.

Hubs and Bearings

Once the hub is separated from the rim, the bearings, seals, and any spacers should be removed, inspected, and replaced as necessary. Inspecting the bearings is self-explanatory. About 85 percent of the wheel bearings come out in a straightforward manner. Some are secured by threaded retainers, which might be either right- or left-handed, depending on the manufacturer's whim. Some are held in place by snap rings.

The other 15 percent are those installed in /5/6 and /7 BMWs using a drum brake. The shop manual provides explicit instructions on their removal and installation. Follow them to the letter and you'll have no problem. Skip one step and you're going to end up with a very expensive paperweight.

BMW Bearing Removal

Basically, BMW wants you to heat the hub and remove both bearings and their spacers as a unit. Sounds easy. Actually, it is, once you get the hang of it, but the first time can be a real pain.

Start by removing the bearing retainer from the left side of the wheel. Leave the bearing in place and insert the axle from the right-hand side. You'll need to make up and install a spacer on the left side of the axle. The spacer needs to be long enough so that when the axle nut is installed the spacer butts up solidly against the bearing. Make sure that when the axle nut is tightened the axle has no free play.

Heat the hub until spit bounces off it (OK, it's crude, but that's a good indication). Tap the axle and bearings through the hub from right to left as a unit. After repacking the bearings, store them in a refrigerator until it's time to reinstall them. Reinstall the bearings, again as a unit, by installing them from the left side to the right. Get the hub good and hot and the chilled bearings should slip right in.

By the way, BMW bearings can be shimmed to compensate for routine wear. Install the bearings and spacers on the axle; along with the spacer you made up, remove the assembly. Again, the idea is to position the bearings as they would be in the wheel. Check the central spacer for play. It should be free to move from side to side without being able to move up and down. If there is up and down play the spacer should be replaced with a slightly smaller one (allowing the bearing to sit deeper in its race). If the bearings are too tight, a slightly larger spacer will be required (forcing the bearing to sit higher in the race). Alternative spacers are listed in the parts book.

GENERAL WHEEL INSPECTION

Once the hub is stripped, a thorough cleaning and inspection is needed. Be on the lookout for the usual cracks, particularly if the hub uses a flange to locate the spokes. Check for wear marks or scoring where the spokes pull across the hub. If they are very deep they'll need to be built up; otherwise, the spokes will "fret" against the score marks and eventually break. Some hubs can be flipped to let the spokes pull in the opposite direction. Pay particular attention to hubs used on vintage racers, particularly MXers. These hubs take an incredible amount of abuse and have a nasty tendency to break at inopportune moments.

On rear hubs check the sprocket bolt holes and repair any threads as needed. If the bike incorporates a rear-hub cush drive, the rubbers should be inspected and replaced as required. Shaft-drive bikes should have the drive splines inspected. Stripped hubs are uncommon, but not unheard of. By the way, if the speedometer is driven from the wheel, now is the time to check the drive gear; the teeth should be evenly worn and unchipped.

Inspect the wheel bearings and races as you would any other. Commonly wheel bearings get rusty from wash and rainwater forcing its way past the seal. While you might be able to clean and grease a bad bearing into something like a serviceable state, the smart money is on replacement. If a wheel bearing lets go at speed, it won't be pretty.

Seals should be replaced as a matter of course. Some of the older bikes might use a seal that's more of a suggestion than a seal. It's not uncommon for such seals—usually felt or cloth—to leak from new. Owners planning to actually ride their masterpieces might want to consider an upgrade to a modern seal.

Once the hubs are cleaned, inspected, and presumably found free of any defects, you can paint, polish, or powder-coat them. A quick caution here: Because some of the hubs will

require a little heat to install the bearings, you might want to install them before you paint the hub. Of course if they are installed prior to refinishing, you won't be able to powder-coat.

As a side note, the last BMW hub I did had already been powder-coated before I got it. The heat did little damage, just a little discoloration around the bearing seat. On this particular hub the hubcap hid the damage. The moral? Try it; you never know what you can get away with.

Bearings, Seals (and Saving a Few Bucks)

By now you know—or should know—how to properly inspect, remove, and reinstall bearings and seals. If not, you are definitely in trouble. I'm not going to tell you not to hammer on the outer race, nor will I tell you not to spin a dry bearing up to 20 grand with compressed air. And you should know that the open end of the seal always faces whatever it is you're trying to seal.

What you might not know, or might have overlooked, is the fact that most, if not all bearings and seals are generic. Sourcing the bearings and seals through your local bearing supply shop can save a considerable amount of money. Before we fly off the handle, I'll tell you that I don't recommend substituting an OEM bearing with a generic replacement when rebuilding the engine and transmission. The reason is that bearings using the same number might have different internal clearances. If you end up with a C-1 (standard clearance bearing) where a C-3 (looser than standard) bearing is required, you can do a considerable amount of damage to an engine.

On the other hand, wheel bearings, steering head bearings, and so on generally run standard clearances, though there are some exceptions. Some Triumphs and BSAs spec a looser-than-standard wheel bearing. The bearing and seal will have a code stamped into them describing their physical characteristics. The bearing house can supply you with the correct seal or bearing using that code. They can also supply you with the correct ones based on dimension, if the numbers have been obliterated.

Typically the savings on generic seals and bearings approaches 50 percent or better. One other thing: When you take them in for sizing, make sure the old parts are scrupulously clean, unless you want them thrown at you by an irate counterman.

The hub on the left has grooves worn into it from the spokes. Because this hub is symmetrical, it can be flipped over and relaced so the spokes pull in the opposite direction. Next to it is an unused hub.

Rims and Cast Wheels

The rim should be free from dents, relatively straight, and as rust-free as possible. Rechroming a rim—while not out of the question—is somewhat impractical and fairly expensive. Since there are several sources for rims, I don't recommend it (see sidebar). If the rims require painting, do it a few weeks before you plan on lacing them to give the paint plenty of time to harden.

Some modern classics might have come with cast wheels. Check these for dents, dings, and cracks. In the main I think you'll find cast wheels to be more or less trouble-free. There are a few shops that specialize in the straightening and repair of cast rims.

Rims: Steel Yourself—or Not

Here's my two cents on rims: If I were restoring a modern classic—say, something built from 1965 on up—and the steel rims were shot, I think I'd replace them with period-looking alloy rims. That's especially true if the bike were a sport model. They're easy to get, relatively inexpensive, and they look great. Besides, they were a popular upgrade at the time. Anything much older than that, or a pure touring model, looks best with replacement chrome-plate or painted-steel rims.

Spokes

There isn't much to say here. If the spokes and nipples are good, they can certainly be reused; if not, they can be replaced with either OEM or aftermarket. You can opt for heavier spokes if you feel the need. If I were restoring a bike meant to be raced, I'd unhesitatingly go for the heaviest available spokes. For general street use I'd recommend stainless-steel spokes, available with either a mat or polished finish, simply because they require less maintenance.

Assembling and Truing

Personally, I find the whole lacing and truing procedure unbelievably tedious and generally send my wheels out to a pro wheel builder. Since this book is about doing it yourself, though, and not UPS-ing parts all over the world, here's how you lace a wheel. To begin with, run a drill bit through the hub to remove any paint or powder-coat that might keep the spoke from seating in the hub.

There are two types of spoke holes, the keyhole—which has a slotted opening—and

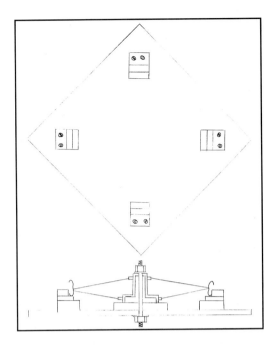

the more common round hole. With keyhole hubs the spokes can be inserted one at a time. Round hole hubs require you to insert all the inner spokes first, then the outer spokes. You'll notice that inner spokes and outer spokes alternate and that the first and fourth spoke, which are respectively an inner and an outer, are arranged to pull in a straight line. You'll also note that spokes are usually arranged in groups of four.

After the spokes are in the hub, place the rim over the hub and then fan the spokes out. Notice that the rim's dimples all face a different direction. Locate an outer spoke that lines up with a dimple, put a dab of grease under the head of the nipple, and run it onto the spoke a few turns. Proceed to the next outer spoke and repeat.

Once all the outer spokes have been connected on one side, repeat the process using the inner spokes. Flip the rim over and repeat for the other side. If the threaded end of the spoke protrudes through the rim too far, try moving it one hole in another direction. To avoid damage to the rim, install a nipple as soon as its spoke is in place. Once all of the spokes and nipples are in place, thread them down finger tight.

An alternative method is to just install the inside spokes into the hub. Lace them into position on the rim and then install the outside spokes. Either way works as well.

A Taverner truing stand as described in *The Vintage Motorcyclists Workshop*. Les Taverner has come up with the perfect way to build wheels. As you can see, he bored a hole in a 1-inch-thick chunk of plywood. Then he bolted the wheel solidly to it. When the wheel was in place, he positioned four blocks of wood at equal points around the rim, effectively locking the wheel and rim in place. The new rim and hub are loosely assembled. The wheel is then placed into the jig. Working your way around the rim, tighten every fourth spoke. When you get back to the starting point, move to the next spoke. Again, tighten every fourth spoke. Repeat until all spokes are tight. When you're done, check the wheel for true in a standard jig. It may not be perfect, but I'll bet it's damn close.

Truing the Wheel

Place the freshly completed wheel in your truing stand. Chances are it'll revolve like a drunk's merry-go-round. The first step is to adjust for offset. If things went favorably, your rim offset should be pretty close. If the rim is too far to the left, tighten only the spokes on the right and vice-versa.

You shouldn't have to screw the nipples down very far to move the rim. If you find them bottoming out, something's wrong. Possibly the left spokes are too tight or the spokes are in the wrong holes.

Once offset has been adjusted we'll have to adjust radial (up-and-down) runout. Mount a pointer to the bottom of your stand. Find the high and low spot of the rim. At the low spot tighten the spokes at the top and loosen the ones at the bottom. You'll probably need to do this a few times until the wheel is true. When your rim is true to about 1/8 of an inch or less, stop.

You may find that the wheel "kicks" or "jumps" at the spot where it's welded. There's not much you can do about it. All steel rims exhibit this behavior; it's nothing to worry about.

Lateral (side-to-side) runout and spoke tension are adjusted at the same time. Move the pointer to the side of the rim; if the rim pulls to the right, adjust the spokes on the left. Repeat until the rim runs true, within 1/32-inch or so. By now the spokes should all have at least equal tension on them. Test them by tapping each with a screwdriver. A snug spoke should have a nice "ping" to it, a loose one a dull "clack."

This heavy-duty wheel truing stand accommodates any wheel I can think of. It's a little much for home use, but it certainly makes the job easier.

This detail shot illustrates the fixing point. The shoelike piece checks radial runout (up and down or hop). The screw pointers measure axial run-out (side to side).

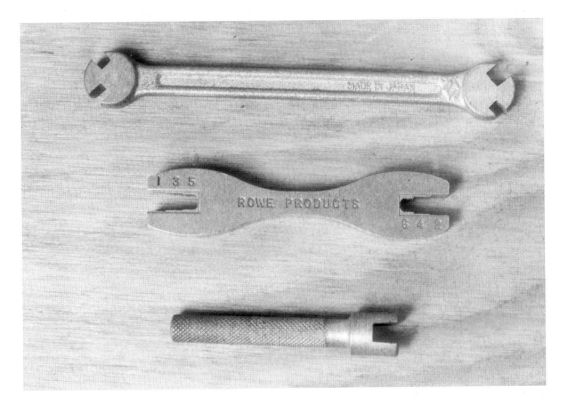

Spoke tools, plain and fancy, from the bottom, which is a standard spoke nipple wrench. (Middle) Rowe makes a wrench that fits most standard sizes from a no. 1 nipple to a no. 6. (Top) Suzuki supplies a wrench that fits all of its wheels—or at least it did in 1971 when I bought this wrench.

Tightening Spokes

Initially, each spoke should only be run down finger tight. Once truing commences, the spoke should only be tightened a quarter of a turn at a time. When the wheel runs true and the spokes are snug, STOP! Overtorquing a spoke will not only pull the wheel out of true, it will make the spoke more likely to break.

Once the bike has a few miles on it—say 500 or so—you can retorque the spokes by giving each one a tug with a spoke wrench. Don't worry if any are loose. This is normal, as the spokes tend to loosen slightly as they fully seat. Tighten them a quarter turn at a time until they are all snug again.

Spoke Tools

What do you use to turn those pesky spoke nipples? You can use a small adjustable wrench. Of course, they are awkward and tend to round off the nipples. A better tool is a dedicated spoke wrench. Spoke wrenches are available in a multitude of shapes and sizes. Some incorporate several sizes in one wrench. Others are cut to fit a particular size.

I usually keep a multi-sized wrench in the toolbox I take to the races and use the single-sized ones back in the shop. If you're

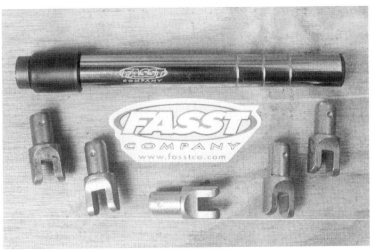

From Fasst Company comes the ultimate spoke wrench: This spoke torque wrench features interchangeable heads and is preset to correctly tension the spokes on your wheels. The wrench also includes complete and foolproof instructions to help you true your wheels. It's a little expensive, but well worth it.

in the market for a high-tech spoke wrench, there is even a spoke torque wrench available with interchangeable heads made by a company called Fasst [sic] (see the appendix). At over $100 it's a little pricey, but it will definitely ensure that all the spokes are correctly torqued.

All it takes is time and patience. This wheel was built from a new old stock (NOS) hub, a new rim, and new stainless steel spokes.

FINISHING UP

I'm a firm believer in mounting the tires as soon as the wheels are done. Grind off any protruding spoke threads and then install a new rim band or wrap the rim with electric or duct tape. Install new rim locks if required and always use a new tube.

Mounting the tires can be tricky, particularly if the rim is painted or alloy. Plastic rim protectors are available from most motorcycle shops and should be used to prevent unnecessary damage. I also use a plastic bucket to support the wheel while mounting the tire.

I'm a strong believer in lots of lubricant (on the tire; I generally wait to the end of the workday before I lubricate myself) and I try to mount the tire using only my own, somewhat limited strength. Failing that I'll use a set of tire irons—not screwdrivers!

14

<u>Chapter</u>
Fourteen

Brakes

Vintage brakes encompass everything from wooden blocks rubbing against "dummy rims" to hydraulically operated disc brakes. Considering the time period we're dealing with, we'll confine ourselves to two types of brakes, disc and drum. While hydraulic disc brake systems have been around since Jaguar popularized them in the 1950s it's only been since the introduction of the Honda CB750 in 1969 that they've really caught on for motorcycles. More prevalent on classic motorcycles are mechanically operated internal-expanding drum brakes.

DRUM BRAKES

All of the drum brakes used on motorcycles since the late 1920s have been of the internal-expanding type. In principle, all drum brakes work the same. Normally, cable- or rod-operated drum brakes come in three variations: single leading shoe, double leading shoe, and four leading shoe. The leading shoe refers to the brake shoe whose leading edge is actuated by the brake cam; the shoe whose trailing edge is actuated is called the trailing shoe. Since the rotation of the brake drum wedges it harder against the brake surface, a leading shoe does most of the stopping.

Disc brakes are found on many modern classics. This is a typical single disc setup used by Triumph.

There are some variations, including hydraulically operated drum brakes. Harley-Davidson used a "juice" brake on the rear wheel of its big twins from 1958 on, abandoning it only when H-D converted to hydraulic disc brakes in the mid 1970s. BMW used a hydraulic drum brake in conjunction with the standard mechanical system on its sidecars. Similarly, some Italian brakes fitted dual-sided, single-leading-shoe drums, but these were mechanical.

Brake inspection and repair comprises several sub-units. Since I'll discuss cables and levers in the next chapter, I'm going to ignore them for now. Suffice it to say that a good brake system begins with a good cable and lever. Worn lever pivots and binding cables can render even the best brakes as useless as a broken crankshaft.

Front and rear drum brakes work on exactly the same principle, so a discussion of one is as good as the other. The work starts with a thorough cleaning and disassembly. (Doesn't it always?)

Some brakes might use a different spring and shoe in the leading and trailing position. A little identifying mark might be in order. If there's any doubt, consult your parts or service manual.

Single-leading-shoe brakes will have one brake cam and one pivot or anchor pin. Before removing the actuating lever from the cam, mark it with a punch or scribe, or at least note its position in relation to the cam. Many levers are offset note which way yours points as you remove it. There might also be an external spring attached to the lever. Again, be aware of its position. Photos help here.

Once all the external hardware has been removed, the cam itself should be withdrawn. Inspection is pretty simple. Look for any worn spots, bent cams, broken springs, and so forth. Normally, minimum brake-lining thickness is listed in the service manual. A brake might look fine and be worn out. The converse is also true. If the lining doesn't appear to be worn out, measure its thickness just to be on the safe

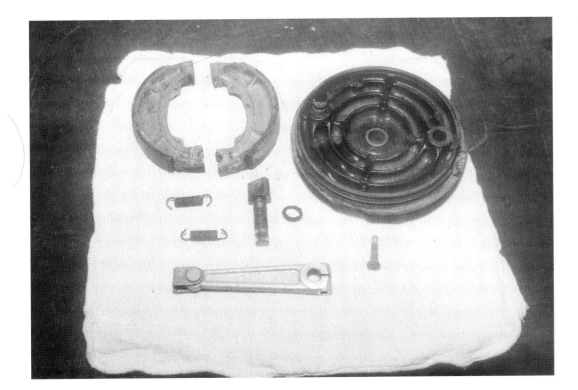

There's not much to a single-leading-shoe front brake. The springs and dust seals should always be replaced, even if the shoes themselves are still serviceable.

side. If its depth is within spec, fine. If not, the brake shoes will need to be replaced or relined.

Brake linings are either bonded in place or riveted on. If your shoes have bonded linings you'll either have to purchase new ones or have the old linings ground off and new ones bonded to the old shoes. Any good brake shop should be able to accommodate you, or check the appendix for a shop that specializes in bikes.

If the brake shoes are riveted in place you might want to learn some new skills. Of course you can always just buy a new pair of brake shoes, but replacing a riveted shoe is fairly easy. Start by drilling out the old rivets and removing the worn-out shoe. Place a rivet punch in your vise. Insert the rivets into the new shoe. Start at the middle of the shoe: With the rivet head resting on the punch, use your hammer to peen over the rivet. Work your way to the edges. Make sure that there is no gap showing between the lining and the metal shoe.

Assembling the single-leading-shoe brake is just as easy as disassembly. Lightly grease the cam; install any new seals inside the drum. Insert the cam, place a dab of high-temperature grease on the faces of the cam and on the fixed pivot. At this point you can either reinstall the brake arm or the shoes; it won't matter. Some

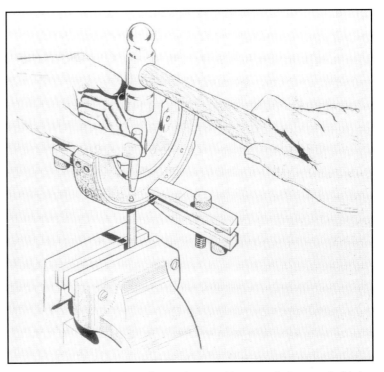

Riveting brake linings is just about a lost art. Use a small clamp to hold the lining to the shoe. Place a punch in the vise to support the shoe, with the appropriate end against the rivet. Peen the rivet over using a center punch or rivet punch.

The threaded rod halfway between the two levers is used to synchronize shoe application on this twin-leading-shoe front brake.

Four-Leading-Shoe Brake

Not many of these made their way onto production street bikes as standard equipment. Early Suzuki GT750s, a few Laverdas, the Benelli 650 twin, and the Moto-Guzzi V-7 Sports used them, but that's about it, though some race bikes also used them. Disc brakes came onto the scene and the four-shoe brakes, as they were called, quickly became obsolete.

The four-leading-shoe brake is nothing more than two twin-leading-shoe brakes in a common hub. One brake lives on the right side, one on the left. Inspection and rebuild is identical to any other brake and shouldn't present any problems. The difficult part would seem to be in the actuating mechanism. After all, both brakes need synchronized application to work effectively.

A balance bar at the control lever handles (no pun intended) synchronization. The balance bar compensates for any slight maladjustment of the control cables. Make sure the balance bar pivots freely on its trunnion. Other than that, cable and brake adjustment are identical to the twin-leading-shoe brake.

like to install the lever first to keep the cam from slipping out. Others like to install the brake shoes first; that way they can align the lever position to the shoe. I favor the latter method, myself.

If you opt to reuse the original shoes give them a light scuff with a piece of sandpaper. If the shoes are new, a slight chamfer of the forward edge will help prevent squeal.

Double-Leading Shoes

Essentially the same as a single-leading shoe with two important differences. For starters, you'll have two pivots and two cams. Secondly, they'll need to be synchronized. The cams are dealt with exactly like the one on a single-leading shoe.

Since both shoes of a twin-leading-shoe brake must contact the drum at the same time, they need to be synchronized. Methods for synchronizing the two shoes vary. Some brakes use an adjustable rod. The shoes are held against the drum and the rod length adjusted. BMWs use an eccentric adjuster. BSAs and Triumphs equipped with conical hubs utilize car-type internal adjusters. Some Japanese bikes have holes drilled through the brake levers that correspond with holes in the hub. The adjusting rod is removed, a drift inserted through the lever and into the hub, and then the rod adjusted to fit.

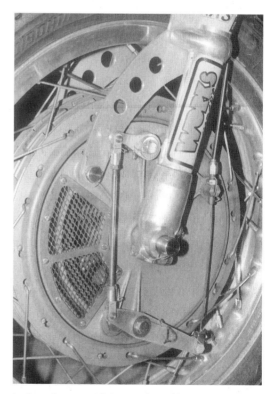

It doesn't get much better than this: a very trick four-leading-shoe front brake fitted to the Britech 750 Triumph vintage racer.

Adjustment

While most drum brakes are adjusted by spinning the nut at the end of the cable or rod, a few are adjusted via automotive-style adjusters. Conical-hub BSA and Triumph brakes, for example, as well as a few other British bikes, incorporate internal adjusters. Likewise, Harley-Davidson's hydraulic drum brakes utilize an automotive-style adjuster, though it's external. In general, turn the adjuster until the brakes start to drag and then back it off a turn or two. Both types of brakes are adjusted in the same manner; neither should drag when the lever is released.

HYDRAULIC DRUM BRAKES

"Juice" drum brakes aren't found on too many motorcycles. Most commonly, they're found on Harley-Davidsons. The big twins and Servi-Car were both equipped with hydraulic rear brakes. The repair and inspection process is the same for both.

Obviously, if you only plan to replace the shoes and hardware, you don't have to drain the brake fluid. If the brakes were working and no leaks were apparent, a good cleaning with brake wash or an alcohol-flushing agent is all you'll need. The parts can then be painted and reassembled.

If the master or wheel cylinders were leaking, they'll need rebuilding. Before pronouncing the hydraulics sound, lift the rubber end covers; if there's fluid behind them, the cylinders should be rebuilt. In fact, a rebuild is a good idea if the bike is very old or has high mileage on it. Always give the cylinders a light hone and de-burr the master-cylinder bypass port afterwards.

Before starting any hydraulic work, completely drain the system. Once the system is drained, the individual components may be broken down and inspected, and worn parts can be replaced. Brake fluid is corrosive—it'll eat your fresh paint in a heartbeat—so keep painted parts out of harm's way. It's also hydroscopic—it absorbs moisture—so if you're not sure how long it's been in there, you should probably flush the system with new fluid. Use only DOT 3 or 4 brake fluid to refill the system.

Drum Inspection

Putting new shoes into a scored or warped brake drum is not only stupid, it borders on insane. If the drum is less than perfect it should be skimmed or turned on a lathe.

If it's a bolt-on drum, turning it is no problem. If it's part of the wheel hub you'll

This hub needs to be cut; rust and time have ruined the surface.

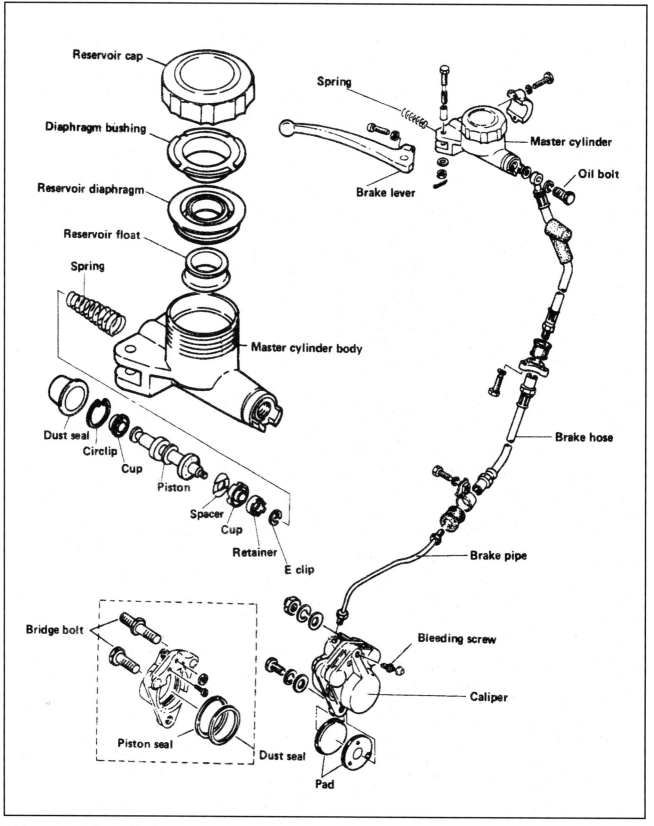

Reservoir cap

Diaphragm bushing

Reservoir diaphragm

Reservoir float

Spring

Dust seal

Circlip

Cup

Piston

Spacer

Cup

Retainer

E clip

Master cylinder body

Spring

Brake lever

Master cylinder

Oil bolt

Brake hose

Brake pipe

Bridge bolt

Bleeding screw

Caliper

Piston seal

Dust seal

Pad

While master cylinders and brake systems may vary in detail, they are basically all the same. This is a typical front brake master cylinder and plumbing. A rear-wheel master cylinder differs in external mounting and actuation but is essentially the same internally.

have two choices. The first is to break the wheel down, remove the hub, chuck the drum in a lathe, and cut it. Lace the wheel back up. If your plans include replacing the spokes or rim, great, although some will argue that lacing the rim and truing the wheel might warp the drum.

The other choice is to find a lathe big enough to skim the drum with it laced in place. Some mechanics prefer this method, but finding a lathe big enough may be difficult. Some dedicated brake drum lathes might have enough clearance, but securing the hub to the spindle could be a problem.

In theory, the advantage of cutting the drum in situ is that you don't have the hassle of relacing the wheel and possibly warping the drum. My feeling is that during a restoration the wheel is probably coming apart anyway. Besides, the factories didn't cut the drum after the wheel was laced. They cut the drum and then laced it to the wheel. If they can do it so can you.

DISC BRAKES

After the introduction of the Honda CB750 in 1969, the front disc brake became a standard fitting for most high-performance street bikes. In fact, within a short time it became the standard brake for everything from scooters to dirt bikes. Since front and rear disc brakes work identically, a discussion of one is as good as the other.

Disassembly

Because they are hydraulic brakes and the fluid does nasty things to paint, every effort should be made to drain the system before removing it from the bike.

The brake system should disassemble into two main groups: the caliper, brake pads, and their attendant hardware, and the master cylinder and brake hoses. The brake pads themselves should have wear indicators on them, usually a notch or painted red line. If the wear indicators say replace, then do it. Inspect the pivot pins, sliders, and retaining hardware for any signs of galling, corrosion, or damage and replace as needed. Some brakes, the ATE discs on /6 and /7 BMWs and the discs on many Hondas, use an adjusting screw or eccentric pin to center the caliper on the disc. Note the adjustment before it's removed.

The calipers themselves might need rebuilding. As I noted, brake fluid is hydroscopic, and the water has a tendency to settle at the lowest point in the brake system—the caliper. Rust might—and often does—form in the caliper bore, causing the brakes to seize or at least drag. A brake cylinder hone and a cleanup on the piston will usually cure the problem. If the caliper is heavily pitted, it will probably need replacing.

Rubber brake hoses—particularly the ones fitted to older bikes—have a tendency to swell when pressure is applied. This gives the brakes a mushy feel. If strict originality is a

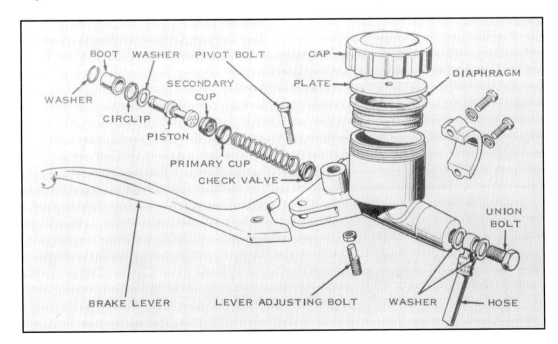

Hydraulic master cylinders are pretty much the same the world over. As long as the bore isn't rusted out and parts are available, they can be easily rebuilt.

This Lockheed master cylinder is typical of most handlebar-mounted master cylinders. The bubbled-up paint is caused by brake fluid seeping past the reservoir joint. On this type of master cylinder the reservoir screws into the piston/lever assembly. It can be unscrewed and sealed with a little Teflon® paste.

concern, then by all means use the originals if they are in good condition—chances are they won't be. Otherwise, replace them with new old stock. If good brakes are more important, read the sidebar.

The master cylinder will either be good or bad. If it's good, flush it out and set it aside until you're ready to reinstall it. If it's bad, it too will need rebuilding or replacement. If it's shot and unobtainable you'll need to find a substitute. Several aftermarket manufacturers offer replacement master cylinders. By matching the bore size (which affects brake pressure) you should be able to come up with one.

REBUILDING MASTER CYLINDERS

Rebuilding kits for most master cylinders are available. In general, expect to pay about one-third the price of a new master cylinder for the kit. In many cases peripheral parts such as the reservoir and cap should also be obtainable. Start by giving the master cylinder a complete and thorough washing in brake cleaner, followed by a thorough drying with compressed air. If the cylinder bore is in good

condition, a light pass with a brake cylinder hone should be all that's needed to recondition it. If it's heavily rusted or pitted, you have nothing to lose by running the hone through it. If after honing the bore still looks like the surface of the moon, my recommendation is to bite the bullet and replace it. Even if you successfully rebuild it, it will remain suspect. If it decides to let go at an inopportune time, life may get real exciting. At best, you'll probably blow brake fluid all over your fresh paint job; at worst, well, I'll let you imagine what happens when you pitch a bike fast and powerful enough to need disc brakes into a turn without them.

Use light oil, WD-40 for instance, to lubricate the bore during the honing process. Again wash out the cylinder and blow it dry. No point in leaving little bits of grit in there to ruin the seals. Most mechanics like to lubricate the seals and cylinder bore with fresh brake fluid. By and large this is an excellent idea. In fact no master cylinder should ever be assembled dry. But some of you, myself included, don't like the feel of brake fluid on

This caliper was taken apart for your viewing pleasure. It looks pretty grim and the piston is frozen in place like a politician's grin.

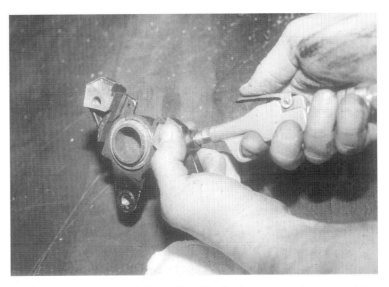

your hands. In that case you may be tempted to assemble the master cylinder with white lithium grease. It can be done, but you must be exceptionally careful to use very small amounts of the stuff to prevent it from plugging up the ports. A better solution is to use one of the brake assembly lubricants sold in auto parts stores and often found in automotive rebuild kits. Or consider wearing gloves.

Rebuilding Calipers

The caliper is the area most likely to cause problems. Because any moisture that finds its way into the brake system will settle in the lowest part, and the caliper is the last stop on the brake fluid trail, the calipers on older, poorly maintained bikes are often frozen solid from rust and corrosion. Your first job will be to disassemble the caliper. Start by removing any dust seals or bellows surrounding the piston. If the caliper is in decent shape the piston should be easily removed; in fact, it may come out with the dust seal. If not, first try pulling it out with your fingers. If that fails, try using a pair of internal expanding pliers to remove it. Of course if there's still fluid in the system and the master cylinder is still connected, just pump the lever

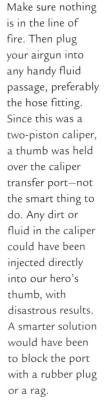

Make sure nothing is in the line of fire. Then plug your airgun into any handy fluid passage, preferably the hose fitting. Since this was a two-piston caliper, a thumb was held over the caliper transfer port—not the smart thing to do. Any dirt or fluid in the caliper could have been injected directly into our hero's thumb, with disastrous results. A smarter solution would have been to block the port with a rubber plug or a rag.

Out pops the piston, and the caliper is now ready for rebuilding.

until the piston pops out of the caliper. Which is a good argument for starting at the caliper and working your way backwards. I generally lack the foresight to do that, though. What if the piston just won't budge? There are two reasons: The first is that brake dust and grit have built up a ridge around the perimeter of the caliper that prevents the piston from slipping by. The second is likely that the piston is stuck fast to the caliper bore, rust being the prime culprit here. The easiest way to free a frozen piston is to use compressed air. Stick the nozzle of a blowgun into the line port of the caliper and blow away. Usually the piston makes a large BANG and pops out of the caliper. If it doesn't, inject penetrating oil into the caliper—or better yet, let the caliper spend a day or two soaking in the stuff and then try again. Be extremely careful, though; when those pistons come out under air pressure they do so with a vengeance. If your finger gets caught between the caliper and the piston, it's your finger that's going to come off second best. Better to aim the piston into a box of rags than toward a workbench top or other solid object.

Rebuild the caliper as you'd rebuild the master cylinder. First hone and inspect the caliper. Any rust divots are cause for rejection. If the caliper bore is nice-nice, and the piston surface polishes up, install the seals and bolt the whole thing back together.

Rotors

Rotors need to be inspected for true, heat damage, and scoring. I'd also recommend checking for any heat cracks, loose rivets, or eccentric mounting holes. All brake rotors are stamped with a minimum allowable thickness. Measure the rotor with a micrometer. If the rotor is undersized, bin it and find a replacement.

If the rotor is heavily scored it might be possible to cut it. I've had varying degrees of success here [but it's always worth a try. Likewise, heat spots—blued areas on the disc—should be removed via resurfacing.

Assembly

Reassembly of the brake system commences with the caliper. Make sure that any and all shims and squeal plates (thin metal or fiber plates that attach to the back of the pads to prevent brake squeal) are in place. All hardware should be given a thin coat of anti-seize or high temperature brake grease. All copper sealing washers should be renewed. Connect the hose and install any hydraulic brake line switches, again using new washers. Once the master cylinder is in place, fill it with the recommended brake fluid—probably DOT 3 or 4—bleed it, and you're good to go.

Bleeding Brakes

Most of us bleed brakes using the old "pump-hold the lever down and open the bleeder screw until all the air is expelled" method. Ninety percent of the time that works fine; the other 10 percent of the time it doesn't work at all. This is because air has become trapped in the line somewhere and just can't be expelled. To start with, make sure that you've got enough lever travel. I had an R65 BMW once that simply would not bleed. When I slid the master cylinder further down so the lever went past the end of the handlebar, I obtained enough movement to bleed the air out in a few quick strokes. Once the air was removed I was able to return the cylinder to its normal spot.

The rear rotor on the author's dirt tracker has seen better days. It'll need replacing at some point, but for now it's still serviceable.

Occasionally you can remove the entire system from a bike, hang it up in a straight line and bleed it. Don't forget to put a spacer between the brake pads to keep them from popping out as the pressure builds up. If you don't want to go that far, tap the caliper and wiggle the lines between bleedings to move any trapped bubbles, then try bleeding at the caliper, banjo fittings, or master cylinder connection.

You may need to "back bleed" some systems. Auto parts and tool supply shops can supply you with a large plastic syringe designed to inject brake fluid into the system from the caliper end. The syringe is filled. A plastic hose is fastened to the bleeder screw, which is opened up. The fluid is injected in until it fills the master cylinder—careful here, you can overflow the master cylinder. The bleeder screw is closed and the brake bled in the normal manner.

Another method that works well is to use a vacuum bleeder. These are small manual vacuum pumps that connect to the bleed screw at the caliper. The master cylinder is filled and the bleed screw opened up. When the pump draws a vacuum, any air in the system is sucked through, along with the fresh fluid. When the screw is closed you should have a good brake. If not, bleeding the brake a time or two in the conventional manner should soon set things right.

Centering Calipers

Some older calipers needed centering on the rotor. BMW used an eccentric pin. Remove the cap and spring located under the caliper-mounting pin (you need to do this to remove the caliper anyway). Rotate the pin while spinning the wheel. You should feel the wheel drag slightly as the pads contact the rotor. Adjust the caliper to the position where drag is least. Pump the brake a couple of times and recheck. If the caliper adjustment feels good, lightly grease the cap and spring and reinstall them, torquing to spec.

Honda used a bolt that passed through the caliper and fork leg. The procedure is similar to that of BMW. Loosen the lock nut. Turn the adjuster clockwise while spinning the front wheel until the brake drags. When the brake drags, turn the adjuster counterclockwise until the dragging stops. Give the bolt an additional 1/8 to 1/4 of a turn (ccw) and lock the nut down.

Brake Fluid

This may seem a little out of place in a book about vintage restoration, but since many of you might be restoring or refurbishing bikes from the 1970s, I think it's in order. Brake fluids come in a variety of designations: DOT 3, DOT 4, and DOT 5. The first two, 3 and 4, are polyglycol based. They are also hydroscopic, meaning they absorb water. It's for this reason that brake fluid should be changed frequently, like once a year. DOT 3 and 4 also have a tendency to remove paint, which is a real drag.

DOT 5 is silicone based, it doesn't absorb water, and it doesn't attack your paint. Unfortunately, it also doesn't lubricate very well, so lever return may be a problem. It's also incompatible with some types of rubber, particularly the type found in older brake systems. If the manufacturer specs DOT 3 or 4 use it and nothing else. If DOT 5 is called for, use only DOT 5.

STOP WHERE YOU ARE

While originality is desirable, there are times when practicality—or even safety—may be preferable. Case in point: brakes.

Realistically, few vintage bikes really need upgraded brake systems. In fact, some upgrades—dual discs on your Gold Star, for instance—not only look out of place but actually provide way more braking than you'll ever need. If your intent is to simply ride the bike and occasionally show it, I'd advise against any serious brake modification.

If you plan to use the bike as a regular rider, however, you might want to consider certain upgrades. For disc brakes, steel braided brake lines, particularly on the front, are definitely in order. If you're concerned about the appearance, cover them with a black outer cover, either by using shrink tubing or ordering them premade in black.

A lot of early single-disc models had provisions to add a second front disc, and manufacturers offered them as OEM accessories. Many builders of "bitsa bikes"—so called by the English because they're made of bits of one bike or another—convert from drum to disc, or from single- to twin-leading-shoe drums, or even to four-leading-shoe brakes. Nothing looks better to my eye than a period cafe racer with a big four-shoe-drum front brake.

Upgraded pads and linings, aftermarket calipers, rotors, and master cylinders—you name it, it's out there. Of course if you're restoring or building a vintage race bike you'll have to see what's legal for the class and build accordingly. Bottom line? If you plan to build a rider, by all means attach the best anchors you can, more so if you plan to ride quickly.

The rear brake on this H-D Sprint custom has been replaced with a cable-operated disc.

The front brake has also been replaced with a disc. A nice workmanlike job.

Nothing says "trick" like a carefully drilled brake. This one was painstakingly modified—both inside and outside—by Jaye Strait at BRITECH.

$\underline{15}$

Chapter
Fifteen

Handlebars and Controls

Right off the bat I'd be willing to bet that your bike has tweaked handlebars—either that or they've been replaced. In a way handlebars are sacrificial. Any time the poor bike hits the ground, the handlebars take the brunt of it. In the process, you hope they kept some of the more important bits and pieces—the fuel tank, for instance—from damage.

Handlebars that are only slightly bent can be straightened, but I think it's more trouble than it's worth. After all, there are literally thousands of handlebars available through the aftermarket. I'm certain you can find either an exact duplicate or some alternative bend that you'd prefer.

HANDLEBAR SIZES AND TYPES

Over the years handlebars have been produced in a range of sizes and more bends than I could or would care to count. As far as sizes go, there are four that are commonly available: 1-inch, which fits most American motorcycles including H-D and Indian; 15/16-inch, which are peculiar to some Triumphs; 7/8-inch, which fit almost everything in the world; and 22mm, usually found on BMWs or other European machines.

Those of you who can convert inches to millimeters are probably thinking that 7/8-inch is pretty damn close to 22mm, therefore the handlebars and controls should be interchangeable. You're right, kind of. Because these are nominal sizes, the bars do interchange. Unfortunately the controls may or may not.

For instance, the one-piece lever perches fitted to older BMWs will have to be pried onto a 7/8-inch handlebar—and may break in

The high buckhorn style bars are from a U.S. model 1979 Triumph Bonneville, the lower ones from the same bike intended for the U.K. market. I say, mount whichever pair feels most comfortable.

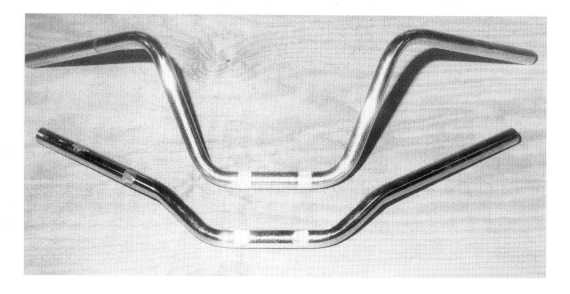

168

the process. The lever perches on a 7/8-inch Norton handlebar will be a loose fit when installed on 22mm bars.

If your bike had 7/8-inch bars to start with, I'd recommend sticking with them, especially since there are so many different bars to choose from. Conversely, if your bike has 22mm bars—and one that comes to mind using that size is BMW—I'd also recommend staying with that diameter.

If you decide to go with the OEM handlebar, finding it should be as easy as picking up the phone and ordering it. If you decide to go with a non-stock bar it gets even easier. Bars are measured in four dimensions: width, which is handlebar tip to handlebar tip; rise, which is the lowest surface to the highest when the bar is in the normal riding position; pullback, measured from the front of the bar to the rearmost portion of the bar; and center width, the total flat surface of the bar's center. Pick a bar with the dimensions that suit your needs and order away.

If your intent is to restore a bike to catalog specs, your handlebar choices are fairly limited—limited, not nonexistent. Most manufacturers offered alternative handlebars for different markets. British bikes, for example, had short "touring"—what we'd now consider sport bars—for domestic and European sales. Bikes bound for the United States got high, buckhorn bars. A quick stroll through the parts book should list at least one alternative to the standard bar.

CONTROL LEVERS

Levers present few problems. If they're bent, broken, or missing, they'll have to be replaced. This means new OEM or aftermarket. Unfortunately, many of the aftermarket OEM-style levers sold are of poor quality, especially the ones intended to replicate those on American and British bikes. The chrome is poor, the fit between lever and perch is poor, and the perch-to-handlebar fit is terrible. There are

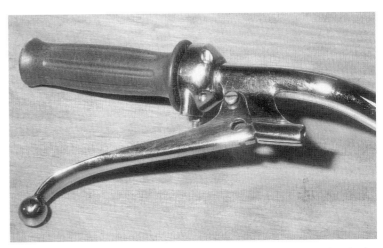

A few bikes used handlebars with welded-in-place control levers. They look neat but a tipover that bends the bars or lever mount means replacing everything. These bars were on the author's Montessa Cota. Since the bike is regularly ridden in vintage trials events, the bars, which are tough to find, were replaced with an off-the-shelf pair and aftermarket levers. These are only installed for shows.

Barnett throttles, levers, and cable have an excellent and well-deserved reputation. They make the perfect alternative to the OEM stuff.

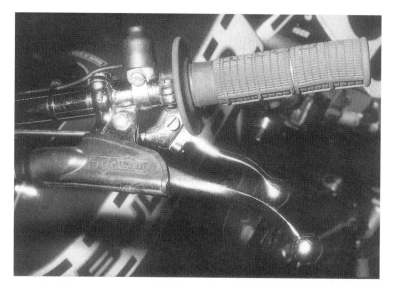

Lots of old bikes use multiple levers. Make certain that each lever has enough room to operate. Vintage race bikes may be required to use a kill button. This restored and raced Bultaco Astro has a period-correct Magura kill button installed as well as a compression release. Because the bike is raced (and occasionally crashed), the original and expensive alloy clutch lever has been replaced with a Barnett lever assembly.

If you plan on racing your restored dirt bike, you may want to consider a throttle like this Magura 314. It's inexpensive, it works exceptionally well, and it's available at every motorcycle shop in the world.

some exceptions—Barnett levers being the most notable.

The Japanese-bike restorer has a somewhat easier time of it, in part because chances are that the aftermarket supplier is the same as the OEM source. German bikes invariably use Magura levers, and as far as I know these are only available through the manufacturer or from a Magura dealer. Likewise, the Italian bikes, which generally use controls made by Domino, Tommaselli, or Brembo. British bike controls were made by either Doherty or Amal. Both are available either as new old stock or through a few select dealers as new.

All levers—replacement or otherwise—should be checked for fit. The first place to look is where the lever mounts in the bracket. The pivot hole should be perfectly round and the lever free to move without binding. If the hole in the lever has worn oblong, the lever should be either bushed or discarded.

Another source of potential trouble is where the lever bracket mounts to the handlebar. Aftermarket levers frequently have a slight gap between the lever perch and the handlebar. The gap allows the perch to flex when the lever is pulled. The flex gives the brake or clutch a mushy or uncertain feel, and can actually interfere with clutch disengagement or brake feel.

THROTTLES

The throttle, or twist grip, as we motorcycle riders like to call it, is subject to the same wear and tear as the rest of the bike. As with levers, there are dozens of shapes and sizes available besides the original equipment.

There are internal throttles, common to older American and some vintage Japanese bikes. The internal throttle has the cable running to a sliding piece mounted in the handlebar itself. The twist grip drum has a spiral cut, which engages the slider. With this system your handlebar and throttle choice is limited to the original equipment.

A note of warning: Be especially careful with Harley-Davidson internal throttles, since the spirals are cut for either a push or pull throttle cable, depending on the carburetor used. If you're keeping the stock carburetor, it should be no problem, but if you're changing over to a different carb, you might have to change the throttle drum as well.

I've never actually heard anyone refer to them as external cable throttles, but that's what they are. Plain old-fashioned twist grips. The cable runs directly onto a drum that rotates when you turn the handle. There are a couple of variations on the theme. BMW's side-pull throttle, for example, uses a pair of timed gears and a tiny chain and is a wonderfully complicated little piece of overkill. Otherwise, all throttles using external cables are more or less alike.

As long as there is no cracking or other physical damage to the drum or housing, or any completely worn-out parts, there should be no reason to replace the average throttle.

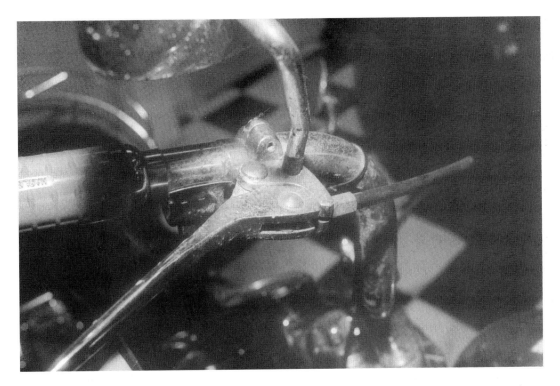

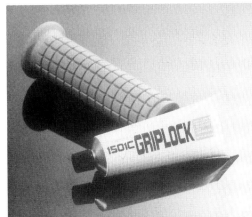

Grips, especially those used on vintage race and MX bikes, should be glued into place. *Photo Courtesy of Three Bond Corporation*

Obviously, cosmetic repair might also require replacement on catalog restorations.

REFINISHING

Since most of the original stuff was chrome-plated to start with, refinishing should present no problems. I've had tons of levers and throttle housings replated; if anything, they fit and worked better after a dip in the chrome tank than they did when I took them apart. Just be sure to mask any external threads and chase the internal ones with a tap. Polished aluminum parts should also just require a quick buffing, since normal use keeps them pretty shiny.

ALTERNATIVES

Unless you plan on a catalog restoration, there's really no need to be locked into the OEM handlebar levers and throttle. What the heck, lots of these got changed when the bikes were new. In fact, if you're restoring an old MXer, dirt tracker, or roadracer, chances are the original equipment is long gone and may be unobtainable.

For my money, any off-road bike would probably get suitable, period accessory parts. Including perhaps the obligatory quick-pull throttle and trick levers. In fact, if I were

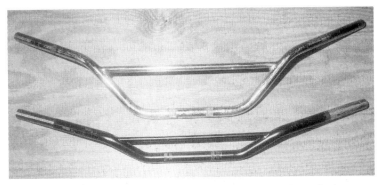

Here's a dilemma: Most new dirt bike bars, such as the pair on the bottom, are too short for vintage use. While there are some manufacturers replicating the old bends, an alternative is to use ATV bars (top).

171

An aftermarket throttle like this "Whirl-pull" makes a nice period-correct addition to a restored MX or enduro bike.

Cable Maintenance

In the first place, make sure the cable is the correct length and properly routed—check your original photos or vintage road tests for the correct routing. When the handlebar is swung from side to side, the cables should have enough slack left in them to maintain free play at their respective levers. They should hang freely, without draping themselves in big loops. If they kink or bind when the bars are swung you'll need to install longer cables or find a better way of routing the ones you have. If the cables are Teflon- or plastic-lined, your maintenance chores are limited to greasing the nipples, inspecting the inner wire for any frayed spots or broken wires, and adjusting the free play. Older non-lined cables need to

This cable lubricating tool cost about five bucks new, and it's paid for itself at least a hundred times over. Use one regularly and cable replacement will be a thing of the past.

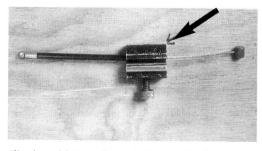

Slip the cable into the tool, tighten the clamp, and insert the straw from your favorite can of lubricant into the hole (arrow).

judging a show the MXer with the most period accessory parts would probably win.

CABLES

Cables are either good or bad; there is no in between. Normally a cable will exhibit the most wear and be most likely to break at the lever-end nipple—except when the inner portion of the cable can break off in such a manner that you're forced to pull half the engine apart just to retrieve the broken bits. Unless the nipple is kept well lubricated, it has a tendency to bind in the lever hole. The binding nipple causes the cable to flex. Eventually the cable strands part, and ping! the cable breaks, leaving you stranded somewhere to ponder the unfairness of life.

Unless the cables are known to be brand-new, they should be replaced as a matter of course during the restoration. Even brand-new cables have been known to break.

be lubricated on a regular basis. Over the years I've tried every method of oiling cables ever devised. The only sure-fire, genuine, guaranteed-not-to-fail method I've ever come up with is to use one of those little clamp-on pressure lubricators. Use one of these little dandies on a regular basis and I can just about promise you that you'll never have another cable failure.

Rolling Your Own

Every rider of vintage/classic/custom or old motorcycles should know how to build his own control cables and be prepared to do it. In the first place, the correct-length cable might not be available to fit your motorcycle. In the second place, even if the correct cable is available, it might not be in stock at your friendly local dealership. "Sorry, but Gold Star clutch cables are temporarily out of stock" are words you really don't want to hear on a sunny Saturday morning, especially the day before a planned Sunday ride.

Cables are easy to make—the parts are cheap and the skills required are minimal. Once you've done a few of them you'll be amazed at how quickly they can be built. Cable supplies—nipples, cable, and so on—are available through a wide variety of sources, and any motorcycle shop should be able to order up exactly what you need. Since a picture is worth a thousand words, just follow the photo sequence.

Making Cable Ends

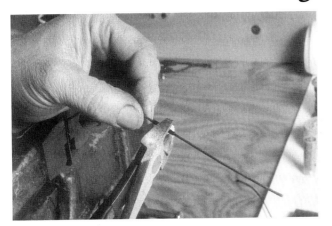

Start by measuring—twice in fact—and then cutting the cable to the proper length. A piece of tape wrapped around the cable will prevent fraying.

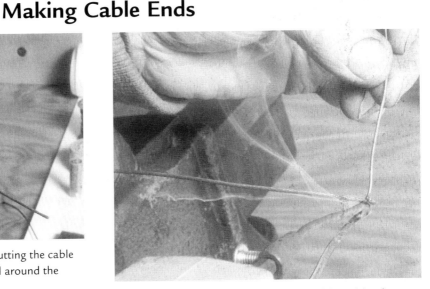

Use flux and 60/40 solder tin on the end of the cable. If you tend to get a little sloppy with the solder, or the nipple is a tight fit, you may want to install the nipple on the cable first. Just let it slide down out of the way for the moment.

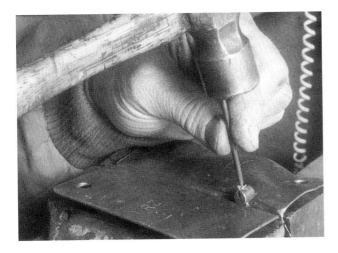

Pull the nipple over the tinned spot. Using a nail or center punch, spread the cable ends out until they fill the groove in the nipple.

Making Cable Ends (continued)

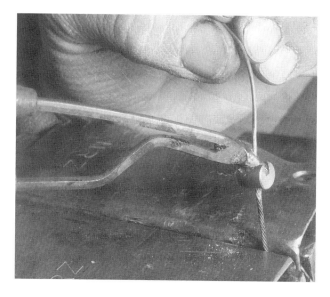

Fill the groove in the nipple with solder.

File off any excess to prevent the nipple from binding.

All done!

Wiring and Electrics

Let's have a quick show of hands. How many of you really hate electrical work? I thought so. Electrical work—specifically trouble-shooting—can be a real pain in the butt. Part of the problem is that you can't see the electrons scurrying to and fro through the wires. Actually, there are times you can see them. Unfortunately, it's usually when there's a dead short and the wires are glowing bright red.

Fortunately for the vintage enthusiast, older motorcycles—and by older I mean those made before 1978—have, at least for the most part, simple, straightforward, and easily repaired electrical systems. Why the 1978 cutoff date? Starting with the 1979 model year, many new motorcycles had electronic ignition systems as standard equipment. The new ignitions complicated the motorcycles' electrical system slightly, and the situation has gotten worse ever since.

At first glance the wiring might seem complex—wires run hither and yon, and there are odd-looking devices all over the place. But don't fret. There is a logic to it. I think you'll find that between removing all the bits and pieces, and inspecting and reinstalling it all, you'll gain a considerable amount of confidence in working with motorcycle electrics.

MOTORCYCLE WIRING BASICS

Here's most of what you'll need to know, at least as far as wiring goes. Bad connections and/or bad grounds cause more electrical problems than anything else. Make certain that the connections are clean and tight and the grounds are perfect.

Repaired wiring harnesses should be avoided. Let's face it, you've already sunk a bunch of cash and time into your "dreamsickle." If the wiring harness looks like a patchwork quilt and a new one is available, bin the old one and install a new one. Otherwise, the wiring harness itself should be inspected for breaks, improper repairs, and plain old wear and tear.

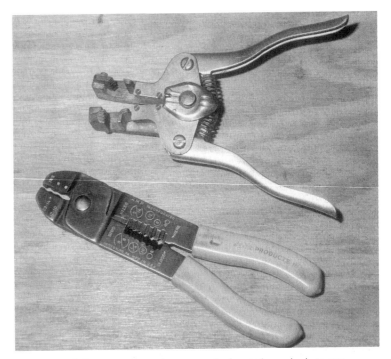

The only satisfactory way to crimp a terminal or strip a wire is to use special tools. The tool on top is an automatic stripper. The wire is inserted into the appropriate set of jaws, the handles squeezed, and the insulation removed from the wire. The bottom tool is used to manually strip the wire, and the "pliers" end of the tool is used to crimp the connector in place.

Clockwise from the top: The conical twist connector is fine for hooking up doorbells, but it has no place on a motorcycle. Insulated and uninsulated spade connectors. The insulated butt connector is used to splice two wires. A Scotch-lock® connector is used to splice a wire onto another or to repair a break. Finally, a shrink and solder connector. The wire splice is made and the connector slipped over it. A heat gun is then used to shrink the tubing and melt the solder into the joint at the same time.

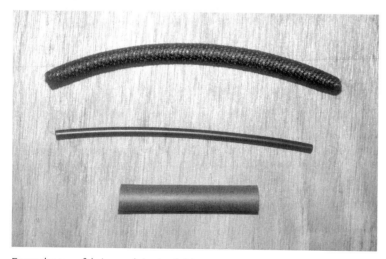

From the top: fabric conduit. Available at most auto parts stores, this type of fabric insulation was in use for many years prior to the advent of the rubber-covered harnesses now used. In the center: a small piece of rubber insulation. This is used to cover and protect individual wires. Bottom: heat-shrink tubing. Slip a hunk of this over any electrical joint you want to protect and heat it up with a heat gun or torch. It will shrink to fit. Available in every size from gauge 22 to 000, it can be bought in most hardware, auto supply, or electrical supply stores.

Most of the repairs will be at the terminal ends and are easily checked. Replace any after-market crimp-on connectors, regardless of their age. Look for damage any place the harness bends—the steering head, for instance, or around any portion of the frame.

Older cloth-wrapped harnesses are susceptible to a variety of damage, the main one being deterioration of the cloth covering. These harnesses, while desirable if utter authenticity is your aim, leave something to be desired from a position of practicality. I generally replace damaged cloth-wrapped harnesses with PVC covered ones if the bike is going to be ridden regularly.

Connectors, Wiring Diagrams, Repairing Wiring Harnesses

While major "open-loom surgery" should be avoided, minor repairs to the wiring harness are certainly permissible. What constitutes a minor repair? Replacing a bad terminal, splicing a strand or two of wire, and repairing minor harness damage are all perfectly acceptable.

Terminal Replacement

Crimp-on terminals are popular for good reason—properly installed, they provide a sound connection without a lot of fuss. Crimp-on terminals are the current (no pun intended) standard of the industry because they are easy to install and resist vibration better than a soldered-on terminal. The best type uses brass connectors that double-crimp onto both the internal wire itself and the external insulation. If originality isn't an issue, you can also use the soft plastic terminal insulators, like those found on modern Japanese bikes.

Make sure that the terminal is correctly sized for both the wire and its intended application. A bit of heat-shrink tubing will seal the terminal and give it a finished look.

Harness Repairs

Broken wires, provided there's only one or two of them, should be spliced together either by adding a short jumper or rejoining the broken ends if there is enough slack. The connection can be made with a crimp connector or by a good old-fashioned "splice and solder" connection. Or you can combine them both by using one of those combined solder/heat shrink connectors. The finished

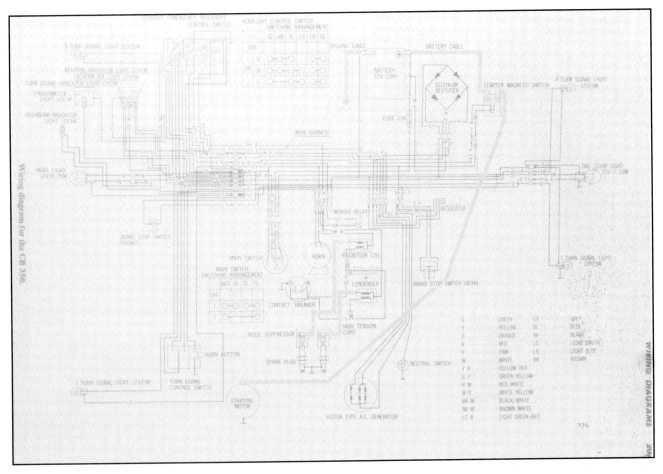

repair should be covered with either heat shrink or electrician's tape.

Wiring Diagrams

The wiring diagram found in every service manual represents a road map of the circuits. The odd little symbols scattered throughout the diagram are pictorial representations of the devices that transfer, control, or use electricity. Japanese, American, and British diagrams generally use pictures that look like the objects they represent.

European manuals usually use the German DIN symbols (DIN stands for Deutsche Industrial Norms, the German standards committee that sets regulations on everything from the size of a piece of notebook paper, DIN-4, to sizes and shapes of gears, DIN 3960).

DIN symbols can be a little confusing. However, the ever-efficient Germans specify a terminal designation and wire color code for each component. For instance, anything built to DIN specifications—lawn mower, motorcycle, car, truck, or airplane—uses the same terminal designation and color code for its electrical components. For example, terminal 15 is always an ignition switch, a green wire (or grün, if you're a stickler for accuracy) always runs from the 15 terminal on the switch to the 15 terminal on the secondary ignition coil, end of discussion. Would that we were so efficient here.

Unfortunately, there is no real standardization otherwise. Each manufacturer is free to do as it pleases, though thankfully certain conventions have been adopted. It's safe to say that manufacturers generally find a system of colors and symbols they like and stick with them. For instance most manufacturers in this country use red to indicate a "hot" wire and black to indicate ground.

Take a few minutes to familiarize yourself with the particulars of your bike's wiring diagram. You don't have to memorize it, but at least take a look at it, which leads go where, what colors the individual circuits look like, and what the pictures represent—preferably before you have to look for an electrical fault at 2 a.m. in the rain.

Honda has always been known for its easy-to-follow wiring diagrams. This CA/CB/CL 250-305 diagram is no different. Clearly labeled and easy to trace, it can help you repair, replace, or remanufacture the bike's wiring without much trouble.

Wiring should be secured with plastic ty-wraps if they are appropriate to the make and year of the machine. A nice alternative are these chrome clips that came on some British bikes.

WEAVING YOUR OWN WIRE HARNESS

If you opt to make your own harness—and lots of restorers do—just make it easy on yourself and those who will follow. Use one color of wire for each circuit: Red for power, black for ground, blue for lights. I think you get the picture.

Most electrical supply shops can provide wire in every color of the rainbow, as well as solid colors with tracers, just like the OEM stuff. They can also supply harness sheathing. You'll find it's a simple job to lay the harness out on the bike and tape it at crucial junctions. Once it's done remove it, wrap it in tape, or insert it into conduit or shrink tubing and reinstall it. Don't forget to draw a diagram with the correct colors, too.

Neatness Counts

Wiring—and control cables, for that matter—should always be properly secured. You can use plastic tie-wraps, although they might look out of place on some bikes. British bikes used a variety of rubber "John Bull" type clips, chrome steel clips, and soft aluminum straps to secure any errant cables or wires. American bikes generally run their cables and wires through the handlebars, which both protects them and does away with the need for external clips. Make sure that no matter how you secure things, the clips you use are period correct if you plan to show the bike.

COMPONENT INSPECTION AND REPAIR
The Battery

If the bike has been sitting for any length of time, chances are that the battery is shot. An inactive or underused battery will go south faster than you can say, "holy $49.95 for a 6-volt battery, are you nuts?" Or words to that effect. So the first task should be to ascertain the battery's condition.

A visual inspection is as good a way to start as any. Are the terminals broken, bent, or damaged in any way? If the battery case is clear, check the plates. If they've gone white or gray from sulphation, the battery has or is about to expire. Check the outer case for damage. If some of the cells appear to be filled to capacity while one or two—particularly the end ones—are bone dry, the outer case might be cracked.

If the visual inspection reveals nothing seriously amiss, remove the fill caps and top off the battery to the correct level using distilled water. Remember, never top off a battery that's been in service with anything but water, preferably distilled water. Adding acid to a battery that's been in use is strictly verboten.

Warning! Assault with a Battery

A quick warning: If your motorcycle uses a battery, and most do, remember that you are basically dealing with a plastic box full of highly corrosive acid—one that gives off explosive fumes. When working with batteries the smoking lamp is always out.

If you spill battery acid on your clothes, tools, or paint it will ruin them in short order. If you get battery acid in your eyes, you could easily end up blind.

Take the proper precautions: Keep some baking soda handy to neutralize any spills. And wear the proper protective gear—including eye protection—whenever you fill a battery.

Assuming the battery shows no physical damage, it should be charged and tested. Motorcycle batteries are rather delicate compared to the average car battery; fast charging one is a certain way to ruin it. The battery should be charged at the manufacturer's recommended amperage rate. Usually the rate is stamped on the battery case. If it isn't, the rule of thumb is to charge the battery at no more than 1/10 of its amperage rating. In other words, if your battery is rated at 10 amps, charge it a 1 amp per hour for 10 hours; 20 amps, 2 amps per hour; and so on.

In some cases it might take the battery a day or two to come up to full strength. Test the battery with both a voltmeter and hydrometer. If it's up to snuff, wash it down and store it in a cool location until you're ready to reuse it.

Battery Maintenance

Batteries, particularly those used in vintage and classic motorcycles, have a tendency to go flat through lack of use. Since dead batteries cause a multitude of problems and are more likely to freeze and crack during cold months, I'd recommend keeping them regularly charged.

An inactive battery should be charged every 30 days. Better yet, use a small-demand charger—the Battery Tender is one of the best. Always top off a battery with distilled water, available in grocery stores—never with acid. Always slow charge a battery. If you're not planning on using it much, I'd remove it from the bike entirely. Remove the battery, wash it down, top it off, and slow charge it over the winter.

Battery Replacement

For the most part, modern batteries will replace older batteries in all aspects except appearance. Any decent motorcycle shop will have a battery crossover chart showing which battery fits which bike. The chart should also catalog batteries by dimension, terminal placement, and vent-hose location. If a battery is not specifically listed for your bike, find one of the appropriate dimensions that has the terminal style and the vent tube location in the right place.

Watch the terminal placement, particularly on British bikes that locate the battery under the seat. Lucas batteries used a flush terminal with a short screw to secure the leads. Late-model replacements might touch the seat base or the frame—with predictably disastrous results. An old inner tube cut to fit or a rubber battery tray as used on some bikes can be placed over the battery top to prevent any electrical meltdown.

The vent tube should be run as far from the chain as possible. Battery acid can actually crack the case-hardening on a chain, weakening the links tremendously. In fact, on most of my bikes I normally extend the tube past the rear wheel.

If the battery is out of sight or the bike is being built solely as a rider, it makes no real difference what's in there. If you plan to show the bike and the battery is visible, however, appearance becomes a concern. In some cases reproduction batteries are available. I have also seen others painted black to replicate the old rubber-cased batteries. I've also seen a small, modern battery hidden inside a defunct, hollowed-out vintage piece—a neat trick, provided you're fortunate enough to find an old donor battery.

Short-Circuiting Lucas's Revenge

One problem the restorer consistently runs into is the unavailability of certain batteries—or at least the unavailability at a reasonable price.

This very nice reproduction battery is available to fit a wide range of vintage machines. It's built by Charles Williams (310) 538-1620. *Charles Williams*

In most cases finding a new battery won't be a problem. You'll find a modern substitute from Yuasa or GS or whoever. Pop it in and off you'll ride. But a word of warning: I've seen several British bikes burn up their wiring harness because the replacement batteries didn't quite fit properly. In two instances the batteries were able to move around in the holder until the terminals contacted the frame and caused a dead short. In the other instance the battery was too tall and shorted on the seat pan. Now you know why the original Lucas battery used those flat screw-in terminals.

Obviously, the first step is to make certain that the battery fits the holder properly. I also fit a rubber mat over the top of the battery just in case the hold-down comes loose. Finally, install a fuse on the ground side of the battery as well as the hot side. If the battery does short

out, both fuses will blow, protecting the wiring harness.

GENERATORS AND ALTERNATORS

If the bike was running and in more or less regular use when you acquired it, then any charging problems were probably self-evident. The operative word here is "probably." If so, then the charging system should need nothing more than a general tidying up. If the bike was dead or a basket case, then I'd advise running a few preliminary checks on the charging system while it's apart.

GENERATORS

In general, DC motorcycle generators are as straightforward as their automotive counterparts. The inspection, repair, and testing procedures are identical in most respects. In my experience if the generator spins freely it's probably OK. If it looks decent and seems to revolve smoothly, I'd take it to the nearest starter-generator-alternator shop—check your local Yellow Pages—and have them spin it up. Save yourself some grief, though, and let the tech know if it's for a positive-ground system!

If the generator feels rough or sticky, it's probably rebuild time. Most of the time the bearings are shot. Once in a while you might find that the armature overheated and threw some solder from a connection. This is a repairable condition, so don't panic. If the rest of the armature looks good, resolder the bad connection and then test the armature.

There are a couple of simple ways to bench test generators. These are "quick and dirty" tests. For comprehensive trouble shooting you'll have to head for your manual.

You'll need an ammeter and a battery—use a 12-volt, even if the generator is for a 6-volt system. Connect the ammeter in series with the battery, either terminal, and then attach two test leads, one to the opposite terminal of the ammeter and one to the other battery terminal. Warning: If the needle on the ammeter reacts during any of the following tests, break the connection instantly to avoid damaging it.

Remove or insulate the brushes from the armature. Touch one test lead to the "F" terminal of the generator, ground the other to the generator frame (outer case). The ammeter shouldn't move.

Touch one test lead to the "A" terminal, ground the other. Again there should be no reading. If you get a reading on the ammeter in either case either a field coil is grounded or a terminal is grounded.

You can test the armature for a short by attaching one lead of the battery to the armature shaft and then running the other lead around the commutator segments. A spark indicates a shorted armature. You can also test the armature for a short by using what's called a "growler," if you can find a shop that still has one.

The next test is to check the commutator—the copper segmented rings that the brushes contact. Visually check that the commutator hasn't worn down so that the brushes can touch the mica insulators between the segments—the mica should be undercut about a millimeter or so. An open commutator can be found by touching the test leads to adjacent segments of the commutator, no reading or a low reading on the ammeter means that particular segment is open.

You can also apply battery current to the terminals and try to get the generator to "motor," or spin, although that's no guarantee that it will generate current. To "motor" the generator, connect the "F" and "D" terminals to the positive side of the battery and ground the negative to the case. If the bike uses a positive ground, reverse the connections. The generator should spin in the direction it's normally turned by the engine; if it spins backwards the field connections are reversed.

The field coils can be tested using an ohmmeter. Measure between the "F" terminal and the case. Your shop manual should provide a resistance figure, which will usually be between 250 and 350 to 400 ohms. If you don't have a resistance figure, don't sweat it. As long as the meter shows continuity you should be all right.

As I said, these are only a few quick tests. They may come in handy if you already have your generator apart and just want to double-check before it's reassembled. In reality the

This vertically mounted generator fitted to the Harley-Davidson model DLD was prone to rapid bearing wear. Its odd, upright mounting position led to the bike's being nicknamed the "Three-cylinder Harley."

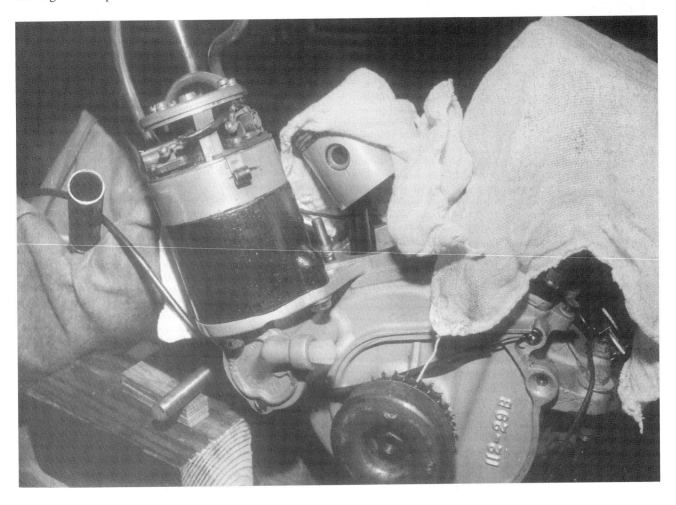

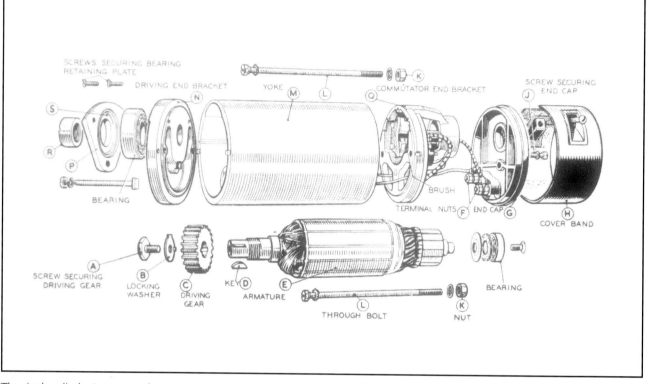

The single-cylinder Lucas magdyno-type generator shown above is typical of most motorcycle units. This particular unit was piggybacked onto a Lucas magneto. During restoration the generator should at least be bench tested, if nothing else. If the generator requires rebuilding, standard automotive rebuilding, techniques are applicable.

easiest way to check most generators is to simply have your local auto electrical rebuilder check it out.

Generator Repairs

For the most part I'd recommend that the home restorer confine his generator rebuilding to bearing and brush replacement and cleaning the commutator. Use contact cleaner or brake clean to wash away any dust and dirt. The commutator can be polished with "00" sandpaper. Avoid using emery paper; particles will embed themselves in the commutator, causing arcing. A hacksaw blade can be used to undercut the commutator. If the commutator shows severe wear, chances are the armature will need replacing.

ALTERNATORS

For most motorcycles, alternators superseded generators sometime in the 1950s. Alternators found on vintage bikes are technically known as internal-magnet AC dynamos, but I'll refer to them as alternators. Their main advantages are higher output at idle and no wear,

since there's typically no physical contact between the rotor and the generating coils. Their one disadvantage is their alternating current output has to be converted to direct current, so they require some kind of rectifier.

The bottom line is that a crankshaft-mounted steel rotor with a series of magnets revolves inside a series of coils. The magnets can be either electromagnets or permanent. The coils are laminated to an iron ring, and the whole assembly is collectively called the stator. AC dynamos are either single- or three-phase and use brushes or not as the case may be. A few alternators use an external rotor revolving around internal coils, but these are more common on Italian singles and later Japanese motorcycles.

In reality, alternators come in so many shapes, sizes, and styles that entire books are devoted to them. For the most part they are relatively trouble-free, the exception being H-D Sportsters. Alternator-equipped Sportsters have their alternators mounted behind the clutch hub. I'm sure that locating it there seemed like a good idea at the time. The

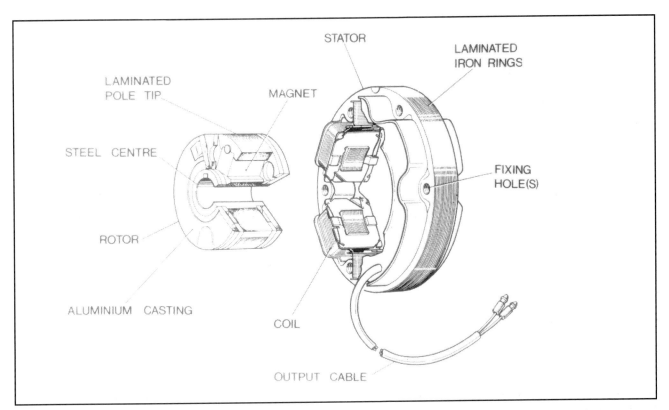

The Lucas RM series alternator common to many British bikes. Early models had a nasty habit of shaking the coil windings apart. Encapsulating them in epoxy cured them. Anytime the stator is removed, the securing bolts should have Loctite or some other thread-locking compound applied to them when they are reinstalled. Always Loctite the rotor securing nut and firmly bend over the locking tab as well.

See how close the alternator wire comes to the chain? Think the chain will have any trouble sawing through those wires? It goes without saying that those leads should be positioned out of harm's way.

183

LOOSE ROTORS AND OTHER SOCIAL ILLS

If you're unfortunate enough to have a rotor come loose on its taper, resist the temptation to Loctite it back on. In the first place it won't work. And in the second place it'll only make things worse. The Loctite will actually prevent the rotor from seating on its taper. Loctite should be used to keep the retaining nut from working loose. A better solution is to lap the rotor onto the taper.

Lock the crankshaft in place. If the engine is together, put the bike in gear. If it's apart, lock it in any way that's practical. Apply a small amount of valve grinding compound evenly around the shaft. Slide the rotor lightly onto the shaft. You want the rotor to turn on the shaft, so don't bolt it down. Using a twisting motion rotate the rotor back and forth on the shaft. The grinding compound will eventually remove the scores and create a new matching surface on both the rotor and the shaft. Inspect your work every few minutes. When you have a smooth, uniform surface, clean everything thoroughly with solvent and assemble, making sure to torque the retaining nut or bolt to the proper torque. This method works on most tapered shafts, rotors, clutches, countershaft sprockets, or whatever, provided the damage isn't too severe.

The zener diode needs to be mounted where it'll get a good blast of cooling air. The finned "egg" is actually the heat sink. The diode itself is mounted inside the heat sink, under the plastic plug in the center.

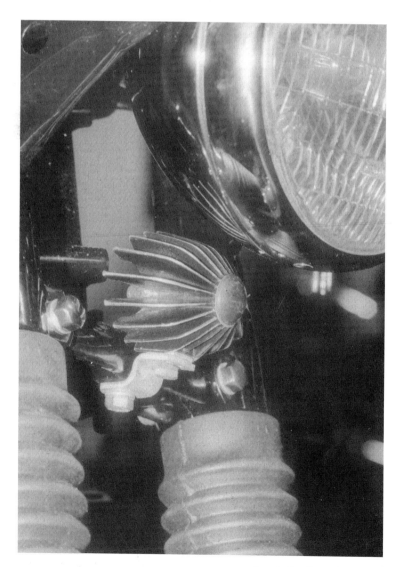

problem is that clutch debris finds its way into the works and shorts them out—bummer.

Anyway, most alternator problems boil down to one of three things: mechanical damage, bad peripherals, or damaged wiring.

Mechanical damage is generally confined to the rotor. It might come loose on the crankshaft taper, in which case the crank end itself might be damaged. The magnets might loosen in the rotor or if the rotor is an electromagnet type, it might develop either an open or a short in the windings.

Trouble Shooting

As always, check for mechanical damage. An ohmmeter will let you trace continuity. Always check the wire leads for signs of chafing and damage, especially where the wires run under the primary chain or gears. When reinstalling the stator be sure to securely tighten the hold-down bolts—a little dab of Loctite won't hurt. The rotor nut should also have a dab of Loctite and of course a new lock tab. Always renew the grommet where the leads pass through the cases. In fact a little dab of silicone there won't hurt, particularly if the bike is going to be used off road.

Voltage Regulators

In most cases the voltage regulator (as used in a DC generator system) will be adjustable, but not repairable. The regulator should be checked for any mechanical damage and internal corrosion. Adjustment procedures

Rectifiers are fragile and easily damaged. Never turn the securing bolt that holds the plates together. Always hold the bolt and turn the nut.

vary from model to model. In my experience, if the bike isn't charging at all and everything else checks out, you're better off replacing the regulator.

Zener Diodes

The zener diode is the simplest form of regulator. Essentially the zener functions as a sort of electronic pressure valve. Under 14 volts the zener won't pass any current; above 14 it starts to pass some current to ground. At 15 volts it passes all the current to ground. It has no moving parts and normally requires no maintenance.

Zeners do need a good ground, however, and a good heat sink. The mounting stud should be torqued to no more than 2 foot-pounds. Occasionally you'll find one that shorts to ground, causing the fuse to blow instantly. The check is to disconnect the zener; if the fuse stops blowing you've found the problem.

Rectifiers

Rectifiers are used to convert the alternator output from alternating to direct current, so that it can charge the battery. Normally they require no maintenance and are not serviceable.

A rectifier can be tested by using an ohmmeter. Set the meter to the ohms x 1 scale. Apply one lead to any tab and the other to the input terminal. Your meter should read about 10 ohms. Swap the leads around and the meter should read infinite. Don't worry if you get something more or less than 10 ohms, that's

just a rough guess. The actual reading will depend on the make of the rectifier.

If the battery won't take a charge or if it loses its charge after sitting for a short time, suspect the rectifier. Lucas rectifiers are easily damaged by improper installation—usually someone breaks the connection between the plates by twisting the center bolt when they're installed. Most others are fairly robust.

Capacitors and Battery Eliminators

I wasn't sure if I should mention capacitors under charging systems or ignition systems. Since they replace the battery, I figure I'll lump them in with the charging system. Capacitors were fitted to British bikes intended for off-road use, but they were also available

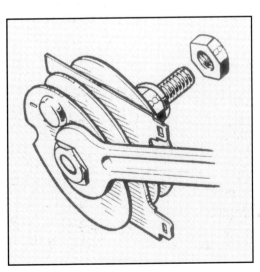

Always hold the rectifier by the through bolt and turn the end nut. If you try to turn the bolt, there is an excellent chance of ruining the rectifier.

Enough horns to satisfy the Boston Pops. The ones held together with bolts are easily disassembled. The riveted ones are a little harder. The selection shown here are all OEM Triumph.

from the aftermarket. The idea is that the alternator charges the capacitor, which then supplies the coil. You can remove the battery from the system and use the capacitor to run the bike.

There are a couple of ways to test the capacitor; the best way is to simply disconnect the battery and try to start the engine. If the capacitor is working, the bike should start. Stock capacitors aren't found on all bikes, only on those intended for competition use. If your bike has an aftermarket battery eliminator, I'd suggest going back to the stock battery system since there's no real bench test for them and they can fail without warning.

Alternatives

As with ignition systems there are alternative charging systems available. There are 6- to 12-volt conversions, which I highly recommend if the bike is going to see a lot of real world riding. There are several systems available to eliminate the regulator/rectifier/zener diode, or you can adapt a late-model regulator/rectifier from a modern bike. MAP Cycle Enterprises of St. Petersburg, Florida, has

some very nice pieces that will let you design and build your own charging system. See the source list for details.

HORNS, LIGHTS, AND SWITCHES

Since most of us are restoring bikes that were intended for use on public roads, horns, lights, and the switches that control them are going to need repair or replacement. For the most part these components either work or they don't. While switches and horns can often be coaxed back into service, a blown light bulb is just that.

Horns

Horns are pretty tough little devices. If they've got current and a good ground they'll usually work. If they don't, try using the adjusting screw to restore the tone, failing that I'd opt for replacement. As in most cases, if showing the bike is a priority, look for a new old stock or exact reproduction.

If riding the bike is paramount, find one you like and bolt it on. There are lots of aftermarket and original equipment horns available—Fiamms are usually a good choice. A few older horns can be disassembled and cleaned. These horns generally unbolt in layers. Chances are the inside will be filled with a mixture of dust, rust, and bugs. Remove all the extras, reassemble, and give it a try.

Lights

The lights themselves—at least the headlight shell and the taillight body—will be covered under bodywork. The lenses should be checked for cracks. Some older models might have a mechanical high/low beam. If so, you'll need to check the sliding focal point, its cable and actuator. Admittedly these are rather rare, and if you've got one you're probably way ahead of "how to" books.

Resist the temptation to polish the headlight reflector with any type of abrasive cleaner. The reflectors are silvered, and chances are you'll polish the backing right off. If you must, use a little glass cleaner and a soft rag to clean the reflector. There are alternative lights available if you intend to do a lot of night riding. Feel free to use them, but make sure your electrical system is up to the challenge.

Switches

My inclination here is to tell you to replace a bad switch with a new one. But—and take this with a grain of salt—there are an awful lot of switches in resto-land that need nothing more than a good cleaning. If the switch goes south during the cleaning, it's no good anyway. Since you've nothing to lose, you might as well take it apart and see what you can do.

When disassembling a switch, work carefully; there might be small spring-loaded components in there. Most of the problems I've encountered were caused by corrosion. A little WD-40 and some crocus cloth might save the switch. The second most-common problem is probably a broken wire, or more accurately one that's broken away from its terminal. These can generally be resoldered with a pencil point-type iron. Italian and German switches often have small screw-posts for connections, and the set-screws might simply be loose. Much more than that and the switch should probably be replaced.

All switches—be they ignition, turn signal, headlight, and so on—are treated the same. And all might be replaced by their generic equivalents if you are so inclined. In fact if I

Replace the bulb, clean the reflector, and make sure the lens is in good condition. Resist the urge to polish the reflector with an abrasive polish; all you'll do is scratch it up and maybe remove some of the silvering.

THROUGH ROSE-COLORED LENSES

When I was a kid, novelty taillight lenses were all the rage. Triumph guys could buy tiger's head lenses. There were Maltese cross lights available, peace signs, you name it. I always thought they were cool—course I was about 16 at the time. But you know what? I still like to see stuff like that, especially the ones that just light up and say "STOP."

were restoring an older Italian motorcycle to ride I wouldn't even consider installing the standard switches.

Kill buttons were more commonly seen on off-road bikes and magneto-equipped bikes. The one on the left is a Magura; it works well and has been used for the last 30 years or more. The one on the right is a Lucas. It was used on British street and off-road bikes like the Triumph TR6C. The Magura retails for about $10 and is available just about anywhere. I use them on all of my off-road machines. The Lucas, last time I bought one, went for about $70. I'd only use it if the bike were going to be shown or ridden on the road.

The speedometer on the right is a Smith's Chronometric. I'd leave its repair to a specialist. The one on the left is Smith's Magnetic, and is still available as new.

INSTRUMENTS AND DRIVES

Instrument repairs are one of those gray areas. My personal opinion is that any instrument overhaul is best left to a specialist. But before you ship your stopped clock off to a rebuilder, there are a few things to check.

Speedometers

Most speedo problems can be traced to either the speedometer cable or the drive. You should always inspect these first if your speedometer is malfunctioning. The drive might be taken from either wheel or from a separate gear drive. If the drive is taken from the rear wheel, normal practice is to use a gear drive. In most cases—particularly on British bikes where the speedometer drive is taken from the rear wheel—the speedometer and gear drive ratios are matched to each other. Likewise BMW speedometers, which are driven from the transmission, must be selected based on the numerical ratio of the final drive.

If the speedometer fails to register at all, first inspect the drive cable. If the cable is in one piece and spins when you turn the wheel, the problem is most likely in the instrument itself. I have run across drives with stripped gears that would spin a loose cable, but would slip under the load imposed by the speedometer. In theory you inspected the

speedo drive during disassembly; if you didn't, take another look now just to be safe. If the cable and gear drive check out, the problem is in the speedometer.

Instrument rebuilding is not for the faint hearted. There are several problems to overcome before you can even get to the guts of the clock. First, the bezel must be removed. Older instruments have a screwed-on bezel, which might or might not come loose. Newer ones are crimped or rolled on. Either way, special tools and skills are required.

Problem number two, parts are a little difficult to come by. Needles and new faces are available, but anything else must come from either an instrument shop or a donor. The final problem is that some instruments—particularly Japanese ones—just aren't rebuildable in the commonly accepted manner.

For what it's worth, I'd recommend that you leave any major instrument repair to the pros. Minor work—replacing the needles or face—can be done at home, in some cases quite easily, dependent on the design of the instrument.

TACHOMETERS

Tachometer repair is identical to speedo repair. If you can remove the instrument works from the housing, you can probably replace the face or needle without too much trouble. Other than that, call in a specialist. Tachometer drives are usually pretty straightforward, though unlike speedo drives, they are a potential oil leak. British and Italian bikes usually use a gearbox, although some mid-1960s Triumphs took the drive direct from the camshaft. Some—Harley Sportsters, for instance—took their drive from the magneto. Japanese models usually use a worm gear cut into the cam and an adapter drive. Another common drive source was the oil pump.

Tricks of the Tach

The tachometer drive found on most British bikes has a small Welch plug fitted into the back. The plug keeps the tiny driveshaft from falling out. Unfortunately, it's usually the plug that falls out, followed shortly by the shaft.

Your first indication that all is not well is a tach that's not working and a monster oil leak. About 75 percent of the time the shaft lodges against the crankcase or stays inside the tach drive. The problem that remains is how to reseal the drive unit? I thought you'd never ask. Use a nickel. A good old 5-cent piece fits the hole perfectly, drift it in, peen the end over, and you're back on the road.

Spin Doctoring

When installing a new speedo or tach-drive cable there are a few simple rules to follow:

Lightly grease the inner cable except for the last 6 inches before it enters the housing. The reason we don't grease that last little bit is so that grease won't enter the instrument. Excess grease will attract dirt and eventually gum up the works.

Let the cable follow a gentle arc; use cable ties only on long straight sections. Cables that are too tight will cause the gauge to "flutter." Also pay attention to the cable routing, particularly at the drive end. The straighter the entry, the longer the cable will live.

Repairing a Smith's Tach Drive

The time-honored shade tree method of repairing a Smith's Tach drive. Assuming that only the Welch plug has gone missing, you'll just need a nickel and a 5/16-inch ball bearing, and you can forgo the ball in a real pinch.

You'll probably need to file the nickel down slightly.

It should fit right into the tach drive.

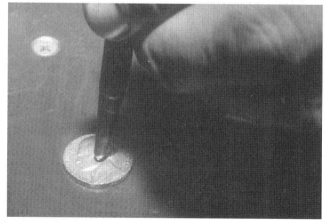

Center punch a divot as close to the center of the nickel as possible.

Repairing a Smith's Tach Drive

Epoxy the 5/16-inch ball bearing into the divot; this will act as a bearing for the shaft.

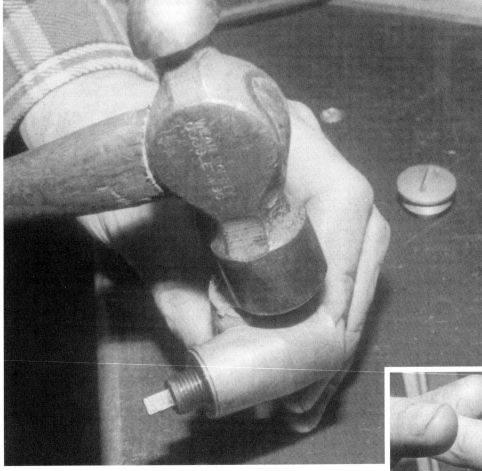

Assemble the tach drive and carefully drive in the nickel.

Use epoxy or silicone seal to prevent the plug from coming loose and to prevent oil leaks. Personally, I like to use clear silicone; that way my handiwork remains visible.

17

Paint and Bodywork

The ultimate goal of any restoration should be to end up with a bike that runs and looks as good as, if not better than, the day it left the factory. Sadly, this isn't always the case. I've seen many otherwise-credible restorations spoiled by a poor finish, sloppy metal work, and inattention to detail. Conversely, I've seen lots of bikes that looked fantastic but were close to junk under the glitter. Of course none of the dolts doing those restorations had this book as a guide.

Under the generic heading of paint and bodywork we'll cover the stripping, repairing, and refinishing of the cycle parts. Some sections might seem repetitious, for instance engine refinishing. I'll try not to repeat myself, but if I do I hope the editors will catch it. Before we dive into this chapter let me digress a bit and tell you a short story.

A few years ago I was helping judge a show dedicated to British bikes. I came across a very pretty Triumph T100C. It was a purple 1970, one of my favorite years. It looked great. The cases were polished, the paint was flawless, and the engine shone like a new penny. The owner/restorer mentioned that it had undergone a complete resto, had never been started since the complete engine rebuild, and was for sale, at a price that made my nose bleed.

The bike had a few detail items lacking, which made me question the owner's veracity. The cables were old and worn, and the Pozi-Drive screws holding the breather tube to the rear fender had been replaced with slot heads straight from the hardware store, but all in all it didn't look too bad. As this book was nearing completion I went to look at an original, unrestored 1967 T100C that a friend had purchased with a gang of other bikes. Lo and behold, that pretty purple job was there as well and it, too, was for sale at a very affordable price.

I was instantly smitten and struck a deal, conditional on getting it running. Here's what we found when we started it. The oil lines had been reversed, preventing any oil flow to the motor. Since we started it for the first time no real harm was done, but it could have been a disaster.

We also found as the bike warmed up that the beautiful high pipes had been dented, repaired with solder, and then rechromed. Have you ever watched a pipe melt in front of your eyes? It's not a pretty sight. We also discovered that the swingarm bushings were non-existent, the steering-head bearings shot, and every major bolt was loose. To add insult to injury the wiring harness had all the integrity of a politician. In short, this once-proud motorcycle had been reduced to a static, albeit very pretty, display. Of course once the engine warmed up and the solder melted out of the exhaust, some of the bloom came off the rose.

My point in telling you this should be obvious, but since I've been known to belabor the obvious, here goes: Only the rankest amateur or the most dastardly snake in the grass tries to hide an improperly restored bike with paint and shine. Ben Franklin once said about something or other, "Look how it resembles a dead fish in the moonlight; it both shines and stinks at the same time." I think Ben would have liked old motorcycles.

This original Triumph tank will be easy to refinish. It has all the factory stripes in place and is still in the factory colors. If it weren't, traces of the factory finish might be found under the knee pads, emblems, or the center trim strip.

STRIPPING AND PREPPING THE BODYWORK

Before you start stripping the bodywork down to bare metal you'll need to thoroughly document the standard paint job, if it still exists. Clear color photographs are good for starters. Note the width, style, and location of any pinstriping, as well as the location of any decals. Don't worry too much about that metal flake peace sign stuck to the oil tank; I'm pretty sure they're still available.

If the paint job includes scallops à la 1970s Triumphs or other distinguishing features, measure and note them as well. If you're concerned about losing the pattern, you can make paper patterns with tracing paper. Make certain you also note the width and color of any painted bands that might separate two adjacent colors.

The colors and paint schemes of the popular bikes are well known, and just as well documented. For instance, if you need to know the correct color and layout for a 1935 Indian, a glance through the Indian Motorcyle Buyer's Guide has a complete rundown. Since Indians are commonly restored, it's a simple matter to obtain the correct shade of paint. For some bikes, though, the original paint is either no longer available or there is little documentation to go by. If that's the case, you'll need to do a little detective work to determine the original color so that it can be matched. The paint color itself can be problematic. If you can get a paint code from the manufacturer and the paint is still available, great. BMW, for instance, uses a three-digit paint code. Code

#511 is Havana Gold—which sounds more like something illegal that you'd smoke than it does a paint color. If you were to restore a BMW in that color, all you would need to do is trot on down to the local BMW shop and order up some #511.

Where can you find the code? The first place to start is in your parts book. My 1972 BSA parts manual lists the correct color for a 1972 Lightning as Firebird Red #261. Now you might not know what Firebird Red is, but if you can locate a paint tin marked with either the name or the paint code, you're in.

The problem that crops up most often is that not all manufacturers coded their paint. Lots of them just gave the paint a part number and a name and let it go at that. And by the same token, having the paint code is no guarantee you'll be able to match the old paint with a modern equivalent. After all, who ever thought we'd be restoring old motorcycles?

The predicament the budding restorer now faces is exactly what color is Hi-Fi Flamingo pink (H-D Sportster color for 1967) or Aubergine (1967 Triumph Bonny). With the more popular bikes, paint can usually be found through either the dealer or restoration network. Less popular bikes will most likely need to have the old paint matched with a substitute. Besides, what the hell color is flamboyant metalflake orange, anyway?

Even rusty, crusty, or repainted bikes generally have some of the original paint left lurking somewhere. Look under pieces of trim, bolts that hold on the fenders, fuel-tank emblems, or anything else that might cover up a small section of paint. Two excellent spots to find traces of the factory paint are on the fuel tank, or under the petcock or kneepads. If the bike has been repainted in a non-standard color or scheme, you might need to carefully scrape or sand away until you find the original paint.

Beware when playing motorbike archeologist. I've seen several new tanks and fenders that were repaints from day one. Apparently, too many of a particular color tank would be run off. Instead of warehousing them, the manufacturer sent them back to the paint shop to be redone in a color more in demand.

Once you've got an original color chip, you can have it matched by any good paint dealer specializing in automotive finishes. There are also several dozen shops scattered throughout the United States dedicated to

NEW PAINT FROM OLD CANS

When I was a mere stripling I was spray-painting some wooden ship model I'd hammered together in the back yard. Halfway through the job the nozzle plugged up and the can stopped spraying. No problem, I thought. I'll just puncture the can, remove the paint, and brush paint the rest of it. Accordingly I drove a nail through the top of the can. The ensuing explosion covered me in white enamel that stayed on for a week.

Occasionally you'll run across OEM touchup spray cans. The paint is presumably the correct shade, but there are two problems. First, the paint may not spray. Second, it may not be enough paint for the job.

The solution to both problems is simple. Remove the paint from the can, have it matched, and spray it with conventional equipment. If the quantity is sufficient for the job at hand, use what's in the can, again spraying it with shop equipment.

The trick is to get the paint out of the can without wearing it, or worse, losing it. The solution is to turn the can upside down, puncture it, and let the propellant escape, then remove the bottom with a can opener.

repainting motorcycles. They can generally be counted on to supply the correct color finish, at least for the models they specialize in.

If you know what color the bike should be but can't match it for some reason or other, all is far from lost. Occasionally NOS paints, often in old touchup-size spray cans, will surface. I've also run into boxes of one-pint tins for sale, usually at swap meets. I wouldn't recommend using the aerosol cans as sold but the paint can be extracted and either matched or sprayed with conventional equipment (see sidebar).

Color brochures and old magazines can also provide the correct scheme and color, as can others who've restored similar bikes. Try to maintain a sense of perspective about your need for perfection versus reality. Few new motorcycles looked as nice as their restored counterparts. Even with new models on the showroom floor, paint shades varied between identical bikes. When I commented on the exquisite paint on one fellow's immaculate plum purple Commando, he mentioned that he'd painted it nine times to get exactly the right shade. Since the bike looked 100 times better than any of the new ones I'd ever seen, I wondered how on earth he'd decided the first eight were no good.

PREPARATION

Overall, about 99 percent of a good paint job is in the preparation. Consider the initial phases—stripping the old finish, repairing any damage, and priming the bare metal—as the foundation on which to build your paint job.

As with any good foundation, a lot rides on the initial excavation and site preparation.

STRIPPING THE OLD FINISH: CLEANING AND REFINISHING METAL PARTS

We're trying to overcome a couple of problems here. The first is to remove the old finish so that we can inspect the parts for hidden damage. The second is to remove any and all traces of rust and corrosion. And third we want to give the new finish a solid base so that paint adhesion is uncompromised.

One advantage a motorcycle restorer enjoys is the comparative ease with which the entire bike can be broken down into relatively small and easily transported pieces. Just imagine what an antique tractor enthusiast goes through, for instance. Because the parts are so easily handled, the stripping process becomes that much easier. Rather than have a sand blaster come to your garage, it's a lot easier, cheaper, and neater to drop the parts off at his shop.

Small delicate parts or light-gauge sheet metal should be chemically stripped if possible. Blasting, no matter how carefully done, might warp or hole thin, light parts. Aluminum tanks, such as BSA Victor fuel tanks, are also easily damaged by blasting. Steel fuel tanks and oil tanks can be bead blasted or chemically stripped, depending on the circumstances.

When it comes to removing old paint, rust, and years of baked-on grime, there are a few different options. If the parts in question are painted or naturally finished and sturdy, you can media blast them clean. Sand and glass beads are used on heavy-duty parts such as frames, fenders, and heavy brackets. Varieties of less intrusive shot such as walnut shell, plastic beads, or water vapor are all used on naturally finished parts, alloy pieces, and engine parts. Mask off any openings before you blast it, and thoroughly clean the inside of the tank afterwards.

Chemically stripping paint is messy, smelly, and dangerous, but it is a practical way to remove paint at home if you aren't prepared to buy a glass beading cabinet and compressor. You can always hand strip paint using wire brushes and sandpaper, but this can be incredibly labor intensive, and quite frankly unless the parts are very small, way more effort than it's worth.

Fiberglass pieces should be hand-sanded or blasted with plastic beads. Chemical strippers are also available for fiberglass, but the chemicals can leach into any cracks in the gel coat and create problems down the road. Glass beads can be used in a pinch. Turn the air pressure down as far as practical and hand sand the 'glass afterwards to remove any "fur."

Media Blasting

Not too long ago I would have said that all but the crudest sandblasters were impractical for most home restorers. Nowadays, decent abrasive beading cabinets can be had for un-

der $400. At that price the home restorer can easily afford one. The convenience factor alone makes it worth buying. About the only thing that won't fit into one of the bargain cabinets is a frame. Of course you'll need a good sized compressor to run one, which will up the ante slightly if you don't already own one.

Bead blasting is absolutely 100 percent guaranteed to return your parts to bare basic metal no matter what sort of paint, grease, rust, or scuzz covers it. The pitfall is that using the wrong technique or the wrong media can damage thin material. When blasting, the correct choice of grit will go a long way toward preventing damage. Any reputable shop can make suggestions as to what to use.

When actually blasting, always hold the gun at a 45-degree angle to the work. Mask off all external threads. Protect internal threads with old bolts. The parts should be completely dismantled prior to blasting. Bearing races can be left in place but they must be protected. Wheels can be blasted in the assembled state if you must, but axles and bearings should be removed.

Engine parts that need blasting are going to require some special attention both before and after. Any oil passage must be completely sealed beforehand, and thoroughly cleaned afterward. In fact, some engine builders I know recommend boiling the

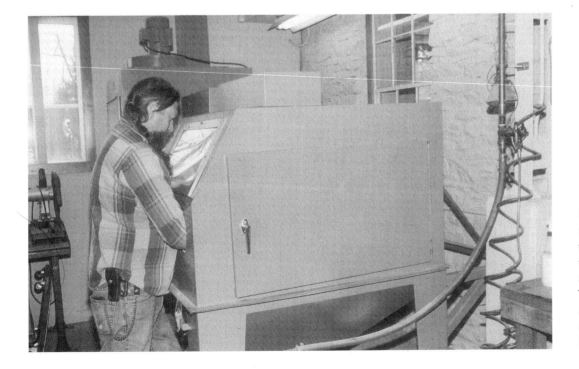

Industrial-strength media blasting is the quickest way to strip paint, rust, and corrosion. This cabinet will accommodate anything up to and including a frame.

Before and after: The parts on the left are ready for priming. Those on the right have yet to be stripped.

TYPES OF GRIT

The following abrasives are a few of the most commonly available. Since new ones are compounded on a regular basis, it pays to check with your supplier to see what's available.

Glass beads: cleans brass, aluminum, steel, etc., leaving a smooth finish: 60-80 grit.

Walnut shells: won't pit or scratch the material surface, providing a very smooth, original-looking finish: 35-60 grit.

Aluminum oxide: imparts a texture but holds up well in the cabinet: 46 grit.

Steel grit: for heavy-duty cutting; can leave a rough finish.

The first layer of stripper has been applied. Once the tank has set for a while the bubbled paint will be removed and the process repeated. Chemical stripping is time-consuming and messy but less intrusive than sandblasting.

parts in water after bead blasting them to remove all traces of grit.

Normally, fine grit, glass beads, walnut shells, and plastic beads won't damage gasket surfaces or threads, but always check with your blaster or supplier beforehand. Finally, any freshly beaded steel or iron surface will

start to rust as soon as it's removed from the cabinet. Unless you're going to be repairing the piece in the very near future, give it a quick coat of primer-sealer.

CHEMICAL STRIPPING

Nasty stuff this, but if you don't have the room or inclination to bead blast it's the only way to remove tough old finish. By the same token it might be the only way to strip some delicate parts. Chemical strippers include spray-on and brush-on types. Apply the remover, let it sit, and then use a putty knife or wire brush to start stripping.

This can be a tedious, unpleasant process. Most of this stuff stinks. The fumes can be overpowering and you always get some on yourself or your clothes. Always use chemical strippers in a well-ventilated area. You'll probably end up repeating the apply-scrape-inspect cycle a couple of times before you're through, which is also a pain in the butt. Once the bulk of the paint has been removed you can use plastic pot scrubbers or fine steel wool to give the parts a final rubdown. Also be sure to get all of it off; it removes new paint even faster than old.

You'll need to wear rubber gloves and some type of eye protection whenever you're working with a chemical paint remover. You'll also have to dispose of the leftover mess—no, you can't just dump it down the nearest storm drain. If it's up to me, I'll blast the old finish off every time.

RUST REMOVERS

There are some chemical rust removers out there that work quite well. Normally, I'd tell you to blast to remove any heavy rust but there are instances where you can't or shouldn't. The best example is probably a gas or oil tank interior. Chances are the oil tank interior is fine—after all it's usually full of oil. Problems occur when they have been left to sit empty for very long periods of time.

Tank interiors that have been previously coated with one of those pour-in plastic compounds are particularly difficult to clean out. Jaye Strait of Britech recommends using caustic soda (lye, the principal ingredient in Drano) to remove the old coating. Pour in a 50/50 solution of soda and water, let sit for a week, and then rinse with vinegar. Phosphoric acid is a good choice if you just need to de-rust the tank. The acid can be rinsed out with tap water. Phosphoric acid has the advantage of leaving a residual coating that protects the surface from further rust.

There are an assortment of other good products on the market, Miracle Rust Remover being just one of them. Miracle has the "advantage" (if you can call it that) of being able to strip nickel plate! Several commercial de-rusting agents are available through your local auto supply house under a variety of trade names as well.

A word of warning: Use rust removers only on steel. Most caustic solutions will destroy aluminum and alloy parts. Caustic solutions are also dangerous to work with. Follow all of the printed warnings and keep plenty of fresh water on hand in case of an accident. Make sure you use whatever protective gear is required as well—eye protection is mandatory.

Once the metal has been de-rusted carry out whatever repairs are needed. Most of the sheet-metal parts on a motorcycle respond well to standard body shop practices and tools. Dented fenders can be pounded out by using a body hammer and dolly or by working them on sandbag, described below. Work from the outside edges toward the center to avoid stretching the metal. Holes should be brazed or soldered closed and then ground smooth.

Dented fuel tanks can be worked with a "planishing ball." A planishing ball is a steel ball welded to a stick. The ball is inserted through the fuel filler opening and used like a dolly. Using one on a fuel tank is not for the faint-hearted, and I'd recommend you leave this job to a pro. Fuel tanks can also be repaired from the outside by using a slide-hammer to pull the dent. Headlight shells are repaired in the same manner as a fuel tank. The obvious advantage is that you have easy access to the inside.

Headlights, fenders, and sidecovers can be worked by using a sandbag as a backing. Find yourself an old truck inner tube. Cut it through one side. Fold one end over and secure it by sandwiching the end between two pieces of wood and nailing them together. Fill the rest of the tube with sandbox sand. Then close off that end. You can work the dented piece against the sandbag. Place the part with the concave side of the dent facing the sandbag. Using your hammer, work the dent toward the bag.

FILLING DENTS

If you must use filler on the gas tank, try to use as little as possible. Bondo has its place, but a tank covered in an inch-deep layer of "mud" won't last long. The art of "leading" is damn near lost and few body shops even know how to do it. But it's still the best way I know to fill small dents.

Leading

Despite the name, leading actually uses solder to fill dents. On cars it's difficult because most of the dents are in vertical panels. Again the small parts of a motorcycle work to your advantage. Position the parts so that the dent is horizontal. Grind the area to be leaded until it's shining, leaving the surface slightly coarse to obtain better adhesion.

The easiest solder to work with is a 30/70—30 percent tin to 70 percent lead alloy—sometimes called "plumber's solder." Plumber's solder flows at a relatively low temperature, about 490 degrees Fahrenheit, making it easy to work with. It also adheres well. The high tin content makes it a little softer, so it has a bit of flex to it as well.

After the metal is ground, warm it with a propane torch and apply tinning solution or paste. Some recommend applying a tinning coat of 50/50 electrical solder to the dent first; this acts like a primer coat and gives the body solder a better grip. The tin coat should spread over the dent with some steel wool held with pliers.

Once the tin coat cools, start to apply your body solder. Build up the solder proud of the tank. Use a file to work the solder down and then sand smooth. The molten solder can also be worked with a wooden paddle—that's how the old timers smoothed large areas. However since we're working with such small areas, I've found it's just as easy to build the solder up in layers.

The most common problem in applying body solder is excess heat. If the base metal starts to glow red, it's too hot. Let it cool before proceeding.

Most tanks can be safely repaired with solder. There are, however, a few older ones out there that have soldered seams. If you are working on one of those you might not know it until the tank separates into a pile of loose panels. You might check with a restoration shop or dealer to find out if you're working with a soldered tank. If so, use of a heat-stop paste, sold in welding shops, and a low temperature solder should prevent any of your repairs from unraveling large sections of the tank.

Plastic

Plastic body filler—"mud"—has its place. The cardinal rule in its use is always to use as little as possible. Follow the manufacturer's recommendations for mixing and spreading the filler. Allow ample drying time. Plastic filler is porous and absorbs water; if you wet sand it, dry the area afterward with a heat gun on low setting.

HOLES

Any holes in the fuel or oil tank should be brazed or silver-soldered shut. The fuel tank should then be coated with a sealer like Por15 or Kreem to prevent further problems. I don't recommend sealing oil tanks; a plugged fuel line is a minor problem. If some of the sealant breaks loose and plugs an oil line, it's going to get expensive.

For the most part, small holes in fenders can be repaired by brazing them closed. Large, rusted-through sections will require sectioning or a repair with fiberglass. If at all possible, replace rusted-out fenders with swap meet, NOS, or reproduction items if they're available.

RUST PROTECTION

If the metal parts are to be stored prior to painting, they need to be protected from rust. There all kinds of rust inhibitors on the market that can be used. Most of the inhibitors are water-soluble; they can be rinsed off prior to painting. You can also spray parts down with

WD-40 or the like. These work well, but the parts will require a thorough degreasing before painting.

If you decide to prime the parts, remember that most primers are porous and won't prevent rust from re-forming below the surface. Instead use an epoxy primer to seal the surface, or a primer sealer. Dupont makes an excellent aerosol epoxy primer, #214. If the parts are going to be shelved use it or some other rust preventive to protect the parts.

FIBERGLASS

To be honest, I hadn't given much thought to fiberglass repair. It's not really something I think about where vintage bikes are concerned. Then I realized some of you might be restoring vintage dirt bikes, notably those of Spanish descent. H-D also used fiberglass touring accessories, which you might need to fix up. Or you may need to do a little work on some of the 'glass tanked Nortons or BSAs. Then again some BMWs use fiberglass fenders.

Anyway, the more I thought about it, the more I realized that many of you could be running smack dab into a wad of the stuff. Major damage is better left to a shop that specializes in fiberglass repair. The solvent resins and catalysts used are noxious and messy. Besides, the stuff makes your skin itch like there's no tomorrow. If it looks like big chunks are going to need replacing, I'd recommend a pro. On the other hand, minor cosmetic damage can be repaired fairly easily. Because fiberglass is woven, cracks don't require "stop holes" drilled at the ends of the crack the way a crack in a metal object does. Cracks and gouges can be "vee'd out" with a grinder, filled in with Dura-Glass or Mar-Glass, and sanded smooth. On structural damage, the broken fiberglass should be reinforced by "scabbing" a piece of new 'glass over the break (on the hidden side, of course).

PAINTWORK

First impressions are the most lasting, and the initial impression of your restored bike is what sticks in most minds. The overall appearance—primarily the paint job—is what grabs 'em. Consider the paint the "jewel in the crown."

In all honesty, because of space, equipment, and talent limitations, I send most of

Freshly prepared parts should be primed and sealed as quickly as possible to prevent rust.

my paintwork to the pros. There are entire libraries devoted to the art of painting. If you intend to do your own painting, I'd suggest you read through some of the available titles listed in the sources section. In the meantime, I'll discuss some of the basic concepts.

Equipment

For home painting you'll need a compressor with enough capacity to handle your chosen spray gun. Typically, paint guns require from 8 to 60 psi at 3 to 22 cubic feet per minute. Most compressors in the 4-horsepower range should be able to handle any spray-painting chores. You'll also need enough room to paint and somewhere to mix and store your paint. Finally you'll need somewhere to clean your equipment and a tank to hold waste paint and thinner.

Before doing any paintwork, you should install a water trap in line with your compressor discharge hose (a good idea anyway). You might also need to upgrade the hose itself. Most compressors sold for home use a standard 1/4-inch hose. To ensure enough airflow, a 5/16- or 3/8-inch hose is a better bet, especially since you're going to be painting some distance from the compressor. Because the paint gun requires something less than line pressure, you also need an air-line regulator.

Good spray guns start at around $100. They can be bought at Sears, auto supply shops, and through the mail. Assuming that this is your first venture into spray painting, I'd recommend buying the gun at the same place you buy the bulk of your paint and primer. A little expert advice as far as the gun

Part Betty Crocker, part Merlin the Magician, modern paint needs to be mixed in the correct proportions. From the left: catalyst, reducer, and paint—in this case a clear topcoat.

The factory paint on this as-found Duo-Glide has held up fairly well. The cracks in the topcoat are the result of time and weather.

and its ability to match what you plan on shooting saves a lot of time and aggravation in the long run.

Spray painting requires a bit of alchemy. You'll find yourself mixing paint and thinner, adding catalysts, and so on. An accurate measuring cup is an absolute necessity. A plain old mixing cup, just like mom uses in the kitchen, works as well as any. I found mine at the local supermarket. Buy the oven-proof Pyrex one; it's the easiest type to clean after you're done.

Primers

Primer is a catchall term that describes the initial paint coat or base. The function of a primer is twofold. Primer creates a bond with the bare metal and fills in surface imperfections. Contrary to popular belief, most primers are water porous. A primed piece that's set back on the shelf for a month or two is a prime candidate for rust (sorry about the pun).

There are numerous types and styles of primers available and to list and describe them all would take another book in itself. In fact, there are even primers formulated specifically for use in California to comply with that state's stringent air-quality laws.

Primers are formulated to work with a given type of paint. For example, if you're going to shoot lacquer, you'll need a compatible primer, something like PPG's Super Combo Acrylic Lacquer Primer. If you decide to go with an enamel finish, you'll need to use an enamel compatible primer. Since the PPG book is open, I'd recommend PPG's Jetseal Primer-Sealer.

Failure to match paint to the correct primer means you'll end up doing the job over. It might be a year later, a month later, or

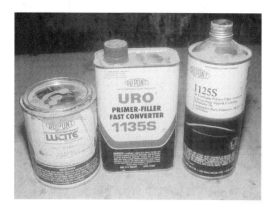

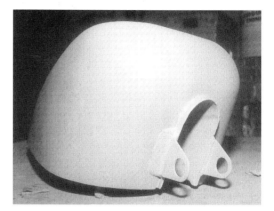

This Sportster tank has been primed and sanded, and is ready for paint.

15 minutes later, but mark my words, you will do it over.

There are four basic primers. Plain old primer—a very thin, light type—is used as a bond between the metal and the fresh paint. Primer-surfacer contains a fair amount of solid material to build up the surface and fill in small scratches. Primer-sealer is used to seal over an old coat of paint. It provides a base for the new paint and it prevents the old paint from bleeding through the fresh primer—which, remember, may be porous—and ruining the new paint. And finally, sealer, which, although it really isn't a primer, is used in conjunction with primer. Sealer, as its name implies, is used after the last primer coat to seal it off from the fresh paint. Failure to use a sealer may result in the fresh paint reacting with any old paint, body filler, or in some cases the primer itself. Anytime you paint over an old finish, which I really don't recommend, you must use a primer sealer or sealer to keep the solvents in the fresh paint from reacting with the old.

Priming used to involve a lot of labor-intensive work. The primer would be applied, allowed to dry, and then a second coat of a different color blown over the parts. When the second coat had dried, you started sanding. The color variations revealed the high or low

spots. The low spots would be built up with body filler, more prime applied, and then the sanding would start over.

Today "high-build" primers are available. Because they contain large amounts of solid "filler," the high-build primers fill in low spots and sanding scratches much better than the old watery primers. They eliminate a lot of the tedium caused by repetitive priming-sanding-filling and repriming. Properly used, they provide a smooth finish and excellent gloss when the topcoat is applied.

PAINT

I suppose you can make a case for there being only two types of paint suitable for motorcycle use: lacquer and enamel. Of course each type has several variants. There are nitrocellulose lacquers, acrylic lacquers, polyurethane enamels, acrylic enamels, and epoxies. In all honesty, there are so many variations of paint out there now that it's difficult to keep up with them.

In reality, if you decide to do your own paintwork, you're going to be limited to shooting your garden-variety lacquers and enamels, particularly if this is your first foray into painting.

Enamel

Originally, enamel was the paint of choice. In fact, at one time only the most expensive motorcycles were painted with enamel. For durability, gloss, and ease of maintenance, enamel, particularly when baked on (stove enamel) was unbeatable.

The problem with nonacrylic enamel is that it's very slow to dry. This gives rise to all

sorts of problems. There's nothing more discouraging to the novice painter—or the experienced one, for that matter—than to apply what looks like a flawless enamel paint job only to return in an hour and find a sag, run, or orange peel in the paint. Usually the only solution is to let the job cure and then sand out the offending area. This is easier said than done. Enamel is also very difficult to touch up if it's damaged.

Another shortcoming with enamel was that, unlike lacquer, it couldn't be rubbed out. Acquire a small scratch and you had to live with it. All of that changed in 1972 when Dupont released its Imron line of polyurethane enamel. In the ensuing 27 years urethane paints have become so good that there is little reason not to use them if you can.

One downside that remains with enamel, however, is overspray. Since enamel still takes longer to dry, the overspray remains wet when it lands, and sticks to everything. (Lacquer overspray tends to dry in the air, and lands like dust.) If you're using enamel, especially in an enclosed space, keep everything covered unless you want it the same color as your bike.

Lacquer

In the 1920s nitrocellulose lacquer became very popular as an automotive/motorcycle finish, particularly for the bodywork. Because it was extremely quick to dry, it was easy to apply on the assembly line. Even today, it is very easy to touch up or repair if damaged. Because lacquer is relatively soft (compared to enamel) it can be "rubbed out"—polished to the nth degree.

Nitrocellulose is currently available only through paint suppliers catering to the vintage trade. It is also quite expensive, with colors going for around $25 a pint.

Today's acrylic lacquers have a lot going for them. They are easy to spray, provide excellent coverage, and are forgiving in use. Follow the manufacturer's instructions to the letter and the job should come out fine.

Spray-Can Finishes

I've seen some excellent work done with a "spray-bomb." In fact, most of the small parts on my vintage Bultaco were painted with an aerosol. If you plan to refinish anything large—a fuel tank or frame—you'll probably want to pick up several cans. Check

the bottom of the can for the batch number: making sure that all of the cans are from the same batch will ensure a uniform color match. As in any type of painting, match the primer to the paint.

Again, because a bike has such a small area that requires paint it's easy to obtain a decent finish. That's particularly true if you use lacquer, which can be shot, sanded, and compounded until you achieve the desired finish.

BRUSH FINISHED

Across the pond you still run into a few restored bikes that have been brush painted. This is an incredibly tedious way to refinish a motorcycle. It involves hours of patient brushing followed by prolonged drying, and then a long session of sanding before the whole process is repeated. If you've got the time and patience—not to mention a strong masochistic streak—you might want to try it as a lark.

POWDER-COATING

To powder-coat or not, that is the question. Powder-coating vintage motorcycle parts still generates some controversy. Its adherents point out that it's durable, almost impossible to damage, looks great, and is relatively inexpensive. Its detractors are just as quick to point out that it's entirely too "modern" a finish. And the temperature involved prevents you from using plastic fillers to smooth a rough surface.

My feeling is that its advantages outweigh almost any argument against its use, especially if the bike is going to be ridden. Having said that, I limit my powder-coating to the frame,

ENGINE PAINTS

Very often engine components—or in some cases, the whole engine—must be painted. Aerosol cans are the perfect way to do it. Factory colors are available from PJ-1, Lubritec, and Kal-guard to replicate the finishes found on most Japanese motors. Black cylinder can be painted with almost any high-temperature paint—personally I like Krylon semi-gloss barbecue paint.

I've also obtained excellent results by spraying small bits with enamel and baking them in the oven at 350 degrees for 30 to 45 minutes. Of course the missus wasn't so happy with the smell that permeated her kitchen for a day or two afterward, but what the hell, the parts looked great.

wheel hubs, various brackets, and engine parts—the bits that look good in black and are rarely examined up close. Tanks and fenders should be painted.

Another consideration is cost. In my neck of the woods it's actually a little cheaper (at least at the time of this writing) to powder-coat a frame than it is to paint one. Durability and low price are strong selling points no matter how you slice it.

SHOULD YOU OR SHOULDN'T YOU PAINT?

Call me a coward, but the only painting I undertake is for very small jobs. The big pieces, especially the fuel tank, I always send to a real painter. In the first place my garage space is limited—basically, a two-car garage. It's also crammed full of bikes, parts, and memorabilia, all of which need protection from overspray. Lastly, my time is limited. If I send the painting out I can concentrate on the mechanical end of things, which is what I really enjoy. Besides, I really don't have the patience to do all of the masking and pinstriping and clearing that most jobs require.

If you decide to do your own painting follow these simple rules and you'll save yourself a lot of grief:

1. Locate and read a book dedicated to the art of painting. Most paint manufacturers offer them gratis.
2. Ensure that the area where you'll be painting is safe and adequately ventilated. Painting in an enclosed cellar near an oil furnace is about the worst scenario I can imagine.
3. Find and use the proper mask or respirator when dry sanding and painting.
4. Read and follow the manufacturer's recommendation on mixing and thinning the paint.
5. Paint only in a dust-free environment.

Wet down the floor and walls if you have to.
6. Wear the proper clothing. A wool sweater or dusty flannel shirt ruin the best paint job.
7. Secure the shop. Lock the doors from the inside—visitors bring in dust, dirt, and fingerprints.
8. Remember, weather affects the paint-to-thinner mix. Excess humidity and high or low ambient temperatures will certainly call for a change in the ratio, as well as a change in air pressure.
9. Always use primer, sealer, and paint from one source, i.e., if you use a Dupont top-coat use a Dupont primer and sealer.
10. Take care of all surface flaws before you paint. Paint won't fill scratches, nicks, or chips—it will actually make them more visible.
11. Afterwards give your spray gun a thorough cleaning.
12. Take your time. The final job is going to be a direct and highly visible reflection of your work habits.

CHROME

Replace or rechrome? Another good question. Let's take a look at what it takes to restore a chrome-plated part. To successfully replate a part, the plater must first strip off all of the old plating. He'll dip the part in a chemical tank to remove any traces of grease, dirt, or stray paint. Next, he'll use reverse electrolysis to remove the chrome plate in one tank, then remove the nickel in another.

Once the parts are down to bare metal they can be inspected for hidden damage, repaired, and then buffed. Buffing the parts is the chroming equivalent to preparing sheet metal for paint. Any surface imperfection must be buffed out. Obviously, this is both labor intensive and time consuming. Once the part is buffed, it's washed with detergent, rinsed, and dipped in a dilute acid solution. The parts are then washed in clear water to remove all traces of the acid.

The part is then immersed in a copper bath for anywhere from 20 minutes to four hours. The copper is then buffed. With luck, the copper will fill in most, if not all, of the pits. Depending on the depth of the pits and the thickness of your wallet, the process continues until everyone is satisfied with the finish. The

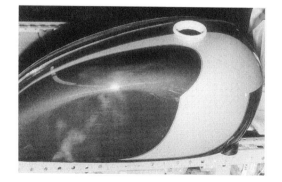

This Bonneville tank is in the process of being redone by BRITECH. When finished it'll be better than new.

part is then bathed in nickel and finally chrome.

As you may well imagine, it's fairly easy to reach the point of diminishing returns. Very often, unless the part is simply unobtainable you'll pay more for restoring old chrome than you would for a new part. If they are too far gone to plate they'll need replacement—and that, as they say, is that. In general, if the parts are heavily rusted or corroded, replating the part is probably not going to be cost effective.

Home Plating Kits

These small, do-it-yourself plating kits are becoming more and more popular, and for good reason. They're convenient to use and relatively cheap to own. While they won't fit a large part they work just fine on the small pieces that make up the bulk of a motorcycle restoration. They work best in restoring the original cadmium-plating on nuts, bolts, washers, and other small parts.

Polishing Alloy

Nothing looks better than a gleaming hunk of alloy. British bikes in particular, with their alloy timing and clutch covers, really respond well to a little TLC. Polishing alloy is as easy as it looks. It's also incredibly dirty, but usually worth the effort.

Buffing wheels are available to fit most bench grinders. If you feel ambitious, you can always salvage a motor from an old appliance. I like to polish big parts like timing covers by hand, the smaller parts on the wheel. I start by working the area with 600 grit paper, then wet it down with light oil or WD-40 to remove any light scratches. From there I go to a coarse rubbing compound. In some cases I'll use a hunk of Scotchbrite with the rubbing compound. Finally, I finish the job with Simichrome or Autosol polish.

If you prefer to use a buffing wheel, you need to match the "mop" size to the motor speed. If the motor runs at 1750 rpm use an 8-inch wheel, at 3450 rpm you can use either a 6- or 8-inch. Normally, soft metals—aluminum, brass, and die-cast zinc—are polished with Tripoli compound first. The wheel is then cleaned and polishing continued with white rouge. Final buffing should be done with a loose section wheel.

As a final tip, there's nothing worse than polishing a brilliant piece of metal and knocking a chunk out of it with the retaining nut on the buffing-wheel arbor. A thick section of rubber tubing or a rubber ball stuck over the arbor's end will protect those finely polished parts.

SEAT WORK

I wasn't really sure where to put this section, but here's probably as good a place as any. After all, the seat on a motorcycle is as much a part of the body as anything else. The bike's saddle has almost as much visual impact as the paint job, and a sloppy recovering job or a seat obviously intended for another make or model really detracts from the overall appearance.

I'm not saying you need to reinstall the OEM seat—after all, it's your motorcycle and you're going to ride it. In fact, there are lots of bikes out there that look a lot better with an aftermarket seat, although if you plan to show the bike, the wrong seat will go against you. Here again, you have a few choices. You can refurbish the original seat, or you can buy a new or reproduced original—often built by the original seat maker. Or you can install an aftermarket or custom seat.

Refurbishing a Seat

Step one, of course, is to photograph the seat, assuming it still exists. Note the seat-cover material and how it's fastened on. Remove the cover as carefully as possible. Then remove the foam base, if so equipped. If the foam is crumbling like a week-old cookie, don't worry, but try to keep it in one piece.

Inspect the sheet-metal pan for any signs of damage, particularly around the mounts. Make any needed repairs. Some seats use captive nuts for the mounts, hinges, or retaining pin; these work loose over time. It might be a good idea to weld or epoxy them into place now. When the base is finished, treat it to a coat of paint and set it aside.

Over time seat foam compresses, gets damp, and eventually breaks down. In fact, in many instances the quality of the foam wasn't that great to begin with. New foam can sometimes be found through the normal channels, but a better bet is simply to have an upholstery shop cut you a new one. Try an automotive/custom upholstery shop, rather than the guy who just did Aunt Millie's sofa. Most custom shops—and every town seems to have one—are well versed in the art of custom-cut motorcycle seats. They should be able to provide you with a new foam base that's equal to or better than the original at a very reasonable price.

The seat cover itself might be held on in any number of ways. Some use sheet-metal tabs that are bent over to catch the cover. Vintage dirt bikes, particularly those with aluminum or plastic seat bases, often have the seat cover stapled on. Or the cover might be secured with small nuts and bolts, which in turn are covered by a trim strip. A portion of the cover, usually the front, is often glued down as well.

Seat covers—for the most popular bikes, at least—are readily available. If you can't easily find one, a repeat visit to the shop that supplied your foam should set things right. I've found that it's easier to insert the foam into the cover first. Then mount the foam and cover to the base. Square the whole assembly up before you start to fasten any portion of the cover down. This step is crucial if the seat has a logo on it—if the logo isn't straight, the bike's never going to look right.

Once the cover has been placed squarely where you want it, clip down the front and work your way to the rear. Check the fit continuously as you go to avoid any undue wrinkles. As a finishing touch reapply any applicable manufacturer's decals to the underside of the seat.

Leather Saddles

If you are fortunate enough to be restoring a bike with a leather saddle, my best advice is to seek out someone experienced in their repair. If you really want to tackle a leather seat yourself, start by visiting your local tack shop. Any place that sells horse saddles should be able to connect you up with the leather needles and twine you'll need to make one.

There is also an excellent book called The Vintage Motorcyclist's Workshop by Radco,

published by Haynes. This book goes into great detail on the procedure and tools needed to refurbish early leather saddles.

DECALS

I prefer to install all decals after the motorcycle has been assembled. That way I can see where they go not only in relation to each other but how they look on the bike as a whole. Some of you undoubtedly feel otherwise, however, so I'll at least cover the basic types.

The first are the pressure-transfer type. These are usually found adorning toolboxes and refrigerators. A paper backing is peeled off and the sticker pressed into place—usually crooked. If you first spray the surface where you attach the sticker with soapy water, you can slide the sticker around until you get the alignment you want. Then squeegee the water out and the sticker will stay put. These are the easiest stickers to apply.

Gold size transfers were common on bikes built from the 1920s to the 1940s. These are the most difficult to apply. The paper backing is first peeled off. A very thin coat of gold-size or clear varnish is applied to the decal. The decal is then left until the varnish becomes tacky. The transfer is then placed where you want it. There's no second chance here, so make sure it's exactly where you want it.

Working from the center out, push out any air bubbles. Let the decal sit for an hour or two then dab the paper covering with water and carefully remove it. Wipe the decal down with water to remove any gum left from the backing. After two days, varnish over the transfer with a clear polyurethane varnish.

Water slide decals are exactly like the ones that came in those model plane kits you built as a kid. The sticker is placed in a saucer of water until it's free to move. It's then placed where you want it, slid off the paper backing and into place. Apply varnish when dry.

Dry transfer decals are also common and fairly easy. Remove the paper backing and place the sticker where you want it. Rub the front with a soft rag or your thumb; if all goes well the sticker will adhere to the surface and the top paper will peel smoothly away.

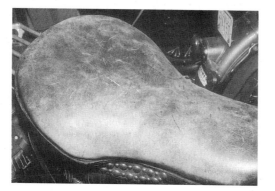

A little saddle soap or Neat's Foot Oil would have this original leather saddle back to health in a jiffy.

Final Assembly, Sources, Mechanics, Endpapers

18

Assembly

At some point in your labors a new day dawns and you realize that every piece of your motorcycle has been rebuilt, buffed, painted, and polished. What you have sitting in various boxes and on every flat spot in your workshop is a brand-new motorcycle waiting to be assembled. The trick now is to assemble all of those painstakingly acquired and lovingly restored bits and pieces into a living, breathing, single entity.

Believe me, if there was ever a time to step back, take a deep breath and count to 10, this is it.

Impatience now can undo all of your work in a heartbeat. A careless slip of a tool, trying to fit the engine without help, or forgetting to torque down a crucial fastener are certain to ruin your day.

Before you start reassembly, sit down, think the process through and—if you have to—draw up a game plan. Does the transmission have to go in before the engine? Can the engine be installed fully assembled? Would it be easier to assemble the complete frame and then install the engine? These and any other questions should be clear before you pick up

Time's up; everything is back and ready to go together—except the brake backing plates, that is.

206

the first part. Also figure out how you're going to protect the freshly painted parts, primarily the frame. And at what stages you'll need help.

Nuts and Bolts

One item often overlooked is the hardware needed to hold everything together. This can be a tough call. If the bike is being restored to ride, my suggestion is to replace all of the hardware with new. I'm also a big fan of aircraft-style locknuts, particularly since the majority of them won't be visible. Source all your hardware from the same place and make sure the dealer is reputable. If the manufacturer's marks are left on the boltheads, take the time to make sure they are all alike. Nothing looks worse than a hodgepodge of mismatched hardware holding a bike together.

If the bike is going to be shown I'd recommend using the old hardware, assuming it's in good condition and has been replated. If the original stuff is long gone or simply not serviceable, you can either try to find something that matches or resembles the original hardware, or install new. Some restorers even take the time to buff the manufacturer's mark off.

Protecting the Frame

The easiest piece to scratch is usually the frame. The engine usually needs a bit of wrestling to get it into position. The swingarm needs locating and so on. I've seen rags wrapped around the frame, taped up newspaper, plastic bubble wrap—you name it.

The best solution I've found is to use long strips of foam pipe insulation to cover the frame rails. The foam comes in long strips precut down the middle and is intended to fit over water pipes. It's nice and thick and semi rigid. Place it over the frame rails and secure it with a piece of tape. Leave it there until it gets in the way.

Assembly

If you were fortunate enough to do the initial disassembly, you probably have a pretty good idea of the order in which you want to reassemble the bike. Before assembly commences, read through your notebook and review your photos. In general I'd recommend installing the fork and swingarm first, followed by the wheels. On some machines—BMWs, for instance—you might find the swingarm installation follows the engine and transmission. So be it.

Once the bike has its wheels under it, it should be fairly stable, more so for being tied down. At that point, with the aid of a helper if need be, the engine (and gearbox) can be installed, followed by whatever you've decided

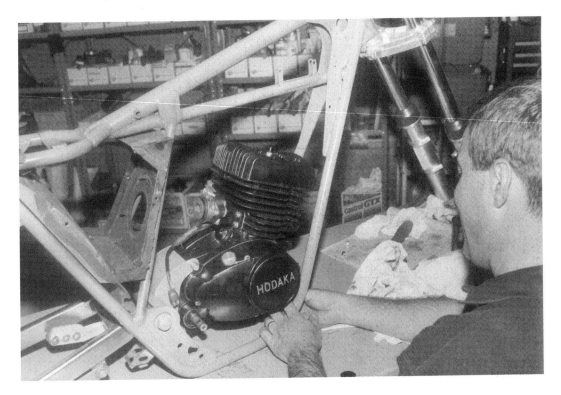

I like to install the engine as early as possible. It helps steady the frame and it's easier to install the mill without a lot of other parts to get in your way.

Then again, some guys leave the engine till the end.

Never leave any portion of the job "intending to get back to it"; bend those lock tabs over as soon as the bolts are tight.

It goes without saying that all parts should be installed in serviced condition. That includes oiling the air filter.

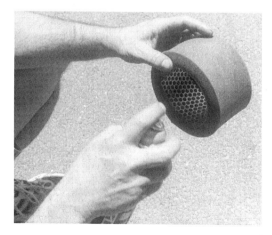

comes next. The advantage in doing it this way is that the bike can be safely wheeled out of the way when you are through working on it for the day.

As an alternative—and I've used this method to good effect as well—the bare frame can be secured to the work stand and the engine bolted in place. Once the engine is in place the peripheral parts can be added. The advantage here is that the weight of the engine helps counterbalance the rest of the parts as they are bolted to the frame. You might also find it much easier, for example, to bolt on the fenders before the wheels are in place. The disadvantage is that in many cases a large and heavy motorcycle will eventually need lifting off a stand. But that's what friends are for, isn't it?

As each subassembly is installed, it's important to complete the task before moving on. For example, when the fork is installed, the steering-head bearings should be adjusted. The forks should have the correct amount of oil poured in (if you haven't already done so), and they should be aligned. Never install a part planning to "get back to it." You may or you may not. You are far better off ending the assembly session a little early than to hurriedly install something and leave it undone.

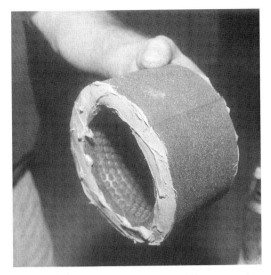

You should also apply a fresh coat of grease to the filter's sealing surfaces.

Anything requiring grease should be well lubricated as it's installed. Likewise, the engine sump should be filled with the correct oil as soon as the engine (and tank, if so equipped) are in place.

Oily Dilemma

The correct weight and grade of motor oil for your classic is always subject to controversy. My advice is to use a modern non-synthetic oil, multi-grade whenever possible. If the manufacturer specifies otherwise, stick with the manufacturer's recommended weight, particularly during the break-in period. Some manufacturers, Harley-Davidson, for instance, recommend a mono-grade oil for many of their models. Again, my advice would be to use it.

I'm also a firm believer in detergent oils, though I think you'd be hard pressed to find a non-detergent on the market right now. Since you're starting with a clean engine I see no rational reason not to use a detergent oil.

Change the oil after the first 500 miles. Change it again after 1,000 miles, and thereafter at the manufacturer's recommended intervals. You may be tempted to change it more often. If that gives you peace of mind, by all means change it more often.

I'd advise against using any full synthetics. In the first place, synthetic oils are often incompatible with engine seals made before 1981. If the engine seals happen to be NOS made before 1981, the synthetic oil may seep past them. In 1981 the seal manufacturers, realizing that synthetics were the wave of the future, changed the composition of the seals to better deal with the new oils. Secondly, you'll probably change the oil so frequently that there will be no practical advantage to using a synthetic.

Any crucial fastener (aren't they all?) should get a little dab of the correct grade of locking compound.

This little Hodaka MXer is almost ready to go.

Bottom line? Use the manufacturer's recommended grade of oil and change it frequently.

If the engine is a dry-sump design, prime all of the oil lines as they are installed and triple-check their routing and connections.

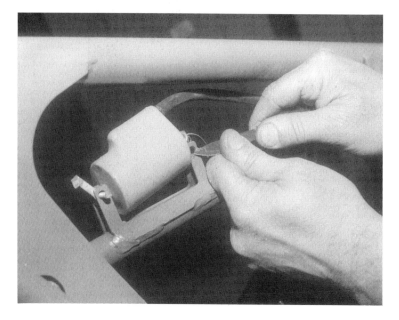

Bleeding Two-Stroke Oil Tanks

Injector tank-equipped two-strokes must have their oil pumps bled before start-up. The procedure varies slightly by brand, but basically you'll need to remove the bleed screw, open the pump manually, and wait for the oil to start flowing. Once you've bled any air from the system, close the bleed screw.

Of course the transmission should be filled. As you install each piece, check its function as best you can.

Once the engine and running gear are in place, run the wiring harness. Ensure that it's properly laid out on the frame and none of the connections are stressed. It's a good practice to test each connection and the function of each component as it is installed. It's a lot easier to pinpoint a problem at this stage than it will be when the bodywork is in place.

Secure the harness to the frame with tie wraps or tape. Check that as the fork swings to

I know it hurts, but scrape that fresh paint off wherever you need to ground an electrical component.

Oops! the bolts are a little long and the wheel alignment is way off, but it's better to find out now.

either side it neither pulls nor pinches the harness in any way. Also watch for any wires that are routed too closely to the exhaust or other hot objects. A common source of trouble on British bikes is stator wires that get caught by the drive chain. A piece of fuel line slipped over the wires where they exit the case can protect them from chafing. If nothing else, it might save you a long push.

Control cables should be routed as carefully as possible. Avoid tight bends; the cables should have gentle sweeps if you want them to work easily. Again move the forks from side to side while checking the cables for free play. Adjust the cable free play as required.

If you're running a bike with dual carbs opened by individual cables, now is as good a time as any to synchronize them. If the carbs have vacuum ports, you can do the final synch once the engine is set up and running. Also, try to run throttle cables for twin carburetors as close to parallel as possible.

As the wheels are installed, the tires should have the air pressure set. Install and adjust the drive chain as you install the rear wheel. Be sure the wheel alignment is correct.

As the front wheel's installed, the front brake might need to be centralized. Different models might use slightly different procedures, but basically the wheel is spun and the front brake applied. With the brake held on—if you're working alone, a zip-tie or bungee can help here—the axle and securing bolt(s) are then tightened up. Check your shop manual for specifics.

When installing the front fender, see that it fits into its bracket and into the fork as evenly as possible. If the fender is too wide and needs compressing to fit, it might cause the forks to bind. Conversely, if the fender is narrow it will bind the fork as the bolts are drawn tight and the fender bows outward. The result is likely poor fork action and ultimately, a cracked fender.

Fitting the Bodywork

The very last step should be the fitting of the fuel tank, seat, and sidecovers. First, double-check every single item that's soon to be hidden away. Nuts, bolts, wire connections,

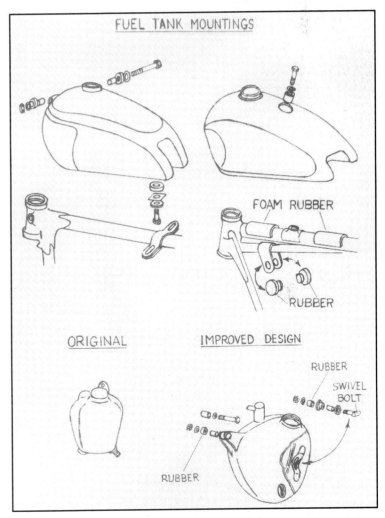

Fuel and oil tanks should always be insulated with foam or rubber strips. Most bikes will have some sort of insulator as standard equipment. If they don't, foam pipe insulation works well.

A piece of safety wire in the appropriate spot adds the finishing touch to this restored vintage racer.

and hose clamps should all be examined a second time and if need be, a third. If the fuel tank requires any insulation or padding beneath it install it now and fit the tank. If you plan to ride the bike, double-check that the tank doesn't contact the frame where it could chafe the paint. This is also a good time to (carefully) check that the fork will clear the front of the gas tank.

Fit the fuel lines as well and add enough gas to test the tank, fuel lines, and connections. Turn on the petcocks and let the float bowl(s) fill. If there's a leak, you'll find it easier to deal with now than later. In most cases it's much easier to slip the tank on and off without the seat.

If the fuel system is intact, install the seat. Before closing the seat make a few checks: If the battery fits under the seat, make sure the seat bottom can't touch the terminals. Some seats use a short restraining strap to keep them from opening too far and denting the sidecovers. If that's the case, check it now—not after the seat has chipped the paint. Everything looks

good, does it? Batten down the seat and install the sidecovers.

STARTING THE BIKE FOR THE FIRST TIME

The magic moment's finally here; presumably the bike is gassed and oiled. All the cables are correctly adjusted and move smoothly. The timing and carbs have been adjusted, statically, of course. There's nothing left to do but light it up.

I start by kicking the bike over a couple of ten times. This ensures everything is free and that the oil is pumping. In fact, if the bike has an oil light, kick the engine over until the light goes out. Make sure the clutch is free—an inherent problem on some British bikes. If the weather is hot, it's a good idea to run a window fan on the engine to help keep it cool.

Take a deep breath and start the engine. Let it run at a brisk idle for a few minutes, and resist the temptation to rev the engine up and down. If it's a dry sump design, check that oil is in fact returning to the tank. It might take a minute or two to start scavenging oil; you can hold your finger over the return for a minute

to build a little pressure if you want to speed things up. If for some reason you suspect the oil pressure is low, stop the engine and investigate before proceeding.

If the engine requires dynamic timing, do it now. Once the timing and carburetion are properly adjusted and you've satisfied yourself that all is well, it's time to take the bike on the road.

THE FIRST RIDE

First, a word of caution: Chances are you're going to be riding an unfamiliar motorcycle for the first time. Take it easy, especially if you've never ridden one like it before. If you've been riding nothing but modern bikes, your first ride on a vintage bike might be a revelation. Vintage brakes, especially, lack the power of modern ones, so give yourself plenty of stopping room.

Chances are the shifting, braking, and power will be totally unlike anything you've ever been on. If you've never ridden an early Norton or Ducati, for example, with their right-side/up-for-low shift pattern, it's

easy to get confused. The first ride should be approximately 10 miles. During the first road test try to make mental notes of any problems or abnormalities.

Assess the power, brakes, and steering. If you're breaking in the engine—and most of you will be—use no more than half of the available rpm. On the other hand, you don't want to lug the engine, either. So try to keep the bike humming. Resist the temptation to ride more than 10 miles.

Return to your garage, check the bike for any leaks and any loose or missing parts. Congratulate yourself on a job well done, and let the bike cool off completely. Before riding the bike again, retorque all the nuts and bolts. If possible, retorque the cylinder head bolts. On some models the bolts will be inaccessible; if that's the case don't worry about it. But if they are, retorque them. Recheck the valves and adjust as required. Repeat this procedure at 500 miles and again at 1,000 miles.

Don't fret too much about carburetor adjustment until the bike has had a chance to break in fully. Once the bike is running, the

You never know what will turn up at a show. This is one of maybe five Hodaka trials bikes ever built. Hodaka never built trials bikes itself; this one and the others were built by dedicated enthusiasts. No, it wasn't for sale!

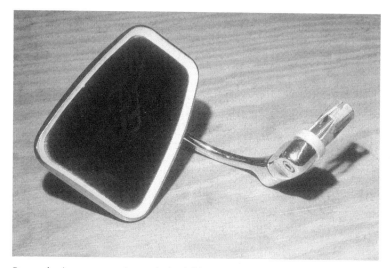

Bar end mirrors are a nice period addition, particularly on a bike fitted with low bars.

A tax disc holder lends that "gen-u-wine" look to a restored Brit-bike!

carbs should be synchronized and the idle speed and mixture adjusted. However, you'll find that as the engine breaks in, the idle speed will probably climb as the engine loosens up. This is normal and will resolve itself after a few miles.

Bear in mind that a restored motorcycle is like any other new bike. As the miles accumulate, routine adjustments and regular maintenance will be required.

RIDE IT, DON'T HIDE IT!

I was tempted to write something pithy and witty here. Instead, I'm going to just tell you how I feel—besides, why change course at the last moment?

There is a tendency to view restored motorcycles as something more than they are, as trophies or monuments, perhaps. I've done it myself. I've seen way too many restored bikes simply carted from show to show, their sole purpose simply being to massage the owner's ego and acquire "Best of Show" awards. Fine, if that's what you want, go to it.

I've won a few best of show awards myself, but I rode my bike to those events. I don't think that any motorcycle, restored or otherwise, should be relegated to a static museum display. Motorcycles are living, breathing entities. The more so for having been lovingly restored. If you want to keep your classic in top trim and ensure that it'll never need re-restoring, ride it on a regular basis. Maintain it, respect it—but most of all, enjoy it.

STORING YOUR MOTORCYCLE

Unless you're blessed enough to live in a climate that allows you to ride year 'round, your motorcycle is going to be off the road for some portion of the year. A classic bike should be stored like any other.

Prior to storage the machine should be washed and waxed; a short trip will ensure that it's thoroughly dried. All of the oils should be drained and replaced with fresh. Remove the battery. The gas tank should be topped off to exclude any moisture, and a fuel stabilizer added. Tire pressure should be lowered and if possible both wheels blocked up clear of the ground.

The bike should be stored in a location that is kept at a constant temperature—in fact, it's better to store the bike in a cold garage than in an area where the temperature rises and falls, such as a basement. If condensation is likely to be a problem, all of the brightwork should be coated with WD-40 or some other moisture repellent. A dust cover that allows the bike to breathe will protect the finish.

Not strictly speaking an accessory, this center stand with pull-up handle was fitted to some Vincents, notably the fully enclosed Black Prince and Black Knight models.

As an alternative, one of those new vacuum bags should work nicely. These are large plastic bags containing a desiccant. After your bike is winterized you roll it inside the bag and evacuate the air with a vacuum cleaner. In theory your bike should retain its pristine condition throughout the winter, vacuum-sealed in its own little cocoon.

ACCESSORIES AND OPTIONS

Opinions vary: Some restorers prefer their motorcycle to be the pure unadulterated item. For them the basic—pure, if you will—motorcycle is the thing. Others like to dress their bike with every conceivable option and accessory. I fall somewhere in the middle.

I enjoy seeing restored motorcycles with period accessories. I don't particularly care for "overdressed" bikes, but tastefully done accessories add a certain something. Besides if you'd bought a Triumph Bonneville new in 1968 it's somewhat unlikely that you'd have left it stock. I know I wouldn't have. Period add-ons include original-style windscreens, saddlebags, and various engine bolt-on bits. If I were judging a show I'd certainly give a little extra consideration to the bike that had a few tasteful period options.

What constitutes a period accessory? I'd say any item manufactured specifically for the bike at the time, or any generic accessory of the time period. For example, a BMW /2 with Albert spotlight mirrors, a factory-optional tachometer and luggage rack, and Flanders crash bars would be a good illustration of a bike with period accessories made specifically

for it. A restored BSA A-10 with a Friedex locking throttle, Ford-Halcyon bar-end mirror, and a tax disc would fall into the generic accessory category. As would a bike with other period gear, like a Bates seat or windshield.

You don't have to track down every single item ever fitted to your bike, but a few period pieces give the restored bike a certain cachet that's hard to beat.

SHOWING THE BIKE

Let's be honest: you're proud of what you've accomplished and rightly so. You'd like to show it off a little, wouldn't you? Maybe get a trophy in recognition of your work? It's show time!

Entering a bike in a show can be supremely rewarding or downright humiliating. First, decide if you want to show the bike for fun or to win (of course, it's always fun to win). I like to show my bikes for fun; if I win a trophy, so much the better.

Because I show for fun I don't take the process as seriously as some owners do. The day before a show I'll wash, wax, and detail the bike. But I'll also ride the bike to the show. If it gets dirty on the way, too bad. I also ride my

As far as accessories go it's hard to beat a tank autographed by a famous rider, especially when the bike is a replica of the one that made him famous.

bikes when I feel like it. On the other hand, hard-core show junkies tend to obsess over every detail. The bikes are fettled for hours and seldom, if ever, ridden. In fact, many of them aren't even capable of being ridden. While they might be beautiful sculpture, they hardly qualify as motorcycles in my book.

If you decide to show your bike competitively, here are a few simple do's and don'ts:

First, the bike should be catalog correct. Common mistakes include using plastic wire ties on bikes that never had them, substituting modern hardware for OEM, and using incorrect peripheral parts. Not all judges pick up on these things, but the good ones do.

Try to arrive at the show early. This will give you time to position the bike to its best advantage and give it a last minute once-over. Some owners will display the owner's manual and tool kit, advertising brochures, and even the original bill of sale along with the bike. Usually a handlebar tag listing any pertinent information is attached to the bike. You don't have to write the history of the bike on it, but do try to hit the high points.

Don't "dog" the judges—let them get on with the job at hand. Don't second-guess them. If you think you were treated unfairly, you have two choices. You can ask to speak to the judges or you can leave. If the judges agree to discuss their decision with you, be reasonable and be a gentleman. I can tell you from personal experience that hot heads always come off second best. Remember that this is supposed to be fun; don't take it too seriously.

Everything is as it should be on this restored BSA M21. All that's missing is the air pump that hangs beneath the tank. Note the mounting of the Lucas mag-dyno behind the engine and the fuel line routing.

Appendix: Sources

I've tried to arrange these in a logical manner by chapter. Like many good ideas, it probably isn't the best solution, but it's a workable one. Many of the businesses listed are ones I've had personal experience with; those I haven't dealt with came highly recommended. I haven't listed any marque clubs because, quite frankly, there are so many of them that I just don't have the space. Obviously, there are some parts sources that fit into more than one category. At the end of the appendix I've also listed suppliers that cater to a specific brand or country of origin. Those are listed by both marque and generic application.

CHAPTER 1: PRINTED MATERIAL

MBI Publishing Company
729 Prospect Ave
P.O. Box 1
Osceola, WI 54020
(800) 826-6600
Publishers of almost anything that pertains to motor sports, including Roy Bacon's Buyer's guides. If it has to do with motorcycles and it's worth reading, chances are MBI Publishing Company has published it.

Motorcycle Days
P.O. Box 9686
Baltimore, MD 21237
(410) 665-6295
Magazines, posters, brochures, books, and who knows what. If it's on paper they have it.

Motorsport
550 Honey Locust Road
Jonesburg, MO 63351
Distributors of Classic Bike and a variety of other British Books and magazines.

Walneck's Classic Cycle Trader
P.O. Box 9059
Clearwater, FL 34168
(800) 877-6141
Want ads and some articles.

The Internet
I know the 'net really isn't print, but this is as good a place as any to list it. You'll find everything you need to know out there in the ether.

Hemming's Motor News
P.O. Box 100
Bennington, VT 05201
(800) 277-4373
Mostly vintage cars, but they do have a large motorcycle section.

Clubs
Antique Motorcycle Club of America
P.O. Box 300
Sweetser, IL 46987

Vintage Motor Cycle Club
Allen House, Wetmore Road
Burton-on-Trent, Staffs
DE14 1TR
01283 540557

American Historic Motorcycle Racing Association
P.O. Box 882
Wausau, WI 54402

CHAPTER 2: VINTAGE MOTORCYCLE SALES

This is a tough call since lots of small local dealers handle vintage motorcycles. Accordingly, I listed the largest dealers nationwide.

Harpers Moto-Guzzi
32401 Stringtown Rd.
Greenwood, MO 64304
(816) 697-3411

Blue Moon Cycle
752 W. Peachtree St.
Norcross, GA 30071
(770) 447-6945
Vintage BMW sales specialists.

Baxter Cycle
400 Lincoln St., Box 85
Marne, IA 51552
(712) 781-2351
A large selection of British and European bikes.

Domi Racer
5218 Wooster Road
Cincinnati, OH 45226
(513) 871-1678
British and European bikes.

Alfa Heaven
Aniwa, WI
(715) 449-2141
Japanese motorcycles.

Hugh's Bultaco
682 Taghkanic-Churchtown Road
Craryville, NY 12521
(518) 851-7184
Bultaco motorcycles—from rough to concourse.

Shipping
The Federal Companies
101 National Road
E. Peoria, IL 61611
(309) 694-3300

Warren Motorcycle Transport
7106 NW 108th Ave.
Tamarac, FL 33321
(305) 726-0494

CHAPTER 3: SPECIAL TOOLS AND HAND TOOLS

Precision Mfg. & Sales Co., Inc.
P.O. Box 149, Clearwater, FL 34617
(800) 237-5947
Precision specializes in supplying tools to the motorcycle trade. They can supply everything from a flywheel puller for your 1969 Ossa to a dyno.

America Kowa Seiki, Inc.
13939 Equitable Road
Cerritos, CA 90703
(800) 824-9655
Kowa supplies metric tools to the big four Japanese motorcycle manufacturers and to some of the car builders. They have some very nice hand tools and a full line of special tools that pertain to the big four.

Sudco International Corp.
3014 Tanager Ave.
Commerce, CA 90040
Although best known for their carb kits, SUDCO carries a good stock of Whitworth tools.

Tip Tools
7075 State Route 446
P.O. Box 649
Canfield, OH 44406
(330) 533-3384
TIP supplies everything needed to restore your bike, from glass beading cabinets and paint guns to replica parts counters.

Lifts and jacks
Lincoln Manufacturing
4001 Industrial Ave., Box 30303
Lincoln, NE 68503
Jacks and roll-around stands.

Western Manufacturing
702 South Third Avenue
P.O. Box 130
Marshalltown, IA 50158
(515) 752-5446
Air and electric lifts, teardown tables, and motorcycle jacks.

Tip Tools & Equipment
7075 RT 446, P.O. Box 649
Canfield, OH 44406
(800) 321-9260
Painting, glass beading, and sandblasting equipment.

CHAPTER 4: EVERYTHING YOU NEED IS AVAILABLE THROUGH YOUR LOCAL AUTO PARTS STORE OR SUPERMARKET.

CHAPTER 5: PRESSURE WASHERS SUITABLE FOR HOME USE ARE AVAILABLE THROUGH RETAIL STORES LIKE HOME DEPOT, SEARS, AND LOWES, OR MAIL ORDER THROUGH NORTHERN HYDRAULICS.

CHAPTER 6: MACHINE SHOP SERVICES AND ENGINE PARTS

Britech Inc.
P.O. Box 371
Southbridge, MA 01550
(508) 764-8624
You name it, they do it.

Mancini Racing
26 Kenosia Ave.
Danbury, CT 06810
(203) 730-0052
Primarily dedicated to current street bikes and drag racing; they can repair any engine problem I've ever run into. They will custom make parts, fabricate a frame, or build you an engine. Mail order is no problem.

SRM Engineering
Unit 22 Glanyrafon Industrial Estate
Aberystwyth, Dyfed
United Kingdom, SY23 3JQ
Tel- 011 44 1970 627771+2
End feed & needle roller conversions for BSA twins.

Bollenbach Engineering
296 Williams Place
East Dundee, IL 60118-2319
(708) 428-2800
Primarily Indian.

Megacycle
90 Mitchell Blvd.
San Rafael, CA 94903
(415) 472-3195
Performance camshafts and cylinder head repairs.

Poweroll
P.O. Box 920
Redmond, OR 97756
(541) 923-1290
Poweroll primarily works on Japanese off road four-
strokes, both vintage and new. They offer a
complete line of engine parts as well as a variety of cylinder and head repairs.

Falicon Performance
1115 Old Coachman Road
Clearwater FL 34625
(813) 797-2468
Crankshaft specialists.

L.A. Sleeve Co.
12051 Rivera Road
Santa Fe Springs, CA 90670
(310) 945-7578
Manufacturers of cylinder sleeves, L.A. can supply a
sleeve for any bike you can think of. They make
vintage sleeves on a one-off basis and can install it as well.

Alloy Tech
608 East Pinzon St.
Tuscola, IL 61953
(217) 253-3939
British parts, sludge trap, Allen bolt replacement.

Dave Quinn Motorcycles
335 Litchfield Turnpike
Bethany, CT 06524
(203) 393-2651
MORGO high-capacity oil pumps and big bore
kits.

CHAPTER 7: CARBURETORS, REBUILDERS, AND PARTS

Sudco
3014 Tanager Ave.
Commerce, CA 90040
(323) 728-5407
Mikuni carb conversion kits, Mikuni parts and
carbs, tech service.

Lund Machine Company
P.O. Box 301
Lebanon, OR 97355
800-295-2915
Amal carbs resleeved.

Bing Agency International
P.O. Box 1, 101 South Main
Belvedere, KS 67028
(316) 862-5808
Bing parts and carburetors.

S&S Cycle
RR2, County Highway
Viola, WI 54664
(608) 627-1497
H-D replacement carbs.

Kokesh Motorcycle Accessories
6529 University Ave. N.E.
Fridley, MN 55432
(612) 571-3863
Linkert carburetor parts.

Cosmopolitan Motors Inc.
301 Jacksonville Road
Hatboro, PA 19040
(215) 672-9100
Dell'Orto carburetors.

CHAPTER 8: EXHAUST SYSTEMS

Circle F
1917 Elmview
Houston, Texas 77080
(713) 467-1488
Vintage two-stroke expansion chambers.

Bub Ent.
22573 Meyer Ravine Road
Grass Valley, CA 05949
(916) 268-0449
Replacement exhausts for all four-stroke bikes.

Aircone
240 Elliot Rd.
Henderson, NV 89015
(702) 566-1077
2&4-stroke exhausts and exhaust pipe parts.

CHAPTER 9: IGNITION SYSTEMS

Jack Hurt
1711 Calavaras Dr.
Santa Rosa, CA 95405
(800) 789-1026
Mr. Hurt rebuilds every kind of mag.

Euro Spares
1451 46th Ave.
San Francisco, CA 94122-2902
(415) 665-3363
Lucas Rita electronic ignition systems, 6v to 12v
generator conversions, and a host of other
electronic goodies for British, European, and
Japanese motorcycles.

Dynatek
164 S. Valencia St.
Glendora, CA 91741
(818) 963-1669
Replacement coils and ignitions for all bikes.

CHAPTER 10: CLUTCH PLATES AND TRANNY PARTS

Barnett Tool & Engineering
9920 Freeman Ave.
Santa Fe Springs, CA 90670
(310) 941-1284
Best known for their clutch plates, Barnett also makes cables, levers, and throttles.

Karata Enterprises
3 River Road
Conshohocken, PA 19428
(610) 825-2070
Belt drive, clutch, and tranny parts for H-D (also magnetos).

CHAPTER 11: FRAME AND REAR SUSPENSION

Buchanan Spoke and Rim
805 W. 8th St.
Azusa, CA 91702
(818) 969-4655
Best known for wheel work, Buchanan has an excellent reputation for frame repair.

Works Performance Products
21045 Osborne St.
Canoga Park, CA 91304
(818) 701-1010
Direct replacement shocks and springs for most vintage bikes.

Progressive Suspension
11129 G Ave.
Hesperia, CA 92345
(619) 948-4012
Shocks, springs, and tools.

Vintage Iron
4774 East Carmen
Fresno, CA 93703
(209) 252-9053
One of the few shops that rebuilds Yamaha Monoshocks.

CHAPTER 12: FORKS

(See the chapter 11 suppliers for springs and dampener kits.)

Forking by Frank
(Franks Maintenance & Engineering, Inc.)
945 Pitner
Evanston, IL 60202
Fork tubes from 1940 on, custom lengths as well.

K&L Supply
K&L supplies tapered steering head bearings to replace the loose balls found in older bikes. Since they don't sell retail, you'll have to order them through your local dealer, which is why no address or phone number is listed.

CHAPTER 13: WHEELS AND RIMS

Buchanan: listed in chapter 11.

Kelly Moss Wheels
3175 Mckee Rd.
San Jose, CA 95127
(408) 254-0440
Kelly laces and trues wheels and can supply any and all components.

Wheel Works
12787 Nutwood
Garden Grove, CA 92640
Wheel builders, these guys also polish, plate, and powder-coat.

Fasst Company
(562) 439-1025
Spoke torque wrenches.

CHAPTER 14: BRAKES

Vintage Brakes
15069 Lupin Lane
Sonora, CA 95370
(209) 533-4346
Ferodo Linings, Grimeca and Lockheed parts.

SBS (Scandinavian Brake Systems)
3501 Kennedy Road
P.O. Box 5222
Janesville, WI 53547-5222
(608) 758-1111
Replacement shoes and pads for more bikes than you'd think.

CHAPTER 15: HANDLEBARS AND CONTROLS

K&N Engineering
P.O. Box 1329
Riverside, CA 92507
(909) 684-9762
Replacement handlebars for street, off road, and dirt track bikes.

Barnett
See above listing under clutches (chapter 10). They also make levers and throttles.

Sunline
7045 Darby Ave.
Reseda, CA 91335
(818) 705-6520
If you're restoring an off-road machine these are the guys to see. Levers, grips, clamps, and so on.

Magura USA
2 Union Drive
Olney, IL 62450
(618) 395-2200
Although they don't sell direct, Magura has such a diverse and well-made product range that I had to mention them. You can source their stuff through your local dealer.

CHAPTER 16: ELECTRICS/ INSTRUMENTS

Deltran Corp.
801 U.S. Highway 92 East
Deland, FL 32724
(904) 736-7900
Makers of the Battery Tender, a must have if your
bike is going to sit for any length of time.

M.A.P. Cycle Enterprises Inc.
7165 30th Ave. North
Saint Petersburg, FL 33710
(813) 381-1151
Mainly a supplier of British parts, M.A.P. is the best
source I've found for battery eliminator kits,
replacement electrical parts, and Lucas magneto repair kits.

MTC
13724 Harvard Place
Gardena, CA 90249
(310) 538-1620
Hard rubber cased batteries in 6 and 12 volt.

Precision Instrument Repair
445 Beaver Ruin Road
P.O. Box 581
Lilburn, GA 30047
(770) 923-5522
British and European speedos, tachs, and ampmeters.

Nisonger
570 Mamaroneck Ave.
Marmaroneck, NY 10543
(914) 381-1952
The source for Smith's instruments.

CHAPTER 17: BODY WORK
Everybody has his favorite painter; these are a few
whose work I've seen.

Hutchinson Cycle
116 Foundry Street
Wakefield, MA 01880
(617) 245-9663
Don Hutchinson is the Triumph paint expert: He
paints bikes, sells paint, and dispenses pithy
advice.

Connecticut Cycle Refinishing
1977 Commerce Drive
Bridgeport, CT 06605
(203) 334-6748
CCR: If it's on a motorcycle and needs paint or
straightening, Sean Lezotte does it to perfection.

Hirsch Automotive Products
396 Littleton Ave.
Newark, NJ 07103
(800) 828-2061
Hirsch can supply nitrocellulose lacquer, rust removers, tank sealers, and variety of paints,
parts washers, and solvents used in the
restoration process.

Essex Motorsports
244 Middlesex Turnpike
Chester, CT 06412
(203) 526-2060
Essex can provide some of the best powder-coating
and chrome on the planet; expensive, but
worth it.

In general: sources of supply by make, country of
origin, and anything else that struck my fancy. This
is a very limited list, and should be used only as a
starting point. Again, these are people I've either
dealt with or have direct knowledge of and that
haven't been listed elsewhere.

American-made motorcycles
Charleston Custom Cycle
211 Washington
Charleston, IL 61920
(217) 345-2577
NOS parts for H-D lightweights.

Nostalgia Cycle
15681 Commerce Lane
Huntington Beach, CA 92649
(714) 891-6263

"45" Restoration Co.
P.O. Box 12843
Albany, NY 12212
(518) 459-5012
Indian.

Starklite Cycle
21230 Gold Valley Rd.
Perris, CA 92370
(909) 780-0857

Kiwi Indian Parts
17399 Sage Ave.
Riverside, CA 92504
(909) 780-5400

Bob's Indian Sales
RD #3, Box 3449
580 Old York Rd.
Etters, PA 17319
(717) 938-2556

British bikes
Collier's Cycle
7401 Charlotte Pike
Nashville, TN 37209
(615) 353-1919

British Only
32451 Park Lane
Garden City, MI 48135
(800) BRT-ONLY

Moores Cycle Supply
49 Custer Street
W. Hartford, CT 06110
(860) 953-1689

EUROPEAN

See listings under chapter 2 for Hugh's, Harper's Blue Moon, and Domi Racer.

Capital Cycle
45449 Severn Way, Suite 179
Sterling, VA 20166-8918
(800) 642-5100
The source for BMW parts.

Syd's Cycles
6600 Haines Road
St. Petersburg, FL 33702
(813) 522-3333
Syd Tunstall is one of the world's leading experts on bevel drive Ducatis.

Parts Is Parts
RR3 Box 3095C
Stroudsburg, PA 18360
(570) 629-1940
Moto-Guzzi parts; the catalog alone is worth the price of admission.

JAPANESE

Speed & Sport, Inc.
305 Montour Blvd.
Bloomsburg, PA 17815
(717) 784-6831
Yamaha parts.

Paul Miller Motorcycle
72 Whispering Brook Dr.
Kensington, CT 06037
(860) 828-1220
Paul specializes in Suzuki parts and bikes from the 1960s to the mid-1980s.

The Dream Merchant
(805) 928-2001
Honda & Suzuki
115 West Chapel Street
Santa Maria CA 93458

Off Road
Penton Imports Co.
1115 Milan Ave.
Amherst, Ohio 44001
(440) 988-4474
Among other things Jack Penton imports PVL electronic ignitions.

Enduro Classics
Lover's Lane
Culpeper, VA
(540) 825-0822
As their name implies, Enduro caters to Yamaha Enduros.

VINTAGE IRON: SEE CHAPTER 11.
Hughs Bultaco: See chapter 2.

Strictly Hodaka
3 Seneca Trail
Charlestown, RI 02813
(401) 364-3427
As the name might imply, Paul Stannard is the source for Hodaka and Hodaka only parts.

Metro Racing
224 Park Ave.
Bristol, PA 19007
(215) 785-3673
From A (Ariel) to Z (Zundapp) Metro is your one-stop source for T-shirts, off-road vintage riding gear, hats, and whatever else strikes Don and Peg Millers' fancy.

Speed & Sport
Long Beach, CA 90806
[need street address]
(310) 490-0012
Parts for your vintage trials bike.

Neil Keen Performance
Wentzville, MO
(314) 639-1586
Vintage track stuff from the man himself, "Peaches" Keen.

I realize that the listing above is far from complete. Hopefully, if you can't find what you need from one of the businesses listed, they will at least point you in the right direction.

Index